A L M O S T
AMERICANS

A QUEST FOR DIGNITY

Patricia Justiniani McReynolds

R·E·D
CRANE
BOOKS
SANTA FE

FIRST EDITION

Manufactured in the United States of America
Front cover collage by Daniel Kosharek
Front cover photograph by Michael O'Shaughnessy
Cover design by Beverly Miller Atwater
Book design by Beverly Miller Atwater

Library of Congress Cataloging-in-Publication Data

McReynolds, Patricia Justiniani, 1926–
   Almost Americans : a quest for dignity / Patricia Justiniani
McReynolds. -- 1st ed.
        p.   cm.
   ISBN 1-878610-64-3 (pbk.)
   1. McReynolds, Patricia Justiniani, 1926-   . 2. Filipino
Americans—California—Biography. 3. Norwegian Americans—
California—Biography. 4. Children of interracial marriage—
California—Biography. 5. Immigrants—California—Biography.
6. California—Race relations. 7. California—Biography.
I. Title.
F870.F4M38   1997
979.4'0049921073'092—dc21
[B]

                                              97-37227
                                              CIP

Red Crane Books
2008 Rosina St., Suite B
Santa Fe, New Mexico 87505
http://www.redcrane.com
email:publish@redcrane.com

This book is lovingly dedicated to José and Ruth's grandchildren, great-grandchildren, great-great grandchildren, and all the rest to come.

JUSTINIANI FAMILY

Fourth Row: Sam, Abraham, Matthew, Rich
Third Row: Hannah, Daria, Maria, Kip, Lisa, Amos (Eagle), Moses
Second Row: Michael, Ramona, Cliff, Justin, John
First Row: Benjamin, Naomi Yellow Bird, Mica, Callie, Pat

FILIPINO Family Tree

Enriqueta (Piccio) m. Florentino Justiniani

Manuel (Manong)   León m. Casilda   José m. Ruth   Isabel

Patricia m. (1) Richard Haynes
(2) m. Cliff McReynolds

Daria m. Sam Wohali   Maria m. (1) James Dorr   Lisa m. Kip Winsett   Matthew
(2) m. Richard Langmaack

Abraham (Abe)
Ramona
Moses
Hannah
Naomi Yellow Bird
Benjamin
Amos (Eagle) m. Casie

Eagle Jr.

Mica
Austin

Michael   Justin m. Randi   John m. Clarissa

Phoenix   Caleb

María m. Paul Kosenko   Ramón m. Margarita   Rosa

Florentino (Flory) m.   Conchita m.   Rudolfo (Rudy) m. Baby   Fae
     Lucille (Lulu)   Rudolfo (Ruding)

Jewell   Jed   Robert   Mae

NORWEGIAN Family Tree

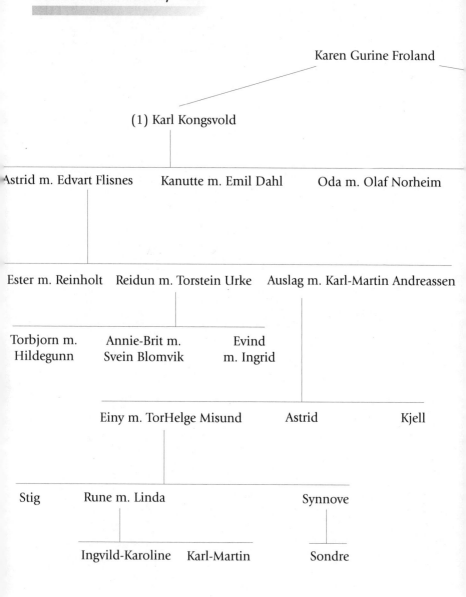

Karen Gurine Froland

(1) Karl Kongsvold

Astrid m. Edvart Flisnes   Kanutte m. Emil Dahl   Oda m. Olaf Norheim

Ester m. Reinholt   Reidun m. Torstein Urke   Auslag m. Karl-Martin Andreassen

Torbjorn m.   Annie-Brit m.   Evind
Hildegunn   Svein Blomvik   m. Ingrid

Einy m. TorHelge Misund   Astrid   Kjell

Stig   Rune m. Linda   Synnove

Ingvild-Karoline   Karl-Martin   Sondre

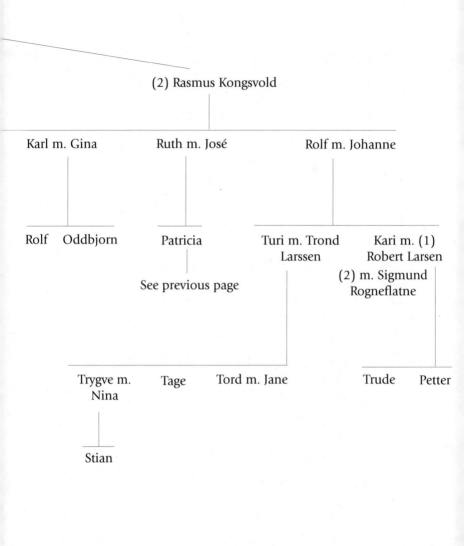

(2) Rasmus Kongsvold

Karl m. Gina   Ruth m. José   Rolf m. Johanne

Rolf   Oddbjørn   Patricia   Turi m. Trond   Kari m. (1)
                                                Larssen   Robert Larsen
                        See previous page   (2) m. Sigmund
                                                                Rogneflatne

        Trygve m.   Tage   Tord m. Jane   Trude   Petter
          Nina

        Stian

One

My eighty-seven-year-old father died sitting on the toilet. I thought it a very undignified way to die and denied it for years.

"That's why he was so heavy when we carried him back to bed!" my husband and son explained to me. In the months after his stroke, they had walked him into the bathroom, supporting him under each arm, so that he could relieve himself and wash. This day, he wasn't helping to walk back, they said, because he was dead.

"No! No!" I insisted. "That's not true! He died in the bed when you took him back!" That's how people die, in bed with dignity, not sitting on the toilet, tugging the toilet paper endlessly and saying: "What the hell?" He had to die in a dignified way because that was his nature—dignified. He sat tall and proud, like any distinguished elder from a noble clan. At someone's house or even on a bus bench, he always sat straight as a pole with his head turning at right angles to the left and the right.

In spite of my need to cling to this shred of nobility at the moment of my father's death, I felt that what my husband and son had said was probably true. Throughout my life, I had made vain attempts to protect my parents from the world outside. They had come from opposite ends of the earth—my mother from Norway, my father from the Philippines—to meet in America. And although we were together constantly throughout my childhood, my parents were an enigma to me. They seemed to know what they wanted and yet were uncertain at the same time. They were so different from each other and from my friends' parents, and still I believed they were the way everyone's parents should be. They were almost always amiable and at times awkward; in comparison, my friends' parents appeared cool and austere. My parents talked of perplexing things, sometimes troubling things in accented English, and were comfortable in other languages that I couldn't understand.

When I thought of them, I couldn't help but liken them to a cat's cradle string game—so simple and yet so complex and easily entangled. In some ways they were innocents, like children who needed guarding; this guardianship fell to me, their one child, and (except for an aunt) only relative in America. We were a tight threesome, despite what I considered their often illogical reasoning, chaotic memories, and unconventional ways of dealing with life in America. They spent a lot of time telling me tales of their homelands, so a story about the three of us in my own homeland of Southern California comes to mind.

It was high noon in The Broadway department store in downtown Los Angeles, and hidden lights illuminated bolts of fabric in the yardage section, heightening their colors and textures.

"Look, Myrtle, is that a Chinaman over there with that white woman?" A hugely overweight woman on a couch leaned her mass into the woman of almost equal size seated next to her, hissing a stage whisper in a broad, California accent.

The friend looked up and both stared at us. Their mouths hanging like dump-truck scoops, they strained to figure out the situation.

Maybe it was their sly voices that intimidated me or maybe their striking similarity to the hefty nurse who had twice wheeled me, on a trolley, into the torture-machine room when I had kidney trouble. My mother had to stay in the waiting room. Perhaps it was their treacherous mass that reminded me of the buxom nurse.

Whatever the reason, seeing that my mother hadn't heard, I went into action: I began shoving her forward toward the next department. Our life was perfectly normal, and I was determined not to let anyone's whispers suggest anything else. I was an American (or thought so most of the time) and knew how to defend against oppressors. My choice between flight or fight was flight, to flee within or away, pretending problems didn't exist.

"Stop pushing me, Patsy! I want to look at this material!"

Despite my prodding, my mother stood there, studying the cloth with her blue eyes flecked with brown that matched the color of her waved hair framing a slim face and delicate nose. I gambled on another solution. I elbowed my father along, saying, "Let's go see that one over there."

"Okay, dear," he answered, pleasantly.

He was taking my mother shopping for sewing materials on Tuesday, his day off, and he was so relaxed I could have blown him like a dandelion along the gray carpeted floor. A slim, energetic man five feet eight inches, he had fleshy lips and a bump on his long nose beneath a shock of thinning black hair. He was enjoying window-shopping in the modern department store.

My mother followed us at last, as I knew she would, inching along, fingering every piece of cloth that caught her eye.

Finally, I got them out of harm's way. It was my job to protect them from the onslaughts of a malfunctioning world, to shield them from exposure to pain, like the pain I suffered at school where I was teased for being different, of two races—white and brown.

Now we were hidden behind tables covered by huge bolts of fabric wound smoothly around cardboard forms, silks and satins, cottons and flannels, in plain and plaids, prints and my father's favorite, paisleys. They may have reminded him of the colorful, wrapped skirt *patadjongs* worn by the women he had seen as a young boy in the Islands. I sneaked a look at the women who now were heading out of the yardage department toward the elevator. I breathed in relief as the bell sounded and the doors closed, swallowing their bulk. My parents were vulnerable, and they didn't deserve more woe than I'd heard them discuss. They surely were not as tried and tested in the fires of racism as I was.

In fact, I didn't think my dad looked Chinese, but very much like the drawing of an Eskimo in one of my school books at home. When I had pointed this out to my mother just a few weeks earlier, she had become incensed.

"No, Patsy! How can you say that?"

I thought the hunter was very handsome, with a strong nose and jaw, and still believed he looked like my father. Maybe, I reasoned, my mother had reacted negatively because the man in the Arctic was behind a sled pulled by dogs through the snow, and that must have been barbaric and offensive. Or perhaps my mother had some prejudice, until now hidden, against Laplanders who herded reindeer in the northern fields of her native land. She had always told me that when she met my dad, he reminded her of the gypsies who roamed through Norway when she lived there, with his dark, wavy hair. When she told the story, her lips, typically pressed together, would relax and curl slightly, and her eyes would brighten. The Eskimo debate, as I came to think of it, noteworthy as one of our few disagreements, may have been the first time I realized that even the closest of people can disagree in the way they see the same things, that the image reflected back to each person had as much to do with the viewer's life experiences and beliefs as it had to do with the object itself.

Later that day, it was my father's turn to shop. He parked the forest green Terraplane in front of a grocery store in Los Angeles' Chinatown, and my mother waited in the car. I trailed at his heels, watching and listening to his explanations of exotic fruits like green guavas and pink papayas, exquisite tins of tea, boxes of cookies brightly wrapped with strange, black writing on them. He bought me, as a special treat, leechee nuts, with their sweet, soft-as-brown-velvet hiding a huge seed. On the way home—a second story flat near the Hyperion Bridge—we picked up a friend from the fourth grade. We played Old Maid while my father fixed dinner and my mother set the table in our linoleum-floored kitchen. Soon, we sat down to plates of sotanghon, long, bland noodles made mouth-watering by tomato sauce and chicken, and *mungo*, tiny green lentils.

My friend wrinkled her nose at both dishes.

"I can't understand what your father is saying," she confided after we finished and were back in the living room playing cards.

"Oh?" I said, feigning great surprise. I could understand my parents easily, even though my mother blended the letters *w* and *v*, and mispronounced certain words, and my father said *b* for *v*, and got *he* and *she* mixed up because Philippine dialects don't discriminate with personal pronouns. I thought my friend a perfect idiot but kept very quiet, thinking that something must be wrong with us, yet I didn't want to know what it was.

It was 1935 and I was nine years old, old enough to believe that when all is going well, I should expect the worst, and young enough to be filled with idealism and hope.

José with friends in Negros Occidental, Philippines, 1911.

José and his family; his brother Ramón and his family in Cebu, Philippines, 1936.

José (holding rifle), Ruth and Patsy in the cart with some of the Sajo family in Saravia, Philippines, 1936.

León on the balcony of the Justiniani hacienda on the sugarcane plantation. Saravia, Philippines, 1935.

Five-year-old Ruth, left, beside her mother, with sisters, brothers, and grandmother on the right. Alesund, Norway, 1908.

José and Ruth's wedding photo, New York City, 1922.

Ruth, José, and six-month-old Patsy.
Santa Cruz, California, 1926.

José and three-year-old Patsy. Carmel,
California, 1929.

Four-year-old Patsy.
Los Angeles, California, 1930.

Patsy on a pony. Los Angeles, 1932.

Pat in Hollywood, 1944.

Ruth and José become U.S. citizens with Certificates of Naturalization.

Dick, Pat, Matthew, Lisa, Daria, Maria. 1964.

José, Pat, Matthew, Maria, Lisa, Ruth, 1965.

Ruth, 1977.

José, 1977.

Pat, José, Ruth. 1977.

Pat, Baja California, 1965.

Cliff, Pat, Lisa, Maria, Matthew, Jim, his mother Ruth, 1975.

Jed, Jewell, Pat, Flory. La Jolla, California, 1995.

TWO

"Oh, I guess I picked May tenth for my birthday because the birthstone is a diamond. Ha! Why not?" In middle age, my father laughed at his continuing search for identification as a rich man.

"Oh, listen to him!" my mother teased. "Always talking about being wealthy and his diamonds from the Islands! But I'm glad I get to wear them!" She spread her hand in front of him, brandishing the gigantic diamond, surrounded by smaller ones, the flashiness contrasting wildly with the simple hair cut just below her ears. He had his largest diamond set into a ring for her, a token of love, Philippine style.

José was telling me a story about his childhood. He guessed that in 1900 he was nine years old. He based his guess on the ages of his siblings. He never knew for sure, since the town hall had long ago burned down, consuming all birth, marriage, and other records so important to the Spaniards then ruling the Philippines. A legal birth date got one jobs and passports, things he didn't need running barefoot through sugarcane fields (stopping to break off a hunk of the juicy sweet stuff) or bathing in the river, splashing the humid heat away—not concerned what the temperature was.

His father, Florentino Justiniani, had been the third son of a sugarcane plantation owner on Panay, one of the central Visayan Islands, just west of Negros. In the sixteenth century, Spanish galleons had cruised into one of the island's translucent inlets and given the main village the name Iloilo. My dad said that in the Visayan dialect called *Ilongo* (one of over sixty dialects of the Philippines), *Ilo-ilo* meant "long noses," the islanders' description of the new arrivals. The Spaniards, ignorant of the local tongue, probably assumed *Ilo-ilo* was the name of the place, and so the capital of Panay was baptized.

Listening to my father, I imagined the Spaniards and Visayans trying to communicate, and the resulting cross-chatter:

"What's the name of this village?" wondered the Spaniards.

"Look at their long noses!" marveled the Visayans.

"Ah!" exclaimed the Spaniards, "it must be called *Iloilo!*"

José loved telling stories of growing up in his homeland, particularly after a long day working at the "House," where he was butler and valet to a rich man, or on Tuesdays, his only day off. The stories always multiplied after dinners my parents gave for their varied and slightly off-beat friends. Alone with my father, I was an animated audience, quick to listen to the stories of his bizarre experiences in the strange and bewildering country. I pictured dirt paths passing through groves of tall palm trees, carriages pulled by horses, islands separated by seas that remained deep azure all the way to the horizon. My mother liked to listen to him too, but had heard the stories so often she sometimes turned on the small radio next to our red plush couch to hear the easy-going Fibber McGee and Molly show, while she crocheted large afghans.

"In the sixteenth century, Ferdinand Magellan was looking for a short way to India," my father would explain to me. "He came from Spain, in those heavy ships going west in a circle—and he discovered the Philippines. That's what they say—and that's crazy! How can you find what is always there?"

Magellan anchored off the first land his ship came to, the central, eastern islands of the Philippines. They stopped at Limasawa, where they met the chief, designated in Hindu fashion *Rajah Kolambu*. Welcomed as guests, the explorers called the group of more than ten islands the Visayan Islands, or the Visayas, Hispanicizing the title *Vishayas*. The Visayas had been taken over by Islamic traders and fishermen from the south (the islands that became known as Indonesia) over a hundred years earlier, a setup that was economically beneficial for both the visitors and the locals. These visitors, who had named the Visayas, did not seek to proselytize nor colonize in large numbers; instead, they simply established *barangays*, communities named after boats carrying Malay emigrants to the islands about 1000 BC or earlier. They also did a considerable amount of construction in Luzon. Any intention they may have had to further colonize was hamstrung by the more aggressive Spaniards.

"You see—after they settled down, the Spaniards named all of the Islands for the king's son Felipe; they called them Las Filipinas. We do not have a letter *F* in the dialects, so it is hard for lots of Filipinos to pronounce. But I always could!" José would proclaim grandly, whenever he told this story.

"Oh, Patsy, your father had so many interesting experiences!" my mother might break in to say. Or, she might just interrupt and plead, "José, come on, now, stop talking, I need you to take me to the store!" Without any delicacy at all, she would conclude his story, just as it was getting to the good part.

For me, one of the best stories was one about our Justiniani ancestor. Around 1849, the commoners were told to pick a Spanish surname, making it easier for the bureaucracy to collect poll taxes. Some kept their original names of Kalaw, Kalupitan, Mabini, and so on, while others picked Lopez, Cortez, or de Leon. My father's family, already named Justiniani, remembered an Italian forebear who married into a land-owning family; their slim proofs were that there were many marriages between Europeans and *principales* (the Spanish title for the wealthy, landed, indigenous people), and that members of our family exhibited a number of mestizo traits such as light skin, tall stature, and less voluptuous features than their neighbors. No one in our family knew who this mystery man was or when he came to the Islands, but that didn't stop my dad from telling me about our family name.

"Justinian was the first Emperor of the Holy Roman Empire. He was the first to codify Roman laws," he would state loftily. José had a singularly authoritative voice that allowed no contradiction.

"Really? How did we get the name? How did he go to the Philippines?"

"Ooh, I don't knooow," he would drawl out, wrinkling his brow, pursing his lips, squinting his eyes, and I would feel as if I had ruined one of his stories—and his day. "I guess he came over on a boat from Italy."

It always wound down there, but I was fascinated. I liked to imagine my Italian forebear a sailor-adventurer. Whenever the subject came up, my mother would pop in with her own stories to tell, remarking, "that sounds like my father—always on boats, always going somewhere far, far away! Oh, he was wonderful! He loved the South Seas, and maybe that's why I liked your father so much, Patsy, I inherited it from my father!"

Later as a teenager, I met a college professor who smiled and said, "you have a very famous name."

"Yeah, I know," I replied. But I really didn't know, or even care at the time.

In midlife my curiosity stirred. The original Justiniani was lost in history, but later, as an historian, I imagined him as a dashing Italian, probably from Venice, center of trade between East and West. On a research trip to the city, I found hundreds of Giustiniani's in the telephone book. (The Italian *giu* equaled the Spanish *j*, the *i* tacked onto the end, in Northern Italy stood for "the family of.")

Out of my daydreams and the history of European and New World art, I envisioned the mysterious ancestor in detail. A man of the sea, he would push his boat away from buildings where the waves slapped and the stains of algae impressed their memory. Stroking through the canal, he would pass the columned, two-story houses of rose, white, and golden marble and the shining cathedrals. He gazed far beyond the canals, churches, and ships toward the open sea. He dreamed.

One blustery evening, he crossed the arched stone bridge called Ponte Giustinian, made straight along the Calle Giustinian, through the broad Piazza Giustinian, toward his home. Life in Venice had paled for him: the city-state's authority undermined by political discord, the economy in shambles. He sat with brothers, cousins, and friends discussing the promise of profit, the excitement of seeing new places and people. Seafaring men and traders, they knew of a route through the Mediterranean, south through the Strait of Magellan, east across the Pacific to Las Filipinas, similar to Venice but languishing in continual summer. There would be trade, land could be easily acquired, laborers aplenty to work the fields, servants to care for the home. Once he had gained wealth and power, he could return.

I was certain young Giustiniani would have entered the Basilica of San Marcos, dedicated to Venice's patron saint. He would kneel beneath the glittering walls and dome of gold and tinted mosaic tile, take the consecrated host in his mouth, and cross himself. Soon, the young man stood on the deck of the masted ship, pensively watching the silhouette of Venice as it sank below the horizon. Then he pivoted, feet spread wide, and looked straight ahead to his new world.

In the Visayan Islands, the beaches were dotted with small huts of palm thatch. Land was abundant. And there were sultry, satin-skinned women with lips like ripe mangos. He was welcome. He became entrepreneur and land owner, a wealthy man. He married one of the Filipinas, giving her his name Justiniani, spelled with a *J* and pronounced with the ardor of Spanish authority: "Hoos-teen-ya'-nee." His cane fields prospered, his family grew.

As my father spoke of our family, I knew that he was Justiniani's heir, a youth who went traveling, so far east it was west, to a new country filled with promise, seeking adventure, wealth, to see something new.

Three

By the 1880s, the family chronicle needed less imagination. The oral history passed on to José and his siblings was that José's father, Florentino, and his mother, Enriqueta Piccio (a Filipina with an Italian surname) were married in Jaro, Panay. Both families were wealthy landowners, raking in profits from the poor peasants, part of which they passed on to the Spanish administrators. The newlyweds moved to the island of Negros, where they had land of their own.

Spain's administration of the Islands began with Miguel de Legaspi's arrival in 1565. He used the local rajahs, or *datus*, and their subordinates to maintain rule over the peasants. The elite families, the *principali'a* or *principales*, became city and provincial leaders and acted as intermediaries between the Spaniards and the subsistence farmers, who paid the Spanish government's demands of tribute once a year after the harvest.

"People with land were fortunate since they inherited it from their fathers," José said. "But maybe not so fortunate. As go-betweens, they received better treatment from the

Spaniards but got anger from the workers who didn't know what was going on—just that they were bossed around by the well-off."

The peasants lived on the land and worked it without ever owning it. Owning the land one worked would be an idea approved, rejected, and kicked around endlessly during the second half of the twentieth century, the century of democracy.

"I'm surprised the poor people put up with all that wealth flaunted around them," my mother would comment later after we visited the Philippines in 1936. "They're such patient, wonderful people."

Forebears of the Justiniani family, with sugarcane plantations on Panay and Negros as their wealth, fulfilled the qualification for *principales* and were allowed to keep their power by mandate of the Spanish Crown, as long as they were loyal to Spain and sent the king taxes.

A true *ilustrado*, my father never talked about money nor was he ever known for the making of it. Like others of his class, his education exposed him to Spanish liberal ideas and national aspirations; as a youth, he was never trained for a profession, and so later in the United States, he was forced to take menial jobs. His work would give little satisfaction, but he would think of himself as successful because he could support his family in an honest way. In his new country, José would call himself a part of the "working class."

"We may not be rich," my pragmatic mother would say to me, "but we get to spend a week in Carmel or San Francisco every summer, and we can go to dinner in Chinatown with friends whenever we want!"

Ruth had one overriding desire—to go "back home" to see her family in Norway—a desire that lost its likelihood year by year. Nevertheless, she was doing what she loved and what my father insisted upon: as most mothers did in the 1930s, she stayed at home with her child. Ruth might have tired of José's diatribes against the American government, but she almost always sided with him. I can remember her repeating to her friends, "he's a good man, and he's been through a lot. He works hard for Patsy and me."

José made an art of his tirades against the United States for taking over the Philippines at the end of the Spanish-American war. Filipinos believed that the revolution against the Spaniards had been won and that Emilio Aguinaldo was the new president. He waited to tell me the grisly details later when I was a teenager. At the same time, he was obviously proud of his ancestors, the *principali'a* who intermarried with the colonizers. With European blood pumping through their veins, they admired pale skin and emulated Spanish customs. Visayan *principali'a* spoke Spanish as well as dialects. By the nineteenth century, Filipinos like the Justinianis considered themselves citizens of Spain, subjects of the Spanish king. Decades after he had left his home, my father would boast that "Manila built Santo Tomas [University] in 1611—twenty-five years before Harvard!"

"Oh, Pat, your father lost a lot coming here," my mother would say, looking up from her needlework when he told these stories. "He was from a well-to-do family and came here to no opportunities at all." She was his rock and comfort; she gave him esteem and dignity.

In Negros, outside of the small town of Saravia, José's parents built their Spanish-style hacienda on the edge of the cane fields.

"*Ai-abao*, yes," my father would recall wistfully. "The hacienda was a big place, big house, lots of land, mostly for sugarcane planting. Seven of us were born there."

From an old, white box filled with photos, he pulled out a picture of a commanding house fronting a circular drive, connected to a dirt road that he said led to Saravia. As he sat there remembering, his soft, brown eyes would stare into a distance beyond the photo, and he would be that child again, playing outdoors with his brothers, running after balls, stealing a ride on a *caribao* in the fields.

The house stood apart, in form, feeling, and geography, from the neighboring houses that were built of simple thatch or wood. Under a heavy peaked roof that covered porches and shutters of the massive painted, wooden dwelling, José and his siblings ran through two stories of rooms. In the mornings, barefoot servant girls rubbed cloths over china and silver cabinets, armoires with long mirrored doors and carved feet, heavy chairs and tables of mahogany and other tropical woods, some ornamented with carved floral patterns in the vogue in Spain, others in Islamic design inlaid with ivory and mother-of-pearl. Other servants cooked and served elaborate meals; still others tended the garden or guarded the estate. No one in the Justiniani family questioned their position or possessions; they, like other *principales*, simply accepted their heritage of wealth and power in the provinces as their due.

Florentino, authoritarian plantation owner, had friendly peers and peerless foes. There were other landowners who owed him money, workers who had grievances with him, squatters who resented his rule. My parents' weathered, black, leather-bound album is filled with an amazing assortment of family photos, alternating tawny brunettes on one page with creamy blonds on the next. In the front, fastened by four black tabs, is a photo of my grandfather, his face gazing sadly out of the pale, washed-out chemicals of early twentieth-century film. He is handsome, with Filipino smooth skin and full lips, a European long nose with a high bump, square jaw, and a receding hairline inching toward baldness, rare in Filipino men. He was over fifty when the portrait was taken, and his face shows the blows of many deaths, the unsuccessful struggle to see his nation free, a son's sudden exodus to a foreign land.

Florentino's house was his stronghold, his wife was his strength, and the lively sounds of children pervaded the house like birds singing in a cage. Maids cared for the children, freeing Enriqueta for other work—bookkeeping, shopping, managing the hacienda, as well as enjoying the various pleasures permitted Filipina women of wealth. There was no picture of my grandmother in the black book. She may have died before photographs were common in the provinces. But a large print of her sister Daida, taken at a studio in Manila around 1910, shows a beautiful, slim woman with a pale, oval face set with regular, delicate features. In the photo, Daida wears a traditional Maria Clara dress with large, crisp butterfly sleeves and a train.

"After siesta sometimes my mother played *pangingi* with other women from the neighborhood," my father remembered. The card game was a favorite of Filipina gentry, who arrived simply dressed in short-sleeved cotton blouses tucked inside wrap-around cotton print, floor-length skirts. Maids served *merienda*, a Spanish-style afternoon meal of thick hot chocolate and pastries.

"Oh, my gosh, maybe nine or ten women came from all around. I stood at the table watching them turn their cards over—and laugh—and talk, so much!"

Young women would nurse babies while older women with glossy hair pulled back in large rolls gossiped; middle-aged matrons, whose hefty figures told of their wealth, sat next to tiny, elderly women quietly smoking cigars as they scrutinized their cards.

"We children also played a lot of cards, and gambling became very interesting to us."

"Yes," my mother might inject at this point, "I know how

interesting gambling was to you!" Sarcasm was not her gift, but she used it at times when a sore spot was touched.

José would generally ignore this type of intrusion and go on exuberantly with his narrative. The most forceful image of Enriqueta emerged from my father's story of the day a gang of bandits kidnapped him and his young male caretaker, Benito.

"You see, these men picked us up from nearby fields and carried us into the mountains on horses. They said to be quiet and they would not hurt us. But my nurse, Benito, a young man, kept asking them to please, take the small child back—I was about four years old. The leader got mad at Benito—he cut him with a knife so that he was bleeding.

"Oh! I did not know what to do—I kept begging the man, 'Please don't, Señor! We will not do it anymore!'"

"How did they find you?" I wondered.

"After a few days my father and a lot of men searching for us found us in the mountains and brought us back on their horses."

"What happened to Benito?"

"Augh, he died of gangrene," my father murmured.

"Ooh! What happened to the bandits?"

"They took them to the jail. And, oh yes, when we were there, my mother came rushing in, screaming at the leader, and oh, my God! She took off the big ring of keys she wore at her waist, and she hit him in the face with it!" He laughed, remembering the shock of his mother's actions.

José always lamented the death of Benito—and explained with disgust the reason they were held hostage. "The kidnapper was mad at my father and asked ransom for me, his small child."

I felt grief for the child who thought he'd done wrong and bravely bartered, not entirely successfully, for their lives.

"Isn't that awful, Mama?" I would say.

"Yes," she would answer, "he was so young to have that happen to him—but I also had lots of things happen to me as a child. I thought I was responsible for a fire that burned down the whole town once, because I was bored and wanted something exciting to happen!"

Occasionally, the story-telling turned into dueling legends. My dad was more persistent and usually won.

Enriqueta glittered in my imagination, her huge ring of keys suggesting authority and, if necessary, weaponry fit for relieving her righteous anger. I imagined my tough grandmother as a composite of her sons and daughters whose photos emerged from my father's cardboard box or the black album: oldest child, Isabel, wise and plain; beautiful Maria, with high cheekbones and narrow nose of Spanish delicacy; youngest, Rosa, round, child-like face; young Ramón, dark skin with Iberian gentility; eldest, Manuel, short and wiry; second son, León, sturdy and responsible; middle child, José, good-natured and irrepressible. I thought my grandmother proficient and fearless and most likely as pretty as her sister Daida.

Enriqueta died a few years after the kidnapping, while giving birth to her daughter Rosa (who would die in her early twenties birthing stillborn twins). With the death of his wife, Florentino lost his zest for life. Children were turned over to nurses or older siblings. In the new century, the patrón became depressed and withdrawn. Embittered by political strife—the painful days of two revolutions throughout the islands—and the loss of Enriqueta, he gave up.

"He gave the plantation to the oldest son, my brother Manuel, Manong" my father said.

But Manong—big brother—did not want the plantation, preferring instead the prodigal's life in Manila. Surrendering to a dandy's existence, he gave his birthright to second son, León.

A large man in size and gesture, León could run a plantation or rule a kingdom. He quickly created a flourishing sugarcane empire and a life of abundance for the younger children.

Four

The years of revolution left a mark on my father, despite his young age. He talked about that period whenever the opportunity arose, showing his deep pain over the Philippines' lack of independence, the anger over injustices he saw, as well as the pride he felt in his people who had fought for social justice and been defeated over and over again.

"We went from one ruler to another," my father sighed, "and from one war to the next. We didn't know what was happening!"

In the late eighteenth century, the *peninsularies* (Spaniards born in Spain) rushed to invest in Philippine land and capitalize on a growing export economy. *Principales*, who wanted control over agriculture, were not pleased, nor were they happy when, in 1813, Spain repealed a law admitting one Filipino representative to Madrid's court. By the 1820s there were complaints of unfair taxation and brutal working conditions for laborers, by the 1850s, there were calls from the Filipino Catholics for a native priesthood. Then, spurred by the successful 1876 revolt in Mexico against its corrupt government, a group of *ilustrados* demanded reformation of their government.

Around the dining tables of *ilustrado* households, families denounced the Spaniards, delighting in plans for ousting the colonizers and liberating their island nation. "This is not right!" was their cry (a saying I can remember my father uttering when reading the newspaper or listening to radio broadcasts). Still the flag of their republic lay hidden in drawers, and revolution lay years away. The firm convictions of José's family and friends planted within him seeds of concern for freedom and justice. But years later in America, the seeds bore a tree of bitterness, and its roots sank deep within him, its branches choking him in unresolved anger.

The *ilustrados'* loyalty to Spain turned to defiance as their requests were scorned. The Spaniards initiated reprisals. Filipino leaders were persecuted, and by 1896 many were imprisoned and executed. Houses were searched, arrests were made, and behind closed doors people talked of *los desaparecidos*. To Spaniards, talk of reformation stimulated rebellion, rebellion meant subversion, and subversion had to be snuffed out quickly.

"My father and my uncles talked about strangers who came to the door and took men away," my father said. Appearing at night, when only iguanas were awake, grunting in the tall grasses, they would pound on a door and without comment carry off a husband, a father, a son.

"Oh, my God, they were never seen again! They would just disappear!" José almost whispered, remembering his family's outrage, the desire for reformation slowly spiraling into revolution.

"They were never seen again?" I asked incredulously.

"No, never," he answered softly, "we guessed they died."

"Lots of our leaders were sent to school in Spain by the Spaniards," José explained, "and they learned how to beat the Spaniards at their own game!"

Nationalists such as Andres Bonifacio, Gregorio Del Pilar, José Rizal demanded fair treatment from Spain. For their demands they were imprisoned and executed, or killed in warfare. By August of 1896 most reformers opted for total revolution and a vision of a republic for Las Filipinas governed by Filipinos.

"They were not just scholars and writers, but statesmen who could lead a republic for our people."

The nationalists swore they would give their lives for the freedom of Las Filipinas—and most of them did. Secret meetings proliferated; whispers of independence flew from hearts to lips, from spoken words to weapons.

School children memorized the political martyr Rizal's farewell to the Islands, *Mi Ultimo Adios*, a long poem the reformer wrote in prison while he awaited execution by firing squad, the fate of subversives. Into his late eighties, my father would remember the way his teachers said the poem had been recovered: Rizal wrote his farewell address the night before execution. He told his sister, "when you come to get my body, look in my shoe for it." They kept it a secret from the Spanish until the Americans came, and then they could publish it.

José had memorized in Spanish four stanzas of the poem. After the first long stanza, I was glad that he couldn't quite recall all of the others—even though for a stanza or so my mother and I did respond to the poetry of the physician and polemic author: *"Adios, patria adorada, región del sol querida, perla del mar de oriente, nuestro perdido Eden... ."* "Good-by, beloved country pearl of the orient sea and realm of the sun, our lost Paradise... ."

As José orated the verses with drawn-out, dramatic intensity, I would fidget until Mother entered and said, "that's

enough. It's beautiful, but it's so long, and we don't understand a word!"

Undeterred, my father would explain, "with Rizal, we were
going to obtain our freedom! But after Spain was kicked out,
American soldiers stayed and U.S. administrators too! They
said the Filipinos were not fit to govern themselves. Too backwards!"

At this point his resentment always took over; sarcasm and
curses consumed the story. I quickly tired of his unrelenting
animosity and went off to listen to Tommy Dorsey records.
Later, during World War II, I did not believe this history that
was not in my school books and distrusted my father—not my
country.

But the facts were these: On June 12, 1898, Filipinos
declared their independence. Six months later, on December
10, at the Treaty of Paris, Spain ceded Guam, Puerto Rico, and
the Philippines to the United States for $20,000,000. On
January 23, 1899, Emilio Aguinaldo was elected first president
of Las Filipinas, but the United States ignored the new government, and American troops closed Filipinos out of Manila. On
May 4, 1899, an American soldier on San Juan Bridge guarding the eastern entrance to Manila shot a Filipino soldier who
didn't respond correctly. Filipino comrades shot back, and the
Philippine war with the United States began. For two days
American warships offshore and gunboats on the Pasig River
shelled *nipa* huts, while onshore soldiers shot or bayoneted
anyone who dared show up in the streets. The bloodshed
spread through Luzon. In forty-eight hours, the United States
Army had killed more Filipinos than the Spaniards had in
three centuries.

In the early 1970s when my father told me of this story
and the atrocities of the Vietnam War were being televised
every night, I groaned, "sounds like My Lai."

"Huh! You bet your life! Worse! Everyday!"

Family and laborers depended on Florentino. But he was helpless against an army with modern military equipment and zealous tactics.

"*Señor!* Patrón! They have set the fields on fire!" A cane cutter ran to the hacienda to tell his employer of American military activity. Hand crushed to his forehead, Florentino gaped unbelieving from the veranda of his hacienda, dark eyes staring at smoking fields.

"Get the people out, Miguel!" he yelled. That was all he could do; he had lost his power. Even though he was a landowner and nationalist, he was no longer patrón, *ilustrado, principal, hidalgo,* Somebody.

If the Filipinos wouldn't surrender to the United States Army, officers were advised to starve them into submission by ruining the crops. President William McKinley declared the expedition had the "twofold purpose of completing reduction of the Spaniards' power and of giving order and security to the islands while in the possession of the U.S.," to "educate" and "uplift" the Filipinos, to subdue the "uncivilized" natives, and to introduce democracy in the name of Kipling's "white man's burden." This translated into atrocities throughout the archipelago. It was obvious the Filipinos needed civilizing, for they fought back savagely.

All classes of Filipinos now angrily craved freedom; women and children resisted in their own ways, burning bridges, cutting telephone wires. Military offensives were continuous and racist (the term "Gook" originated here), as the populace fought back. The United States command employed counter-insurgency methods, including cutting down all palm trees, a source of *principali'a* wealth.

There were moments of grace: An American officer buried reformer Gregorio del Pilar with full military honors, saying he was "an officer and a gentleman." The officer who captured Aguinaldo almost lost a promotion to Brigadier General due to the American public's disgust for his covert methods. The Congress and the people of the United States were split down the center between pro-expansionist and anti-imperialist ideologies. The debate to annex or liberate dragged on for two years in Congress and in 1901 passed in the Senate by one vote. The war continued until 1902, claiming three thousand American soldiers, three-quarters of whom died of tropical diseases, and two hundred fifty thousand to over five hundred thousand Filipinos, depending on who was recording.

"They sent these pictures of half-dressed mountain people to America to say it represented us—oh, my God!" Cluck, cluck, went my father's tongue. "As if we all looked that way! They needed us so they could join the Europeans with American Imperialism!"

Pictures of mountain tribes with numbers on their chests, loin cloths knotted around their waists, and spears under their arms were exhibited as typical Filipinos in books and in the United States at expositions such as the Panama-Pacific in 1915, rationalizing American possession. As if *principali'a*, *ilustrado*, and José Rizal had never existed.

"Oh, José, don't be so bitter. You're all right now! When is the *mungo* supposed to be done? Come in here and check the chicken." My mother called from the kitchen. Usually she tried to console his acrid memories, but at this moment dinner was more important.

Now the United States was a world power with a military base in Asia. The American public knew little of this war, reported mainly in Southeast Asian newspapers, and it was soon forgotten by most. William Howard Taft was elected in 1901 as first Civil Governor of the Philippines, and his benevolent government won an elective Philippine Assembly in

1902 for Filipinos. A congressman from Wisconsin swayed the House to a yes vote after reading what he termed the "lofty" and "pure" words in a translation of Rizal's epic poem.

President Aguinaldo led his army in a three-year struggle for their republic, but after arrest in 1901, he walked humbly to the American negotiation table in Manila. While surrendering, he praised Filipinos: "[Y]ou have loudly proclaimed your love of liberty, and solemnly pronounced before the civilized world, that you would fight for freedom until death." In the hills, guerrillas continued to fight, but by July 4, 1902, most partisans turned in their arms and crossed fields, walking back to houses and huts. Defeated again.

In an American school in the Philippines, José hung his head. Fluent in Visayan dialects and Spanish, he hated studies taught in a language he'd never heard before—English.

Born at the end of the three hundred thirty-three-year reign of the Spaniards, José had attended schools run by Spanish priests; their instruction was haphazard, their cruelty de rigueur, their punishment by switch.

"Sometimes I would wet my pants when they beat me," my father recalled, shaking his head. He hated the priests. "I don't know why they thought they were teachers—when they were only priests. And I don't know why you need something between you and God anyway!"

In the first three centuries of Spanish rule, only the children of *principales* could attend secondary and higher schools. But by the 1860s, Madrid's more permissive period, secondary education was open to all children in the Philippines. The Jesuits' *Escuela Normal de Maestros* placed the brightest senior students as teachers of the younger students. When Spain left the Islands, America took over the schools even as the Filipino-American war continued. For the next ten years, schools often closed temporarily, due to military actions by Filipino resistance forces.

In an attempt to Americanize the Islands, American soldiers were installed as public school teachers. Eventually, accredited teachers from the United States arrived on the ship *St. Thomas*. Most of the Thomasites, as they were called, were ill-prepared—lacking books and teaching materials, debilitated by the climate, inexperienced, unacquainted with local customs.

"We thought the Americans were stinky," my father laughed, "because they sweated so much, oh, my God."

"I'm sure they were suffering!" Ruth said. "I know I would have been!" From a frigid northern nation, she understood the misery of heat.

"Hunh," José grunted. "I hope so! They should not have been there in the first place!"

The disapproval of the American teachers proved as stinging as the whippings of Spanish priests. Asked a question he couldn't answer, José simply smiled in subservient obedience.

"What's the matter?" demanded his teacher. "Are you smiling to cover your stupidity?" José's dark head drooped lower. Deep inside, feelings of dishonor arose.

He lived in a land where overlord Spaniards had deemed Filipinos ignorant and barbaric, needing Spanish culture and Catholicism. With the defeat of the Spaniards, without a skipped beat, Filipinos were whisked into the care of Americans, who found them ignorant and barbaric, needing Anglo-Saxon technology and Protestantism.

"The Spanish beat you up if you didn't know the lessons," José recalled. "The Americans were different, more friendly. But not outside of school. The Spanish said, 'I don't like you, don't come near me.' The Americans said, 'My brother, my friend,' but with restrictions. Outside of school you are a piece of dirt." Best thing, José decided, was to smile, say "yes, sir," walk away, and do what he wanted. He perfected the Filipino ability to adapt, adjust, and carry the burden within.

After a few years, the United States Department of Education gave up trying to place American teachers in the provinces. Instead, retaining the American public school ideal of education for all, the administrators put the oldest and best Filipino students to work teaching the younger ones.

"So then," José said, "the American Normal School continued to train children of *principales* as teachers, as they were used to doing during the last years of the Spanish time." In this way, each colonial order perpetuated and validated the class system of ancient times.

José, María, Isabél, Ramón, Manuel, León, and Rosa completed two years of Normal School which prepared students for American-style elementary and secondary teaching careers. His sisters in stiff piña (pineapple fiber) butterfly-sleeve dresses, he and their brothers in starched high-collar, white cotton shirts, ties and American-style suits graduated from their studies. They stood in a somber lineup with their classmates, row upon row of students, the embodiment of years of training, discipline, and obedience.

José, an instructor at nineteen, employed unconventional teaching methods. "One day—it was Saturday, it was very hot, and I told the children 'let's go to the river!' Afterward, I was going back to open the school, down below, doggone it, I saw the supervisor. Oh, ha, ha, ha! You know we had to use shoes when we were teaching, otherwise if no shoes, then socks and slippers. At that time I was running around without anything!"

He called to his scholars who were splashing enthusiastically, dunking each other in the warm water. Through the bushes he saw the American supervisor plodding along the road in the heat, removing his hat and with a handkerchief mopping off the perspiration running down his face—the face of a man determined to see that educational advancement in the provinces was being carried out as ordered.

José rushed his students back to their thatched schoolhouse, yelling, "come on, let's go!" They flopped like fishes into their classroom, settled before their books, their clothes still damp, their bodies unnaturally upright and at attention, José serene at the chalkboard, just moments before the master teacher appeared at the doorway. "Oh, hello, sir! Glad to see you!" he lied.

José always told this story laughing, but the fallout was not so funny. "On Saturday the supervisor fined me one peso for working with no socks but only slippers. I was making fifteen pesos a month—about seven dollars at that time. I said, 'I was working for fifteen pesos worth of work, but since I am fined, therefore, when I go back, I am going to cut down one peso less work than yesterday!' Everyone laughed but the supervisor. He was very serious. When he asked me if I would sign for next year, I told him I quit now. He said, 'You can't, you signed a contract, and the semester isn't over.' I said, 'Oh, no, I am just as free as you are. I look to go where I am free, can use my own initiative, away from a place like this—that fines me for no socks!'"

In Saravia, an American administrator was seeking six Filipinos to prepare for the career of postmaster and telegrapher in Manila. After a seven-month course, José graduated as a postmaster. "I got an assignment in Isabella, twenty-nine miles from Saravia—forty-five pesos a month! In this small town were four big shots: the president, the vice president, the treasurer, and the postmaster, myself. I received thousands of dollars in postal savings bonds, delivered every three months to Manila. One day three hundred sixty pesos had to be sent, checked, and signed first. Two hours later a Spanish farmer found the young messenger with the pouch, wounded and lying by the river, cut in the neck. Police brought him back, we gave him milk—it came out his throat. He told the judge that the man who signed was to blame—he cut him, when he was bearing the bonds. But, even though the truth came out, I was responsible for the money! The head man in Isabella got it fixed, but I was disgusted, took my vacation, and went on my bicycle to another town. And when I was gone, Isabella burnt down! My trunk with clothes and everything all gone! They assigned me to a place where I sat with twenty-three telegraphers in one corner all day. After two years freedom in management, now I am in the corner. I did not know what to do!"

Five

At home in Saravia, José, age twenty-one, considered the remaining vocations open to him and wasn't pleased with what he saw. As a member of a privileged family, he was an *hidalgo*, a gentleman, so he couldn't by custom, training, or inclination, till the soil or wait on others. His pride or *hiya* meant saving honor in the face of shame, and his independent spirit forced him to flee from orders, criticism, and rules. His American Normal School education had equipped him with skills in math and English, plus the odious teaching certificate, period. The universities of Manila and Cebu were, for all intents and purposes, closed to all but the wealthy students of Manila and Cebu. Now that León managed the sugarcane plantation—settled work José would have rejected, even if it had been offered—teaching or telegraphy were his two options. The first a possibility in Saravia, the latter—an exciting thought hit him—in Manila.

Without much deliberation, he decided to set out for Manila, the Islands' capital, lured by the glamour of big-city life. There, he continued telegraphy, the most technical achievement of his life. During my childhood, my father liked to impress me with his knowledge of the Morse Code. "Tap, tapa, tapa, tap, tap," he would vocalize in a somewhat musical style. "That's the signal for—oh, no, that's not right—tap, tapa, tapa, tap, *Ai-abao*, I cannot remember so much of it anymore!"

One weekend on a day off, he searched out the house of a school supervisor he had known in Saravia and who now lived in Manila, a Mr. Rogers, who had seemed to be sympathetic of the young man's kinetic energy.

"Mr. Rogers? I am sorry to bother you, but is there any way I can go to the United States?"

"Yes, José, why don't you go to America? A bright young man like you would really like it there!"

In 1913, eleven years after the American occupation began, United States colonial policy encouraged Philippine-American educated Filipinos to visit the United States, to grasp the culture firsthand, and to return to the Islands, bringing back western ideas and capitalist methods. (Between 1903 and 1910, about five hundred students went to United States universities; about two hundred returned to become lawyers, doctors, politicians.) José's benefactor helped him obtain a visa and free ship passage; he also gave José a small loan, which the young Filipino promised to pay back once he hit pay dirt in San Francisco.

Impetuously, José sailed away to America. He left, without word to his family in Saravia, confident that they would always be there when he needed them. Besides, family was not the priority calling him now.

"You didn't tell them you were leaving!" I exclaimed. An only child, I marveled at his independence and his cruelty.

"No—I wrote them when I got here," he told me, tightening his jaws.

"Don't bother him about that," my mother said. She had often heard this story since they met, a parallel to her own, and she always comforted him, understanding how much it hurt to leave family so far behind, to hear about their lives and deaths through letters. "He felt bad enough. We had brothers and sisters, not like you," she explained. "It's different when there are so many—it seems like they won't miss you. And you have a lot of freedom."

The idea of children running free mesmerized me. Children not accompanied by adults constantly, not closely questioned and warned of dangers. My parents had only one child, and they believed protection was their primary responsibility. They could take risks, but they didn't risk allowing me to be free.

"Anyway, no use crying over spilt milk," my father added, ending the conversation. He delivered this platitude whenever faced with a problem too late to change or too big to fix. His version of the Serenity Prayer helped him through difficult times, when he remembered it.

In the fall of that year, my father had stood starry-eyed on a steamship sailing through the Golden Gate Strait into San Francisco Bay. Seasick half the way from Manila, he had seen a lot of his bunk in third class. But now he had arrived: he was twenty-three years old and about to make his fortune.

Excitement turned to daze and despair as he wandered streets that weren't paved with gold, where he had no family, and still worse, no money to return home. On the ship he had met a few young men from the Islands, but they continued on to New York.

"I used to cry every night before I went to sleep."

"Really?" As a teenager I was shocked at this story of my grown-up, world-traveler father crying like a baby.

"Sure!" he admitted brightly. He'd forgotten the pain by now.

In San Francisco, just seven years after the big earthquake and fire, he met other Filipinos and formed a new family. A casting agent saw José on the street and chose him to work as an extra in films.

"This was tiresome," José recalled, "but I did it until they said 'now you are going to be a Chinese priest.'" He quit in a huff, believing that by pretending to be Chinese, he would lose face; in the Philippines, as elsewhere in Asia, Chinese were often successful middlemen and moneylenders and, because of that, despised and persecuted. Years later, as an old man, the one-time actor said, "I thought it was an insult! I guess that was really crazy, huh? Geez, look at where I could be today!" He would break into laughter at his youthful behavior and prejudices brought from home that made domestic work preferable to portraying a fellow Asian.

A friend in San Francisco told him about houseboy jobs—easy work, the friend claimed, quick cash, come and go as you please. The Boys, as they were called by their employers, were youthful Filipinos, also called *Pinoys*—a name used originally among Filipinos in the Islands to define themselves in the company of foreigners and later to identify those who entered the United States in the early part of the twentieth century. The Boys seldom saved enough cash to be able to return to the Islands; they died in America, single old men, still called the Boys.

My father told me, "sure, I am a *Pinoy*, but I was not one of the Boys. They were farm people, peasants from northern Luzon—lots of Ilocanos," he said, letting fall his regionalism and his class prejudices against *Pinoys* who had not been raised on the silver spoons of Islamic culture, Spanish prestige, and American education that being Visayan *ilustrado* had assured him. Nevertheless, José joined other houseboys in order to stay in America, and to eat. Working as a servant stabbed his *hiya* to the bone, but he acquired addictions that salved the pain: gambling a little as he had done at home and dancing that he had relished at Saravia's gatherings where guitar and *bandurria* (part Spanish guitar, part Turkish oud) were played all night, but now to different music and with diverse partners. Like the horses wearing blinders that pulled San Francisco's buggies, the *Pinoys* viewed only the city life, the crowded streets flanked by buildings, and the solace of avoiding *hiya* by running home as if beaten by America.

Although he had learned English from American teachers, José's tenses and articles changed with the winds, and idioms were a mystery to him. "One day, the lady of the house said to me, 'José, please go and set the table,' so I did—I went into the dining room and sat on the table."

"When she came in and saw me, she yelled, 'José, what are you doing?'

"'Just what you asked me to, ma'am,' I answered." Years later, he would include this with stories of life experiences—comic, sorrowful, or triumphant—that he related with great verve and embellishment to friends after dinner.

Houseboying was not exactly the American Dream, and so José took a fast train to New York City with his Visayan pals, following impulses of wanderlust and the belief that the bigger the city, the better. On the train they played poker, seven-card stud, jokers wild, penny-ante stakes. They drank coffee, laughed, joked, and fantasized that in New York their work and their pay would be so vastly improved, they would be rich men able to bet much more in the very near future.

But in New York José found the same and only work he could—or would—do. Domestic work abounded, since New York bulged with pre-income-tax rich who needed to staff their new neocolonial townhouses. The abundance of such jobs was a boon for José, since he had no skill in communicating his problems with employers, nor, for that matter, any interest in so doing. At an inkling of criticism or negative comments about his work or person, he would remove his gray service coat, fling it away, gather his belongings, and stomp out of the house.

Surprised, his employers would plea, "wait, José, we can talk it over!"

"Oh no! Not on your life!" José would retort and disappear with pride intact.

He and the other *Pinoys* sought the essence of life in America, big-city style. They recorded in enlarged black-and-white photographs their clowning in Central Park: my father standing on a stone monument, a political orator above his admiring crowd, or lying on the grass under trees, resting on a elbow, one knee up, next to a friend in like pose, feigning the indifference of rich Americans. They dressed in business suits, fitted vests and high, white collars, paisley ties, and silk hosiery. With sweet smiles on smooth faces, these trim *Pinoys* looked like painted mannequins in the windows of Fifth Avenue's glittering department stores.

New York's summer humidity rivaled the tropical heat of Manila. But in winter, winds blew icy, and snow pummeled the Visayans into frigid forms. José, like his friends, would encase himself in a huge woolen overcoat, silk muffler, and dark fedora, like those seen in store windows and in employers' closets.

José was tall for a *Pinoy*, with thick black hair, pleasant, rounded features, and smooth, dark olive skin. He and the other *Pinoys* blended well with all of the races immigrating from Eastern and Western Europe to the American East Coast in the early part of the twentieth century. One Visayan friend named Fred later became my godfather. The two were similar in age and background and soon were inseparable. And true to *compadrizmo* (close relationship of parents and godparents) in the Islands, José felt he had lost a brother when Fred decided to go "back home," through with America's false promises, open now to the real worth of his homeland. A small percentage of the *Pinoys* agreed and returned.

Single *Pinoys* found their entertainment in New York's gigantic dance halls, rectangular boxes encrusted with mirrors on every wall that showed all views of dancers, their costumes, and dance abilities. Dancing became José's passion, dance-hall girls became his white-skinned, light-haired partners, while night became dawn. Often he would dance all night, going to work early in the morning; he wore holes in his patent-leather shoes.

Dances of the day were the one-step, two-step, and the Fox Trot, rocking from side to side in two-four rhythm, from slow and sentimental to fast and furious.

After dancing, a Philippine obsession, José attended to his other Asian habit, gambling. Around card tables he learned sleight-of-hand from card sharks—how to make coins disappear and return with deft, twisting fingers—and how to amaze friends with incredible card tricks. Combing specialty shops, he invested in magical handkerchiefs, adhering coins, disappearing balls, and other hoaxes of surprise and grand illusion.

"I had lots of fun doing these tricks for people and went to lots of parties because they liked to see these things," José remembered. Nevertheless, this wholesome playfulness could twist toward a dark side. He relished practical jokes.

"I got tired doing tricks for these people, and they would keep insisting, so one night I balanced a fish bowl on a broom pushed against the ceiling. I told someone to hold it while I left the room to make the hocus-pocus for the bowl to disappear. Instead I got my hat and coat—and went home!" He laughed heartily at the imagined look on their faces. Behind such a thoughtless joke lurked the pain of a houseboy, restless and miserable.

For a paycheck and the promise of adventure, José signed up for duty in the United States Revenue Cutter Service. The Coast Guard entertained him with a tour of Alaska and the Aleutian Islands on the S.S. *Revenue Cutter Unalga*. Thrown in with cooks in the mess hall, he washed dishes and prepared menus alongside tough career sailors.

"They used to spit into the officers' stew," he confided with a grin.

Off duty and unable to get ashore, on a gray ship mired in gray waters merging into gray skies, the enlisted men played pent-up seamen's pranks. They drank hard, told vulgar stories, and made up ridiculous games. Sometimes, José's mates would put an apron on him and call him Mary! My father joined in the revelry, certain of his masculinity and fully aware of his shorter stature, slender frame, sparse facial hair, and delicate features compared to those of the hulking seamen. (In fact, he was proud of these characteristics. In his seventies, despite my mother's razzing, he used face cream, hoping to keep the smooth complexion that made him appear younger than his years.) Obliging his fellow sailors, he would mince around, hands aflutter, taking a lead role in the makeshift comedy.

Reenacting this tale to friends later would make my mother plea, "oh! José! Do you have to tell that one?"

Her discomfort convinced him this was truly a good story, and he continued to describe the slap-stick show, finally mollifying her with, "oh, it's all right. They were just having a good time."

In 1914, the United States entered World War I. Preparations for combat began in earnest, but not for José. As a "national"—the official status of natives of United States possessions—José couldn't apply for American citizenship, couldn't be drafted, didn't care to serve the Coast Guard in war. War posters of a stern Uncle Sam dressed in red, white, and blue pointing his index finger and saying with knitted brow, "Uncle Sam wants you!" may have charged up other men, but this patriotic pitch rolled off my father like rain off his slicker. In his creed, he had no enemy in Europe and didn't want to kill anyone. He also believed bitterly that "this was just another American war, similar to the Spanish-American, where the U.S. could pick up possessions—like they did with the Islands."

His honorable discharge from the Coast Guard in Seattle tells of a twenty-three-year-old who has progressed satisfactorily from Second Class Boy to First Class Boy in five months, whose Sobriety, Obedience, Proficiency, and Health are stamped Excellent. (No credit was given for female impersonations.) A photo from the white box shows a huge hall in Alaska draped with huge American flags. Standing in the rear and sitting in front is the entire crew, together with ten Eskimo women, four or five white women, and three white men. In the back, my father's dark face looks out inquiringly, pressed in the crowd of tall, white-skinned sailors. Another picture shows a hundred or so at a dance in San Francisco at Native Son's Hall; there are four Filipinos for every white woman, two white men, and my father smiling broadly. He has written "One of the happiest moments in my life" across the top and dated it October 4, 1917, two weeks after his discharge from the Coast Guard.

Released on the West Coast, José never looked across the Pacific toward the Philippines, but hopped an eastbound train heading to New York like a homing pigeon. In the big city, José continued his occupations of dancing, gambling, and employer-pleasing, guaranteeing his bosses the same qualifications the Coast Guard had noted, although their form had omitted any mention of *hiya*.

"These were my 'Happy-Go-Lucky' days," he reminisced. "No worry, no family, not much money—enough for the dancing only!"

But in the fall of 1918, he was hit by the Spanish influenza that raged through the western world like a medieval plague, claiming a third of its prey. The Spanish flu spread through war-weakened Europe and arrived in the United States by shipboard.

"Gosh, I did not pay attention to fever, chills—and then my whole body aching—I thought it was a cold or flu." At the epidemic's height, the *New York Times* reported over five thousand cases in one day, down to four thousand the next, lingering around that level until the epidemic ended in 1919.

"Once in a while they would close movie houses and theaters for a few weeks and then open them again—so crazy!" my father said.

The New York City Health Department warned restaurants about dirty glassware, demanded landlords heat their houses, pleaded for more nurses. But not to worry, this was America, and a vaccine appeared imminent. President Woodrow Wilson reported to the public in newspapers that all possible help would be offered the sick—up to the point of endangering the war effort.

"I lived in a room in a boarding house, run by a landlady who checked out all her boarders," José said of stocky, Scottish Mrs. MacGreber, an immigrant herself, a power-packed lady with arms and calves like bowling pins, who in a photo taken on the tenement-house steps on the Lower East Side sits with legs crossed, as well as she can, smiling demurely. She discouraged drunken, disorderly conduct: "A-o-u-u-u-t!" a rule-breaker would go. Likewise, she encouraged virtue. She hadn't seen José for a few days and knocked on his door. His feeble answer gave her the right to enter.

"My gosh, she came in, and I had this high fever. I did not know what to do, could not go to work—just stayed in bed! She brought me soup!"

Finally, Mrs. MacGreber, fearful of seeing this nice young man—who always paid his rent on time—die, called one of the free ambulances available to the needy and ill. José rode under the screaming siren but never heard it. To others who did hear, the sound of sirens was as commonplace as the obituaries stretched out page after newsprint page. The Spanish influenza was a skulking death figure, seizing those in their prime, skipping over children and the elderly.

In Bellevue Hospital, José was one of the lucky ones to land in a bed. "Oh, my God, even the halls filled up with people on cots," he recalled. "And when no more cots, mattresses on the floor."

Overflowing hospitals turned new patients away, and in Baltimore and other cities, there were no more coffins to be had. Acts of mercy equaled the misery. The wealthy offered their extra houses as elegant hospitals; nurses appeared as Nightingales to attend the sick and dying.

Lying in a ward with fifty other men, on occasion surfacing from his delirium, José would run his hand over his fevered head; he looked at his hand and saw a fistful of hair. "What the—?" Then back into oblivion. After three weeks he left the hospital, thinner of body and wavy, dark locks. In midlife, when his hairline was rapidly receding, he would blame the high fever, since Filipinos don't go bald.

Six

When I was a teenager, my mother and I did everything together; we were as tight as limpets on the rocks at low tide. We sat around talking endlessly—about the clothes we wanted to sew, gossip about our friends, giggling about the latest Frank Sinatra record. Other times—while preparing dinner, window-shopping at nearby stores, or bussing to movies where I got in for a dime—Mother told me colorful stories of a snowbound land of sunlit nights, surrounded by water, her home in Norway. When I was a child, I received them like fairy tales, but as I grew older, we talked woman-to-woman. She would reminisce about her youth in Norway, her family and boyfriends, and her early life with my father in the (to me) equally unknown and mysterious eastern part of the United States.

A couple of times, when I asked how they had met, I remember her telling me it was in New York in 1920. Friends had introduced them. "All of the people we knew back East thought it was so interesting—I had come from an extremely cold country, and your father had come from an extremely hot one! Our friends said we must really have been meant for each other!"

She chatted in her lilting accent as she recalled their dates. "Your father was so much fun in those days, Pat! We went to all kinds of places, and I knew I wanted to spend the rest of my life with him!"

My father told me years later that they hadn't actually been introduced, and I would realize then that she had hidden from me a truth her Victorian sense of propriety denied. But that's what she said much earlier, and before I could get details, the telephone would ring, or it would be our bus stop, and we would have to hurry, lurching to the rear door with the vehicle's sudden slowing to exit down the narrow steps into the street.

Ruth was a seventeen-year-old Norwegian girl who appeared in the early twentieth-century American "melting pot," accidentally giving her own little bit of momentum to the blossoming reality of America as a multicultural nation. She had arrived on a whim, and six months later met my father. She had sailed from Alesund, a town built on a fjord, the largest fishing town in Norway, several hundred miles north of Bergen, which had been a trading center since medieval times. Alesund was a region so enchanting that although (or because) she never returned, she would always be drawn to mountains, forests, and towns by the sea.

"Oh, Pat, it was just so beautiful—I don't know why I left." My mother in her down moods deplored the city of Los Angeles, the perpetual sun, the growing traffic of the 1940s, increasing crowds of people, diminishing natural beauty. She lamented her captivity there. We lived in a suburb called East Hollywood, close to the mountainous woodlands called Griffith Park, and she went there once a week to hike with the women of a gym club when they weren't off to Idyllwild or another wilderness area.

"If it was so good, why did you leave?" At sixteen, armed with city-bred cockiness, I protested the assault on my hometown and center of the universe.

"Oh, Pat, you just don't understand." She didn't feel like explaining; she didn't know if she could.

"Why didn't you ever go back?" I asked, more gently.

"Oooh, we were never able to," she said, dragging out the words, changing the pronoun to include my father, after twenty-some years of marriage, inseparable from any description of her life. "I would never have gone back without you and Daddy." When Ruth boarded the ship in Oslo harbor, she could not have known or even guessed that she would never see her mother, brothers, or sisters again.

My maternal grandmother Kaia smiles with lips pressed together, posing for a black-and-white photograph with my two-year-old mother, the fifth of six children by then. The year is 1904, and both appear weighted down so as not to fly away by heavy straw hats with huge, crushed-cloth flowers. Plump Ruth's gingham dress falls over dark leggings and sturdy, high-laced shoes. Her blond hair and round, piquant face contrast with her mother's willowy form and sage expression. Ruth stands on a brocade couch by her seated mother, twisting her mother's purse by the handle so that the photo blurs there. Kaia is primly pretty behind her glasses, a sprightly Mary Poppins wearing a ruffled yoke over a tightly fitted bodice, long sleeves running up to a choker collar held in place by a cameo. The photo occupies a corner of the page in the black family album; next to it lies a picture of my black-haired, dark-complexioned aunts in Saravia around 1915, attired in black piña-cloth, butterfly-sleeved dresses and long skirts, seated in an open field, dressed for their father's or their sister's funeral, my mother didn't know which.

"The same year this picture was taken," my mother went on, "when I was two years old, the entire town, built of wood, burned down. But the Kaiser helped us. The first Kaiser—Wilhelm, of Germany—came to Alesund every summer. It was his favorite vacation hideaway."

After the fire, the Kaiser sent four ships loaded with building materials, so that by 1907 Alesund was rebuilt almost entirely of stone, organized by an architect who turned the town into a designer's guide to Art Nouveau, the current European vogue. Alesund began the twentieth century known for its unique architecture, with rowhouses topped by domes, towers, and turrets and faced by curlicue wood and ironwork on medieval facades bearing Norse mythology.

Ruth flipped the black page. In 1912, my grandmother Kaia gazed solemnly into the studio camera lenses, mouth pressed into a smile, sitting straight with the dignity and acceptance of a difficult life. While she is at least twenty pounds heavier, she is grande-dame handsome. As in all other photos she wears dark clothing accented by a cameo or white ruffles, and her heavy Lapp eyelids droop—a family characteristic that becomes more prominent with age. Flanked by older daughters on her left, next to her sit the three children from her second marriage, two sons Karl and Rolf, one older than Ruth, the other younger than their five-year-old sister who hangs onto her mother's chair. By this time, Kaia had weathered even more than the storm of six children might ordinarily demand.

"She was just a saint," my mother sighed.

Three older half-sisters, Astrid, Oda, and Knutte, daughters of Kaia's first husband, Karl, are garbed in plain-colored, tucked and gathered, full-length cotton garments of the day. Oda's crossed legs under a long skirt end in high-laced shoes. All present secure, attractive faces. These studied portraits gave the impression of all the sitters as oaks—an expression of how they lived. The daughters grew into women whose personalities matched their faces; they followed their mother's example in fortitude and devotion, becoming wives and mothers and remaining in Alesund.

"Aaay, look at all of those Norskies!" my dad would gaily remark as he came in from the kitchen to peek at the album our noses were buried in.

"What are Norskies?" I had asked the first time he did this.

"Nothing!" my mother continued. "He's just trying to be funny. It's really 'NOOORskeh'"—pronouncing the word *Norske* for Norwegians, so that it sounded like a song.

Young Ruth watched her older sisters glide through rooms, their finery sweeping the floors; before a mirror they adjusted matching hats of great drama. "How I loved their dresses!" she would recall. "I couldn't wait until I could wear clothes like that! But when I was their age, the fashion had changed, and we wore those silly short skirts!" (The 1920s existed for the daring—women who were challenging the status quo, scorning rules, and living freely after the war. This characterization did not describe my mother.) Ruth hated her legs: "Even in flapper days, my skirts always covered my knees. I was a fat baby, and I walked so early, everybody was impressed. But I think that little meat and a mainly fish diet bowed my legs."

When Ruth's mother was young, she married Karl Kongsvold, a good-looking, quiet and religious man who was an officer on a three-masted ship based in San Francisco. While the Kongsvolds of Alesund were now seamen, their forefathers had milked cows and cultivated the earth.

In the Middle Ages, the name Kongsvold—King's Meadow—came about because the family managed a farm in central Norway. This farm developed into the inn that lodged the kings, serving them feasts, cakes, and cream when they traveled north and again when they returned home to the capital at Oslo.

The Kongsvold family migrated to Alesund at the edge of the Norwegian Sea, where men earned a living fishing, netting, or selling varieties of fish, dried cod a specialty. In the nineteenth century, merchant seamen continued the tradition of northern European trading that had begun in Bergen in the eleventh century. When maritime trade faltered, they simply picked up and went to other seas. As Viking meant "Son of the Fjords," these sons were businessmen on the high seas, sailing in fast, streamlined schooners doing the world's business. By the 1880s, times were hard in Norway as the country changed from farming to industrialization. The California coast was where the jobs were. The Pacific coastal merchant fleet was dubbed the Scandinavian Navy, due to the preponderance of captains and crew coming from Sweden, Finland, Denmark, and Norway. Some took out American citizenship papers, but others retained Norwegian status, returning home regularly. Wives remained in Norway nurturing land, family, and children. Norwegians loved the sea and ships: they would go where they could fulfill this calling. Kaia's husband Karl sailed from his San Francisco base to ports in the North and South Pacific for four years at a time, returning to Norway for a year after each duty.

The American ships owned by American entrepreneurs carried coal, lumber, and building equipment, some to Alaska, some to Asia, some to the South Seas. They worked hard, facing the whim of storms at sea, fires, attacks by pirates, and conflicts arising from many men confined in a small space. In a lifestyle common to port cities, Kaia and Karl were reunited for a year every four years; a child would be born before he sailed or sometime later.

My mother said, "after three children and about twelve years of marriage, suddenly, mysteriously—my uncle Karl—who was then captain of his ship, died."

Kaia received word, unbelieving. When had she last heard from him—just six months earlier? How had it happened? In Nordic stoicism, Kaia never discussed his death. And Ruth was always more interested in hearing about her absent father than about a man who was simply her uncle (four more were still living nearby). Bits and pieces of family scuttlebutt passed down through the generations to great grandchildren reporting that Karl contacted beriberi in Valparaiso, main port of Chile, died, and was buried there.

Kaia went on without obvious change in her life. But to Rasmuss, also a sailor, identical twin of Karl, the change loomed large, and he began the courting of his late brother's widow. Accustomed to the bizarre life of a sailor's wife, in a short while Kaia turned toward the attentions of her children's uncle and married him.

"They said Rasmuss had always been in love with Kaia!" My mother would sail off into the sea of her parents' romance, entranced by the siren call of her mother's magnetism. "He would have waited for her forever!" Ruth said rumors that she heard at home or around town added that while Rasmuss loved Kaia, Karl had also asked him to look after her if he should die abroad. To hear my mother, her parents' marriage was as flawless as a Norwegian traditional *blotkake*, strawberry cake, her mother's courage the batter holding the family together, her father's sense of humor the whipped cream topping.

While Karl Kongsvold had been quiet and reserved, Rasmuss Kongsvold was an extrovert and if not irreverent, at least improper. Joking and poking fun at others' serious business came as naturally to him as hoisting a jib. And although Rasmuss was the mirror image of his twin, with poetic good looks, brown eyes, dark hair, and a sweeping handle-bar moustache, he could dismay Kaia with his humor—a quality his daughter Ruth would later require, admire, and rue in a husband.

"When she was cooking dinner for us, he would come along, grab her, and dance her around the kitchen," my mother said, "and she would say 'oh, stop it now, I've got work to do!'"

Kaia had three more children with Rasmuss. "She raised my brothers Karl, Rolf, and me just about alone. I can't imagine how she did it," my mother would say in awe, since the duties of a mother to one were overwhelming her. "And always so sweet and good—she really was a saint!"

In an uninterrupted continuation of her existence as a mariner's wife, Kaia went down to the docks to wave good-bye to her new husband, first mate in line for captaincy, and like Karl, based in San Francisco. "It seemed like he was never there!" my mother lamented. "He came home every so often for a while, and then suddenly he was gone again."

My mother had a picture book she brought from Alesund that showed scenes of buildings, boats, fjords, and the sea. The center opened into a two-page painting in black and white of white-capped, rough waters that made me dizzy and fearful as a child. I would pull it from the drawer and dare myself to look at it. Dozens of small fishing boats tossed about on a swirling sea, where as many whales rose above the water's surface spouting white water and moving through and away from the boats. That was the only visual momento of her sea town that she had. As a teen, I imagined my grandfather sailing in those ships and on those seas and thought him a hero from another world—a Theseus, a David, a monster slayer, or giant killer of a man.

Grandmother Kaia raised her six children—each group of three neatly spaced at four years—with a full network of family still intact in the small town: two sets of grandparents, myriad aunts, uncles, and a profusion of cousins and their spouses. It might have been my imagination, but it seemed that Ruth's eyelids became heavier, much like my grandmother's, as she spoke of those years. And she might suddenly say, "let's not look at these pictures anymore; let's go down to the drug-store for dinner—wouldn't that be fun?"

Kaia had stomach pains that made her scream in the night; she also had no tear ducts, making emotional release difficult for her. This strange ailment mystified me when my mother described it, but Ruth insisted it was true, and so my grandmother never cried. (In later years, a doctor I asked confirmed that such a condition, although rare, does exist.) Kaia's pain tortured Ruth. Ruth suffered, too, toothaches from poor diet and no dentistry, worms that surfaced in the night, making her shriek, "Mama! Wrap me up!"

Her mother would enter the darkened room, saying, "quiet, Ruth, it will stop soon." Kaia would wrap her tightly in blankets, the only treatment at the time for pinworms, which children eventually outgrew. Added to these torments lay the craving in her heart for a father seldom there.

Kaia also suffered through money problems. Often, the checks from her sailor husband, thanks to the vagaries of mail delivery across the seas, were late or lost. Ruth said, "my father would have been dismayed to learn about this, due to his conscientiousness and his love for us. Sometimes I had to hurry across town to my grandparents' house to borrow money until the ship with the check came in. 'Go quickly now, Ruth!' my mother would say."

Ruth believed she played messenger to relieve Kaia from facing her parents. She had been raised in comfort by well-to-do parents—possibly her marriages endured through frowns of disapproval.

But Kaia was a strong, silent woman. My cousin Turi, daughter of my uncle Rolf, once heard our grandmother Kaia ruefully sigh, "it feels as if the mountains are closing in on me." Whether this signified Nordic angst during the frigid, dark months of winter, her own personal despair, or a genetic predisposition to depression remained my grandmother's secret.

Most of the Kongsvold family stayed and raised their children in this northern landscape. Their spirits flew at the gift of snow-frosted mountains and finger-shaped land masses that trailed out into the sea, marveling at their good fortune. But for some, walking in circles around the town, ever ending up in the same place, brought a crushing sense of suffocation. Later, both Ruth and Rolf, with the soul of Kaia, would follow a call to leave Alesund, her brother to Oslo, following an artist's career, and then Ruth to the land where her father spent three-quarters of his adult life.

While Rasmuss' absence from Alesund was a common-place occurrence at that time and in that town, he missed his family, and their presence in his mind grew stronger with the passing years. He sent his young daughter Ruth gifts from his travels, including a necklace of exquisite triachna shells, animal homes as tiny as fly wings, the same iridescent color, unwittingly bartered into extinction through avid trading by Fiji islanders with sailors. The necklace lay crumpled in a small tortoise-shell box with a domed lid, along with other small presents.

"I didn't bring much when I came from Norway, but I had to bring these!" my mother said, showing me how the necklace changed color in the light and uncovering cloth-wrapped spoons that said FIJI scattered among Norwegian silverware bearing her initials and a hand-colored postcard of a lovely brown-haired girl who must have reminded Rasmuss of Ruth, with a message on the back telling her how much he missed her and to mind her mother.

The Kongsvolds knew that Rasmuss loved the South Seas. His heart throbbed for those islands shimmering in the sun— like Nordic fjords wrapped in warm blankets of steam and heat. He maintained his family with his seafaring, enjoying the tropics, but dreaming of his pension and the day he could create a small business in Alesund.

Ruth's childhood of tobogganing in winter, hikes in the mountains, and lone fishing trips in small boats in the summer mirrored her independence. Rowing and fishing delighted her; that she couldn't swim seemed no limitation.

"From Alesund, a good rower might go south all the way to Storfjord—some people say the most beautiful fjord in Norway, with waterfalls and narrow places where the mountains come so close together! I didn't go that far, but I was very independent and brave in those days! I don't know how they let me go out into the ocean all alone—I would never let you do anything like that!" But apparently no one worried about Ruth out in her boat. The people of Alesund were used to the sea, and her independence was routine.

Christmas Eve celebrations meant the usual quarrels with brothers, visits from relatives, and a special gift such as a rare and coveted orange plunged into a stocking filled by the fat and jolly Juliesen. Relatives greeted each other with *God Jul!* and *Gladelig Jul!* as the night of *Julehilsen* was celebrated with singing and joy, and sometimes anger and tears.

"One Christmas dinner, my brother Karl pulled the chair from behind me as I sat down with a new doll with a porcelain head!" Down they went, the doll scarcely surviving, its head shattered into pieces (although mended, never the same) and Ruth nursing a broken heart and a deep-seated resentment toward Karl. "We didn't have much money to spend on presents—and such a surprise to get a doll! Oh! I was so mad at him!"

Observing Christmas Eve was one of the few Norwegian customs Ruth would maintain throughout her life, singing "Silent Night" in Norwegian for our family and friends. We urged her to sing the beautiful song until the Christmas Eve came when we had to force her. Bored at Norwegian clubs, she had made no Norwegian friends and had no chance to practice her native tongue, which eventually became peculiar sounding to her.

"Oh, no, Pat, it just sounds so strange to me," she would moan in embarrassment.

Visits in Alesund from married sisters starred "the beautiful one, " Astrid, the second eldest sister, who struggled with tragedy. "She was madly in love with a very good-looking man who had tuberculosis," my mother told me. She took care of him before they were married, through their marriage, and while he was dying. Kaia often cared for Astrid's children, who filled Kaia's house with bickering and crying to my mother's adolescent distaste. Her mother's role as grandmother puzzled Ruth. "She could have had time to rest, but no, she seemed to like having all the kids around."

Ruth routinely acted out her rebelliousness against her mother.

"I would run out of the house, yelling terrible things at her. I immediately regretted it half way down the street, and I would turn around, run back up the stairs and apologize. I was late to school every time!"

One day in 1915, Rasmuss, now middle aged, stood beneath the arching sails of the schooner, rocking in time to the waves on the slippery deck. He scanned the hills and valleys of the moving seas, the seas that had earned him a good living. The days of the schooner fleet were numbered because of the industrial revolution's introduction of the steam-powered ship. But Rasmuss was ecstatic. This was his last voyage, and he was heading home. After years of saving, he could now leave the sea, start a business, and live with his family.

"I was thirteen years old and so happy!" my mother recalled. "My dreams and prayers had been answered!" With savings, Rasmuss started a bicycle shop in Alesund, riding the short distance from their home on a two-wheeler even during days of snow or sleet. Ruth now had the family life she had longed for, with parents, siblings, security. She often biked to her father's shop to visit, bringing him messages or a hot lunch. These were bright days even in the midst of a white sky's blizzard—hanging around the shop, watching her father fix a bicycle or talk to customers.

Rasmuss' business flourished until the night the fire consumed much of the town, including his bicycle shop. He had allowed the insurance to lapse a day or two earlier; it was as though to him dangers existed only at sea. The family, in a state of shock, soon rallied. It was decided that Rasmuss would go back to sea, catapulting the family back to their former way of life. Guilt burned within my mother: the day before the fire, accustomed to the miracle of her father at home permanently and a tranquil family life, she had wished that "something exciting would happen." A young girl's fantasy became one of Ruth's obsessions, one for which she never forgave herself.

The family's endeavor to remake their lives came to a halt when a year or two later Rasmuss came home to die. Habitual headaches were diagnosed as a brain tumor. Loved ones sought an answer to "why did this happen?" and found it in an early accident: as a young man, Rasmuss had fallen from a ship's mast.

Ruth rushed home daily after school to read to her father. In her sixteenth year, after spending extra time with friends, she arrived home late to find he had died. Her guilt increased with her sorrow. "Why didn't I go home that day?" She would shake her head from side to side.

"But you couldn't have known," I said as I tried to comfort her in my teens, at a similar age. (It wouldn't be my fault, if my father died, would it? I asked myself.)

"Oh, no, I should have gone home right away," she always answered.

After her father died, home and homeland lost its savor for Ruth. Always plumply pretty, she lost her weight to the Spanish influenza of 1918, waking up after a few weeks of fever and delirium to a svelte and streamlined body. With bobbed brown hair, blue eyes, sweetly curving lips, and an elegant nose, Ruth was pleased with herself.

The war, at that point, had little impact upon her and her friends, too young to be enlisted. Since their country was neutral, Norwegians were stunned when German submarines decimated their fleet, killing over two thousand.

Asked about World War I and Germany's march into Norway, Ruth would say simply, "that Kaiser wasn't a good man like his father was," adding, "the war was bad for some women, a few who went with German soldiers. After the war, they dragged them into the center of town and shaved their heads. But I was never attracted by those blond Germans," she finished, with a touch of scorn.

"When I began to go out with young men," my mother said, "I hated the light evenings in Norway. You couldn't walk with your boyfriend in the dark!" English, Danish, and Norwegian men courted her, "but they were all so stodgy and boring." She felt magnetically drawn to dark men. Throughout her life, Ruth had watched with fascination the gypsies who trekked through Norway, shrouded in mystery, beautiful and strongly disliked by most Norwegians. Fleeing nineteenth-century European wars, some gypsies reached Scandinavia. From 1914 to 1954 they were banned from Sweden and found refuge in Norway.

"Stay away from them," the disapproving townspeople told her. "They lie and steal. And they kidnap children!"

She disregarded their judgments and daydreamed about those dusky people pursuing their nomadic lives. "The gypsies were always so happy, always dancing and making music! I wanted a daughter who looked like a gypsy!" she laughed and looked at me lovingly.

The gypsies' lives differed dramatically from Ruth's own,

dominated by the Calvinist Church, which frightened her with threats of a burning Hell and eternal damnation for impish transgressions. Sunday lessons flowed through the day into nightmares. "Oh, it was awful, the minister told stories of punishment in fire and flames, and I would dream about it." She didn't allow herself a spiritual encounter again until a brief flirtation with a California sect, which only intensified her distrust in organized religions.

"I never went to college, like we expect you to do," my mother would say, "but schools in Norway have always been good. A high school diploma is years ahead of what you get here," she added, mocking my country again.

"What do you mean?" I asked once.

She flared, "well, it's true, Pat! When I finished Norway's grammar school, the equivalent of an American high school, I could speak Norwegian, German, and English! But then, of course, without a college degree, the only job I could get was in a state food-stamp store. And it was so boring!"

She recalled her father and his returns from the sea, his tales of visits to strange places and wonderful sights he had seen, and the precious objects he brought back as presents. Her Nordic ancestors had always risked; didn't the Vikings sail south for adventure and acquisitions? Her brother Rolf had just ventured across the Atlantic to America and returned to amaze all with stories and gifts. Yes! She had it in her blood and now was the time to act! She would sail across the ocean to America, where romance awaited. She could come back whenever she wanted—the world was a glowing pearl to observe, touch, and experience! She would tell everyone what she had seen and bring them all presents!

Seven

My mother was standing on deck when her ship passed the Statue of Liberty. The lady's gargantuan size was a promise of what the future offered in this monolithic country, where people got land they couldn't see to the end of, where cows were the size of elephants, and where everyone had to start out at the bottom but soon became a millionaire. Ruth knew, she had heard all of the stories and believed them too.

As the ship sailed to a mooring in the East River, Ruth gaped at the 1920 skyline of lower Manhattan. Buildings veered into the skies—so many, so high! Jostling one another, the passengers transferred onto a lighter that carried them to Ellis Island. Ruth could hear the drum roll of the nearby city's traffic, see the bustling wharfs, see ships nearing the tip of Manhattan, the Jersey dockyards, and wetlands.

After a rough passage from Bergen to Oslo and from Oslo to New York, ten days to two weeks (she couldn't remember later) stuck in a tiny cabin, the young Norwegian was looking forward to docking, sightseeing, and adventure. But now she was held at immigration. The immigration hall on Ellis Island felt like incarceration; it looked like incarceration with its gray walls and high Victorian windows.

Ruth was irritated. "I wasn't an immigrant wearing a scarf and carrying bundles! I wasn't emigrating, and I didn't see why I should have to do all that silly stuff!" Decades later, my mother was still peeved when she remembered her first day in the United States. "I was never an immigrant!" Ruth would often say in Los Angeles. In her mind, Ruth was just a seventeen-year-old visitor who happened to stay. But immigration officials weren't so certain: in the 1880s, immigrants from Norway had packed states like Minnesota, Wisconsin, North Dakota, and Iowa seeking land to till—more than one hundred seventy-six thousand Norwegians, over nine percent of Norway's population.

At Ellis Island, without the sack of food clutched by emigrants, Ruth sat and stared, more and more aware of her own hunger as others dug into their bags. There were hundreds of people from all over Europe speaking unfamiliar languages, women wearing long gathered skirts, long-sleeved blouses, and fringed scarves, men in coats and fedora hats, all eating peculiar foods. Italian couples passed to each other provolone and dried salami; the smell of Hungarian potted cabbage pierced her nostrils; Irish families crunched their soda biscuits; she felt she could taste the Germans' bratwurst and hunks of dark bread. Some were seeking land, others asylum or survival. Unlike them, Ruth hadn't escaped famine, oppression, or death in coming to America; she had sought diversion.

"Then a Greek offered me half of his lunch," my mother related. He wore a dark blue coat pulled up to his day-old beard; his brown eyes were warm as he smiled. (All of their lives my parents referred to strangers as "the Greek," "the Korean," "the Slav," "the Czech." People were known by their ethnicity, because everyone knew that culture told the secrets of a person's life and capabilities, without the bother of looking beneath the surface.)

"Ooh, thank you—I don't mean to trouble you, but yes, thank you!" Dumped into the bureaucratic immigration clearinghouse, Ruth, the visiting Norwegian, found Solon, an emigrating Greek ("peasant," according to her) a temporary ally. In halting English, they exchanged introductions, first, their lands of birth. She, from a fishing town on a fjord; he, a cement worker from Thessaloniki, about to join a Greek community in upstate New York, about to become a rich man in the United States. Together, they suffered through the hours of health checks, paperwork, and fingerprinting.

From early morning until late afternoon, they waited. Once legalities were over, the American experience could begin. Heading toward Manhattan, Ruth looked at the goddess holding aloft the torch of freedom:

Give me your tired, your poor,
your huddled masses yearning to breathe free
The wretched refuse of your teeming shore
Send these, the homeless, tempest-tossed, to me:
I lift my lamp beside the golden door.

At the dock, Ruth waited for an aunt who never appeared. "Oh, Pat, I could see the tall buildings of New York there, it was so huge, so frightening—all I could think of was, I've got to get to my aunt's house!" Later she discovered that her aunt was expecting her the following day! "The Greek invited me to come with him. But I told him my aunt expected me, and I had to find my way there. It was easy."

Ruth, intrepid traveler, took a train from Grand Central in New York, to Bridgeport, Connecticut, using her efficient school-learned English. Having had an English boyfriend couldn't have hurt, I thought smuggly as a teenager.

Eight-year old cousin Mildred met Ruth at the door and became the self-designated steward of her formal introduction to the United States. Her pleasure became Ruth's discomfort.

"She called me 'squarehead'," my mother recalled. "What's that?" I asked. "Just a silly name for Scandinavians in America!" "But what does it mean?" I persisted. "Nothing! Everybody got a mean nickname." In fact, everyone did: mick, spik, wop, kraut, nigger, jap, kike, chink....

"Well, maybe they thought we had square heads," she laughed. She could joke about such things, even though she usually shook her head in dismay at the ridicule that accents of the newly arrived or those who continued to struggle with English.

Sure that there must be cultural bias behind everything, I guessed that earlier Norwegian immigrants had worn square-shaped hats or hair in a four-cornered style or had necks the width of their heads.

A lively rapscallion, the wiry Mildred ridiculed Ruth's Norwegian clothing and stilted English and taught her words that proved embarrassing when unveiled in public. When asked: "what do you think of the weather in America?" Ruth answered, "I think it is damn good!" Eyebrows hiked, mouths dropped. When my mother discovered she was swearing like a sailor in a brawl, she cried, then she got mad. "Mildred was a little brat, but I didn't want to tell my aunt and hurt her. I just had to be more careful—I guess I was a typical greenhorn."

Mildred was the only child of Ruth's Aunt Mathilde. Known as *tante* Tilla, she was widow of one of Rasmuss' five brothers and played the role of receiving relative in the States. *Tante* Tilla was large boned and strong; photos show her standing with legs wide apart, hands behind her back, curled hair cut above the ears, her lips wavy lines that showed the serious core behind her good nature. She worked hard and brooked no nonsense, but as all mothers, she had no idea of what her daughter learned in the street. Her old country ways sustained many strong beliefs that she would hold for the rest of her life.

I don't remember the impetus, but during my twenties, *tante* Tilla and I began a correspondence. After my first daughter was born, she wrote me, cautioning, "always lay your baby on the right side, never on the heart side." I asked my mother why and she had to guess. "Maybe she thinks it's hard on the baby's heart to lie on the left side. I never heard anything like that at home." We giggled about it, but it was really just another sign of my great aunt's love for us. I laid my child on her stomach to sleep as doctors advised us to do in the 1950s.

Tante Tilla welcomed Ruth as a daughter. So far from home, she longed for news. *Tante* Tilla, however, was no Scandinavian tour guide, and as a practical woman living on a widow's pension and the meager profits from a small shop in front of her apartment, she lost no time finding a paying position for her niece. She told my mother she should go into domestic work: "It would be cleaner, easier, and classier than factory work." She did not want her niece in a sweatshop; that was for immigrants! In homes, her reasoning went, Ruth would be around educated people, learning proper English. So Ruth made beds and set out ladies' clothes and, as a child, I assumed that was how she met my father.

"How did you and Daddy meet?" I would ask my mother in my teens, wanting to know the specifics of how people met and married.

"Friends introduced us."

"Who?"

"Oh, Pat, I don't remember."

Once past the boy-meets-girl preliminaries, my mother spoke eagerly of their courtship. "How generous and fun-loving he was," she would sigh. "He never worried about money spent playing one game after another at Coney Island, winning prizes for me."

High in the air on the Ferris wheel, Ruth could see the beach and ocean, then down with dizzying speed, her eyes closed; coming up she opened them to see the red and blue stripes of wool one-piece bathing suits. On the boardwalk, José threw baseballs at wooden bottles, punctured balloons with darts, bet on numbered cards. Ruth tottered away carrying dolls, stuffed animals, boxes of candy.

Besides amusement parks, Ruth and José did all the other things he enjoyed: driving, gambling, sitting on the beach, poking their toes in the breakers in summer, bundling up to walk in Central Park in winter, attending concerts (he possessed a shiny black, wind-up Victrola and Caruso records), and dancing in New York's dance halls. In their album, my mother pointed out black and white photos that pictured Ruth and José as a happy, healthy young couple, posing properly together on a mansion's steps. Other shots, too large for the album, showed them crushed amid hundreds of young people—most of them Filipinos, with a few white men and women—in a ballroom, smiling at a cloth-covered camera, during a *Dimasalang* (Catholic club) celebration for the Filipino community. My dad considered the photo indifferently.

"Oh, *Dimasalang* was for Tagalog speakers from Luzon, but I went sometimes anyway. Before I knew your mother I would wear holes in my shoes dancing!" José laughed as he recalled his breezy single life. Before they married he taught Ruth the rocking two-step, her left hand on his shoulder, other hands clasped, elbows out, fast paced and joyous.

"Gosh, he would dance me from one end of the dance floor to the other! I could see myself coming in the mirror at one end, and then we went so fast, I suddenly saw myself coming toward the mirror at the other end!" Ruth's desire for excitement was met by this dark-haired gypsy dancer.

Although Ruth had copied her brother in making a quick trip to America for fun and adventure, unlike him, she had bought a one-way ticket, sure her return would be as magical as her sudden sojourn to America.

"Rolf went for a little while and came back. It sounded so exciting!" But Ruth's father had died, and nothing such as a romance or a budding career like Rolf's art studies compelled her immediate return to Norway. She began to feel it an omen that out of six children she was the one given an English name.

"Well, Rolf could have been Ralph," I would say, each time she reminisced, since it was obvious to me.

"No, no! It's not the same!" she always protested, as if I were a sort of traitor. And she was right. After her death, I discovered among her papers, a baptismal certificate: her name really was Ruth, not Anglicized from "Rut," the way I heard her say it. The belief in the inevitability of her life with my father and its permanence lay deep in her soul, sparkling like divine fulfillment. For Ruth, sailing to America was like sealing herself off from her homeland with a curtain of sky.

Eight

A justice of the peace married Ruth and José in New York's City Hall in 1922. They had known each other for about a year. Alone at their civil ceremony, a clerk became the witness required. Afterwards, they took a train back to Connecticut for a dinner celebration hosted by *tante* Tilla. A few close friends joined them, and José's employer, Mrs. Harvey, gave them a silver tray with leaves etched on it and said she would give José a good recommendation.

A sepia photo taken the day of their wedding had its spot on my mother's bureau, next to a photo of herself in an ornate oval frame and one of José in a filigreed one. We lived in four houses from the time I was born, and this placement figured in every house. A studio photographer fastidiously posed the couple. Ruth sits in a straight-back chair, a brass lion growling on the open work above; a long string of pearls decorates her dark dress, her left hand lies in her lap, the two middle fingers precisely curled under, her feet crossed and placed on a circular pillow. She stares to the right. José stands, his left hand protectively on the back of Ruth's chair, his right hand neatly hidden in pocket. Dark pin-striped suit, gold watch chain, diamond stick-pin. He stares left. Their lines of sight could never intersect and yet the formal, posed portrait is intimate, conveying youth and attraction.

"A black and white couple got their marriage license the same day that we were there," my mother said much later. "Nobody gave them disapproving looks." Buffeted by many years of double-takes and worn down by whispers that stung like acid whenever she and my father attended PTA meetings, my mother's recollections of New York took on a Utopian sheen.

Ruth and José were in love, and *tante* Tilla wholeheartedly approved the match. She suggested they work together as a couple. "*Tante* Tilla and everyone liked him so much," my mother said. "He was so much fun, so generous, and such a hard worker. Everybody thought he was a wonderful man. And he had beautiful dark curly hair!" She'd laugh and push against him as they sat on the new couch from Sears, gold and shiny. "It's all right, dear," she'd say, patting his balding head and draping her arm around his shoulder.

To this, he'd insist, "well, smart people's brains are so big they push up through their hair!"

After the marriage, Ruth's family in Norway sent congratulations, happy that she was happy and, longing to see Ruth again, urging the young couple to visit so that everyone could meet José. But José and Ruth had no money for a European trip—in fact, they never would. Besides, by 1924, José's wanderlust was aiming him in the direction of California. Lacking white laborers, California had invited Filipinos and others to pick the crops. By 1925, the fields were a polyglot of languages, emanating from Filipinos and Sikhs to Turks and Portuguese to Basques and Mexicans (the largest group of all, numbering around three hundred sixty-eight thousand). All of these dark-complexioned folk worked the vineyards, orchards, and farms that were owned by whites. Japanese would not do stoop labor but leased farm lands (they were not permitted to own land in California) and hired workers. By 1930, thirty-five thousand *Pinoys* filled the fields.

"California has jobs, a Filipino community, good amusement parks at the beach—and warm weather!" my father told his young bride. "I used to live in San Francisco, and I am sure you would like it!"

For the first two years of their marriage, they had worked as a domestic couple in Connecticut and New York, an occupation they resumed upon reaching San Francisco.

"It was okay," José later explained to friends. "Working together in 'Frisco was good, because we could come and go when we liked to."

Come and go, in José's lexicon, meant leaving a job (within minutes) over a trifling criticism or mild disagreement. While this habit upheld his honor, it tore down my mother's sense of fair play. She wanted to negotiate, to settle disputes dispassionately, probably unconsciously to settle down, have a stable home and a child. In José's sense of decorum and pride, moving about was a sign of independence and personal dignity, whereas for Ruth, freedom and dignity were upheld by the security of setting down roots.

"José, can't we talk to them?" she would plead mildly, running behind him as he carried their few bags out to the curb.

"No! I put my foot down on talking to them!" End of conversation.

While they waited for the trolley, both would be silent, for they knew no words to describe the problem or discuss their differences. José would then try to smooth over the division with red roses.

Taking the bouquet in both hands, Ruth would smile and say, "how beautiful. Thank you, dear."

Without further complaint, she would set up housekeeping in yet another apartment or make pleasant the room in a house where they had been hired. She adjusted to what to her was his fiery, gypsy soul, the shadow side to all the fun and games the other side lavished upon her.

For two years they led their free yet confined life. Employers found them engaging. In a brown cardboard box, José kept all his letters of recommendation (among replies from presidents, letters from consulates, sisters, brothers, cousins, praise for good credit standing, legal papers, and a daily weight check of my first three months of life.) José was a "good butler, honest and sober," "an excellent valet, honest and of good character," "a responsible and reliable boy."

Ladies of the mansions mothered Ruth, advising her on clothes, saying, "Here, this dress would become you, Ruth, and I don't need it anymore."

Ruth didn't want hand-me-downs and began her great pastime of sewing, her clothes and mine, from patterns and materials we spent hours selecting, like the comic strip Dick Tracy hunting out criminals with a magnifying glass.

Ruth always deferred to her husband. In this way, she avoided the conflict that would have been too difficult to bear—quarreling with José. When I was having my own questions about a wife's role, she explained that she based hers on her namesake Ruth in the Old Testament, "who never questioned as she followed her husband." (Never criticized as she watched, never nagged as she loved.)

The scripture actually read that the widowed Ruth followed her mother-in-law and her people:

And Ruth said, Entreat me not to leave thee, or to

return from following after thee: for whither thou
goest, I will go; and where thou lodgest, I will lodge:
thy people shall be my people, and thy God my God:
Where thou diest, will I die, and there will I be buried:
the Lord do so to me, and more also, if ought but
death part thee and me. (Ruth 2: 16-17.)

My mother—who throughout her life turned her back on
religion—remembered it as commitment to husband and his
people. For my mother the sacrifice was the same as the
Biblical Ruth's, to leave her people and land of birth forever.

Ruth loved San Francisco. Its bay sparkled like Norwegian
waters, its harbor welcomed all nationalities. A city fashioned
after cosmopolitan European cities, its tightly packed rowhouses in Art Nouveau style painted white and pastel colors
climbed hills like houses in Alesund—both destroyed by fire
and rebuilt around the same time.

"Oh! It reminded me so much of home! I just loved it!"
she often reminisced. "I was at the ocean again, and the city
was so exciting! I saw why my father loved it! I believed my
father had walked these same streets and recognized the similarity to Alesund! I could have stayed there forever, but your
father—oh, he always had to keep moving."

While their marriage began to develop strong roots, deep
within Ruth's heart hope of seeing mother and kin sank like a
stone tossed into San Francisco Bay—now she lived nine
thousand miles from home, three thousand more than her
original destination of New York! Homesick, she concentrated on her namesake, Ruth, who, she said, "promised to follow
her husband."

In San Francisco's Filmore district, inside the small apartment whose bay window overlooked gray days and windy
streets where papers blew and walkers pulled their collars up,
Ruth miscarried, unaware she was pregnant. Hemorrhaging in

the night, Ruth had José call a doctor who arrived quickly and irritably. Paperwork followed the minor operation, followed by the cruel question, "was this an accident?" Ruth cried both for her loss and because of the doctor's disapproval. But Ruth's purity of spirit, like a fine lace handkerchief, was squeezed many years before fraying.

My parents accepted (or rather, my father accepted and my mother concurred) positions as butler and maid with the Musgrove family, a physician and his wife living in Ben Lomand, a pristine village in the mountains above Santa Cruz. The Santa Cruz mountains—lush with pines, laced with streams, scraping a crystal sky—were an American replica of the Norwegian landscape. Ben Lomand was another dream realized for Ruth, her dream and her body expanding with a new pregnancy.

José and the kindly doctor cared for Ruth like artisans tatting Norwegian lace. No more working for Ruth, only months of eating and anticipation. The perfect cow's life. Packed round and firm in abdomen, she was driven down the mountain to Hanley Hospital the day of her delivery; even the good doctor didn't deem himself worthy of officiating over this important event. José was panic-stricken. As a child, he had witnessed too many disasters of rural medicine, times when women in labor died, or if they lived, the baby, he shuddered, "came out in pieces." My mother had her own ideas, picking "the best doctor"—a progressive woman obstetrician—and insisting on delivering without anesthetic to protect her child. (Fifty years later Ruth's granddaughters would be the generation to rejoice in natural childbirth, in a full experience prepared for with classes, exercise, midwives, and a husband allowed to be part of the event.)

Health and welfare were my parents' priorities, and two ecstatic parents welcomed a seven-pound daughter in the early morning of September seventeenth.

"Oh, not having anesthesia wasn't bad. You can put up with it for a while to have a healthy baby," she told me later. A photo of my mother admiring the round-faced, olive-skinned newborn showed a short cropped, prison-style hairdo framing a pudgy face. "And I was so happy to see you, I forgot all about it right away!"

Resting in bed for two weeks, in a private room with private nurse (thanks to the benevolent doctor), she was enjoying herself mightily when in walked José with head and arm bandaged, face and body covered with cruel, red marks. Careening down the mountain to visit his family, he (a new driver) and a friend had flipped over in the Model T, abruptly stopped, nestled by bushes in a ravine. They had climbed out of the car and hitched a ride to the hospital.

Ruth gasped, "oh, my goodness, what happened, José?"

In his thick accent he answered, laughing, "Oh, nothing, just a little poison oak."

Ruth had my name ready, which was just fine with my smiling father: Patricia Corinne. Ruth, with a mind of her own, declared Corinne the American version of her mother Kaia's full name, Karen. My first name had more immediate definition for her. In one of their Eastern houses of employment lived a girl close to Ruth's age, wealthy, friendly, and slinky in a mermaid way. Her name was Patricia. She wore fashionable black shifts with embroidery and a length of pearls that accentuated her long neck under silky, black bobbed hair. The young immigrant Ruth stood in awe of the lovely Patricia. When the time came to name her own daughter, what better symbolic imagery could Ruth choose?

This led to arguments in my teen years that drove her to the brink of tears.

"Why couldn't you give me an exotic name like Delores or

Carmen?" I whined.

"Because *dolor* means sorrow, and Carmen Dela Piña was murdered by a jealous boyfriend." My mother had actually considered these names, but deep, fearful reasons for banning them ruled.

Unimpressed by my mother's logic, I sulked with a yearning for an assimilation of some kind. I couldn't relate to a wealthy Eastern girl, nor was I inclined to interpret so literally the name of one of the few brunette role-models of the 1940s (the Mexican Delores del Rio who starred in Hollywood movies), and I surely couldn't see what the tragic life of one of California's first mestizas had to do with me. (In fact, Carmen's father had emigrated around the time my dad had, but she had been born twelve years before I was, while my father was still wearing his shoes thin dancing.) I lived in a modern age. Clearly, nothing bad could ever happen to me, and my mother's irrational thinking had muddied my life.

She sadly replied, "oh, Pat, I thought Patricia was such a beautiful name."

It means wealthy aristocrat, I thought meanly, locked in my own prison of biases.

In my late teens I resented having to live in the backroom of a mansion. In fact, I balked at going to the "House," and my mother supported me by saying, "José, she has homework to do, piano to practice, and a drawing due for the school newspaper, she has to be at home now."

"Oooh, okay, Boss," he'd answer dejectedly. He needed us nearby.

While I dealt with my mother's superstitions, she dealt with my father's, whose magical thoughts consisted of Asian pantheistic beliefs, such as having the bed parallel the direction of the floor boards for protection. It fitted in fine with furniture arrangements, so I never suspected until I wanted to rearrange my room, and then I heard their whispered dialogue.

"The old people in Saravia said it's bad luck."

"José, you can't do that in America!" My mother beseeched him kindly.

Nine

The year after I was born, Dr. Musgrove died. His widow tried to keep José on, but without the congenial doctor, José lost interest. One of Mrs. Musgrove's guests told him about a job in Los Angeles—a place he had always wanted to see, and with a letter from Mrs. Musgrove, we all moved on.

"Now, José," said my mother, "this time, we will stay put for awhile. We have a child now, you know."

Fatherhood moved José from bucolic to urban life, from nomadic to settled, from butler-valet to house manager for the millionaire Earl C. Anthony, from independent, self-absorbed man to acquiescent, diligent provider for a family. The ensuing eighteen years of intimate living with neurotic people illustrated his response to responsibility.

"A family man has to do his job," José said, and he did, to the best of his ability—even if it meant settling down, saving money, inviting *hiya*. Another change would occur only after I was grown and he saw his shackled life through my youthful, cruelly candid eyes. Then, he would declare he had fulfilled his pledge, hanging up stable employment like a visitor's coat, going back to what he called a "catch-as-catch-can" life. Once again my parents would work as a couple, staying with an employer as long as José could stand it and not a minute longer.

But for almost two decades, my father worked for Mr. and Mrs. Anthony, as we always referred to them, almost an indentured servant, with long hours whenever demanded, no medical benefits or the promise of a pension or Social Security. (The Social Security program, put in place in 1935 as a part of Roosevelt's New Deal program, was closed to domestic workers until a more enlightened electorate required their representatives to append it in the early 1950s.)

Mr. Anthony was about six feet tall, big framed, with an outstanding belly that made him look from my child's vantage point like a gigantic, looming balloon. I would first hear his pounding steps coming down the hall to the kitchen, and before I saw him, hear his thundering voice calling out, "JOE! JOE!" My mother had read to me *Jack and the Beanstalk*, and he sounded like the giant on the top of the beanstalk, shaking the tree with his stomping and shouting. Then he would appear, flushed face, talking a blue streak, eyes darting, occasionally wiping his face with a white handkerchief. He seemed to take up the whole pantry, and my father transformed to a shrunken version of his straight, slim self, nodding, saying, "Yes, sir. Yes, sir, right away, sir," until I thought Mr. Anthony might really be the tree giant.

"Oh! I see you've brought your daughter today! That's nice!" he would bellow. "Is your wife here, too? Why don't they go in the pool? Get me the…and put the whadayacallit … ." He strode around the pantry and into the wine closet, giving orders.

"Yes, sir, yes, sir. Thank you, sir."

I would twist away from my father and run into the help's dining room where my mother was reading.

Mr. Anthony was a prominent Southern California businessman. He commanded the Packard dealership in downtown Los Angeles, and when we turned on the radio, we heard that it was "Station KFI, owned and operated by Mr. Earl C. Anthony, Incorporated." Everyone knew of his importance due to such incidents as one that had occurred nine years earlier, in 1920. A city ordinance banned downtown parking during peak business hours in order to handle Los Angeles' expanding traffic. The first day, one thousand tickets were stuck under windshield wipers. Merchants insisted sales dropped twenty, even fifty percent. Mr. Anthony was furious and promised litigation to prove it unconstitutional and discriminatory against motorists. The *Los Angeles Times* quickly dropped its support of the ordinance and the law was killed. The car (if not Mr. Anthony) became sovereign of Los Angeles.

The Anthonys' alcohol and drug-related problems were a new wrinkle to José. In the 1930s, many of the rich used drugs, and closed-mouth servants were their enablers.

Recalling his early years at the "House," my father would say, "but it was okay for Ruth and me during the Depression." A group of four or five Filipino friends and their wives would be sitting on the couch and arm chairs in our small living room after dinner on José's day off, some smoking, others with an after-dinner drink in their hand or cup of coffee to their lips. My dad was holding forth. "I always had work, because, you know, those dimn rich people always have money to spend even when the working-class people are starving in the street."

"José, do you have to swear?" my mother would ask. My father's profanity usually didn't jar me since it was mispronounced and just sounded like another language.

His observation rang true. José enjoyed a minor financial security from 1927 through the years of the Great Depression and World War II. Working for Mr. Anthony, whose fortune lay in luxury automobiles and national media, José figured he had been dealt an ace in steady work, the joker in stress.

José explained that although he was still in domestic work, he was lucky to have a job after the economic crash of 1929. He hugged his relative security to him amid all the unemployed: the homeless, gaunt-faced men in bread lines, ragged scroungers in "free-food dumps," farmers and office workers turned overnight into strays seeking work, failed bankers and stockbrokers. He had also heard stories from friends about bosses who lost their money, let their staff go, or kept them for room and board without pay.

In fact, he was now manager of a mansion, which he was put in charge of almost immediately upon arriving, the Anthonys recognizing a jewel when it fell into their laps. He directed a long line of gray-coated Filipino houseboys, white-aproned European maids, a starch-costumed Scandinavian cook or two, an Irish chauffeur, and rough-handed Japanese gardeners, who never entered the kitchen but quietly conserved their own community outdoors. (Why, now he could even have managed a sugarcane plantation in the Philippines—if he had been First Son or even Second Son—or if he could remember what a plantation looked like.)

"We like working for José—he's so nice," was a typical remark the maids and some of the Boys would tell my mother.

José and Ruth knew what living with the boss meant, and so, even though they gave up rent-free space and shelled out hard-won money, they rented a house of their own, within walking distance of the twentieth-century castle in the hills above Los Angeles. The rest of the "help" slept in the below-floors rooms, the basement, that entered onto the hall like a train's compartments, near the laundry room.

On the floor above, a main and a secondary kitchen (used during parties) and a pantry glowed with shining stainless-steel equipment (the minor kitchen looked like a laboratory). Heavy chopping-block tables, cupboards, and drawers filled the rooms, wall to wall and floor to ceiling. Through the windows I could see large junipers and the winding, paved road that led to the flat lands where those whom I considered wealthy lived. They were parents of my school friends, had no accents, were professionals, and owned houses with two bathrooms. From below, a car would drive up the left-hand side, which curved twice and met the other road that was one way going back down. If you could see through the trees and look down on it, the road formed a club shape like those on my dad's poker cards. The help approached the "House," parked, and climbed the stone steps to the kitchen area; guests and family drove on to the ornate, heavily carved stone front entrance that I never entered. The treads of the tires crackled, picking up gravel as they rolled along.

Next to the kitchen, the help's pinched dining room was our home when we went with my dad to work. We stayed in this area and ate with the cook, maids, and house boys.

"Why can't we eat in the big dining room?" I would prod, curious and restless. "I want to go into the library and see the books. Can I go in the pool?"

"Be still and finish drawing your picture, Patsy. Daddy is working," was all my mother said, as she resumed reading or crocheting.

I couldn't understand this situation until I was seven or so, when it eventually provoked in me an "us and them" mentality, an underground disturbance that later cracked the surface of our life like one of the region's frequent earth tremors.

When the Anthonys were not home, away on business or holiday, I played in their house like Goldilocks, trying out every chair and sofa I passed in the living room, opening every silver cigarette box and inlaid wood box I came across, counting mirrors in the antique-gold bedroom, the pink bedroom, the blue bedroom, and so on. Mrs. Anthony's had the most mirrors, maybe six, while the others made do with one or two in carved rococo frames. In the bar—a small room my father didn't like to take me into—lay bottles of yellow, brown, and white liquid in frames from floor to ceiling. A genuine saloon with sinks, mirror, counters, metal foot-rod, leather-covered stools, in it I studied with alarm a large black-and-white photograph of a nude female barmaid with cumbersome breasts offering drinks to the viewer. In the great library overlooking Griffith Park, I would plunge into great, soft leather davenports. Then I would peer into the three-dimensional vistas I saw in the steropticon.

During parties, my father pushed me forward (as we tried to stay out of sight at the same time) to see the dazzling visitors in the company dining room, one of the secret peeks the staff could manage. As a child it was ordinary, but as I grew older, it became uncomfortable. I felt a lumbering about in my chest—a rage not recognized until later when I learned how to spot my own anger. I wanted to get away. But from toddler to teen, I did peer in at gala dinners and entertainments in the huge dining room where my father carried great silver trays laden with steaming delights, directing the rest of the staff where to cart what and when.

Colored lights blinked on and off in the pantry signaling the need of a person or object. In two bustling kitchens, fairy-tale visions came true: three huge ovens held turkeys and hams, spitting and hissing, competing with sautéed filets of lamb, Chateaubriand of beef, or slim slivers of salmon and roasted pigeon; meat and vegetables sauced, gravied, creamed, glazed, molded; glints of red pimentos in green olives, rose-cut radishes touching shiny beads of black caviar next to dishes stuffed, puffed, salted, trussed, grated, buttered; followed by desserts *a la Parisienne*, flambé, *plombière*, petits fours; all well-developed foods, teased and tortured beyond recognition.

Meanwhile, Ingeborg, the cook, presented her gift of desserts. Carefully, she would cut French logs, whipped-cream-packed chocolate rolls, sliding each slice onto a golden-rimmed plate decorated with a pink rosebud, one of the many sets of service I unconsciously studied for their color and design. When all were cut, and Pedro and Custodio (*Pinoys* who were family friends) carried them to the guests. I would drop from desire as each wedge traveled to its destination. After my solitary cut, any seconds would be channeled to guests still sitting in the long and high, mahogany-panelled dining room, hung with heavy embroidered tapestries with scenes of a royal court in France or Germany, echoing the chosen few who were there that night. The weighty burgundy drapes were pulled aside revealing the full-length wall of glass and a view of the spot-lighted, kidney-shaped swimming pool beyond. Inside, hovered over by chandeliers, candles glowed on the table and glittered from sconces on the walls—it seemed a medieval knight's banquet hall. Once my father placed me in a discrete, secret spot where I could see a hula dancer wiggling around the long table to *Aloha Oe*. Men's shaven, polished faces were smiling, women's powdered faces had eyes sparkling like their bejeweled necks. By the time I was a teen, to my judgmental mind, it was vulgarly out of time and place.

One health benefit for a servant was gossip. To settle the nerves and improve the digestion, there was always the chance to review drunken behavior and lewd flirtations, to discuss scandals and laugh at fallen-to-earth gods. Politicians, ambassadors, film stars, movie producers, heads of foreign countries, all had a weakness, drink, drugs, other men's women, underhanded dealings, all overheard or told to José. Many nights I listened as my dad told my mother how he had to clean up his boss and put him to bed. Or the well-known one who blah, blah, blah. Disgusted at my parents' interest in this, I would ignore the rumors and slander, believing all the famous, infamous. I forgot the names, the disgraceful activities, and progressed to vacuously despise all of the rich.

In between gorging at their parties, my mother and I waited, she in her housedress, forlornly plain next to my father standing tall and straight, looking dashing and handsome in his tuxedo, with white bow tie above pearl-studded white shirt front. Usually, he wore a pale gray coat and black trousers, but on party nights he dressed like a guest. Late nights when my dad was still working, George, the chauffeur, drove my mother and me home. Outside in the darkness where limousines waited, I saw women, fur coats draped casually over their shoulders, revealing flashing diamond necklaces, echoed by shimmering rhinestones on their Cinderella slippers. Next to me my mother relaxed with curved back in her long, cloth coat, a familiar curve she assumed as she sewed our clothes on her old Singer foot-treadle machine.

Often, from early morning to late at night until I began school and then on weekends, we lived the lives of the Mr. and Mrs. at the "House." Carrying a table-shaped breakfast tray high over my head, my father would then set it, with its omelet and toast on matched, ornamented porcelain dishes, onto Mrs. Anthony's half reclining form on her bed. I was there to chat with her while she ate.

"Thank you, José," she would say in a tired, silvery voice, turning her bored, exquisitely classical face toward me, asking me cautious and routine questions. Her dark hair flowed over the pillows my father propped behind her; her dark eyes deeply set in her pale face watched me as she lay sprawled against giant embroidered pillow cases in a massive bed. I thought she was the most beautiful woman I'd ever seen, but even at four or five, it embarrassed me to sit at her side while she was in a place I assumed for sleep. Around us the bedroom flowed into an all-white dressing room and then into a sumptuous bath with white tile and fancy, embellished mirrors. White shag carpeting lapped at the legs of couches and dressing tables like ruffled waves of a sea. The all-white vista was invaded only by violet colors, all permeated by the mixture of heady perfume and violet sachet.

"How's your mother, dear?"

"Fine."

"Did you bring your kitten today?"

"No."

She took a bite out of her toast and observed me, never pressing for entertainment or invading privacy.

"Thank you, José," she would say a little louder when he came to take her tray and me back to the kitchen. This happened regularly, and I thought she must be ill each time to need to eat in bed; and as an adult I never, except for when I got the mumps at thirty and couldn't get up, wanted to eat in bed; in fact, I feared it.

One day, when I was five, Mrs. Anthony drove me and my kitten to her mother's house in Beverly Hills, or maybe Bel Air. Her dress was bright white with flowers, her car a slinky yellow Packard convertible, and I sat there admiring all. Her mother's home was another mansion, but smaller than the "House." Waiting for the two women to finish their intense whispered discussion (grown-ups had difficult lives), I perched stiffly on a brocade couch, my knees bent at the edge of the cushion, my feet not touching the ground. I felt imprisoned. The room was small, but everything in it was shining and slick and new. Faceted glass teardrops that caught the light hung from table lamps, and painted porcelain dolls and flashing silver picture frames covered the polished tables. Its gleam and comfort contrasted in my head with the drab, dark scenes of people, buildings, and streets we had passed through to arrive here. I didn't know it was the peak of the Depression, but I could spot bright and clean from drab and dirty. I looked down to see the most delicately raised darker designs on the gleaming beige cushion that my kitten was trying to climb down from—possibly scratching it! I knew my mother would disapprove, and I heard them talking about me.

"Isn't she cute?"

"Half Filipino, half Norwegian."

"So good."

"Oh, it's all right, dear, don't worry about your kitten!"

Then Mrs. Anthony returned me to my mother at the castle. She seemed to enjoy brief outings with this small, China doll with dimples and Cupie Doll legs. (Meantime my mother would wait anxiously in the kitchen, drumming her fingernails.)

As a teenager, I avariciously anticipated Mrs. Anthony's Christmas gifts of glossy books, angora sweaters, and a jeweled evening bag. But before greed dawned on my horizon, I experienced her in my child-mind as a lady who was very beautiful, gentle, and sad.

Her handsome son, Kelly, had a strong nose, his mother's dark eyes, thick hair, and white teeth—he was as romantic looking as any mustachioed movie star of the 1930s. When I was around four, he was home from an eastern university and chased me around the vast expanse of the swimming pool, laughing with great whooops. Running as fast as my legs would take me, I dashed for shelter behind my father in the kitchen.

"When we were young, we lived with employers in their house, Pat," my mother said later. "It was bad—no privacy at all, they think they can call you any time of the day or night! Really, they can be so spoiled."

As a teen, I wondered if she, too, wanted to be spoiled like that, with breakfast in bed and servants doing the work. When I was very young, my father often brought her coffee and rolls in bed because she got migraine headaches; on Sundays, he would also set me up in two stuffed chairs facing each other, backed with pillows and covered with a blanket, in grand style, eating Cream of Wheat and listening to my radio programs, comic strips read out loud. Then off he rushed to work.

During the week, my short legs hurried alongside my father on the first block of his three-block walk before seven o'clock every morning to the only house high atop a Los Feliz hill—Number One, Los Feliz Park.

"Los Feliz Boulevard, Los Feliz Park! These people don't know what they're talking about! In Spanish it is either *Los Felices* or *El Feliz*! How can they do this?" my father would bark in disgust.

This long, unforgettable journey alone with my father would end when he stopped to watch my safe return home.

"Go home right now, Pahtsing," his Filipino diminutive for Patricia.

Then he would cross the street to begin his typical fifteen-hour day. The private walks came to an end when increasingly late nights prompted him to drive his latest car—a black, used Ford Model A at that time, with four doors and a running board. (I was allowed to stand on it for a slow, creeping ride from the street into the garage. "Go faster!" I'd yell, to no avail.)

My father crossed the street and watched me walk back. I walked home through a vacant lot filled with weeds billowing around a swath-cut path, dramatized by one or two large, olive-green century plants—a common sight in Los Angeles then. This empty block was my playground: tiny, jagged weeds became the trees lining roads I cut through the dirt for my wood and metal trucks. They rolled along in a clearing between masses of flaxen sticker bushes, white dandelions bursting from green buds, butter yellow daisies, golden honeysuckle tubes waving in the wind, and incorrigible grasses, flattened every five feet by dog droppings. Bugs climbed and insects whirled around these plants, red ladybugs popped about, and sowbugs rolled up section by section, encouraged by my prodding.

One morning a bent old man passed by where I explored. He said, "See these plants? Did you know that they're named century plants because they bloom only once in a hundred years?"

Forewarned, I never wasted my time watching for flowers to blossom, but became conscious of the inconceivable vastness of time in the empty lots behind my house. When I later learned that these Mexican agaves flower at intervals of five to one hundred years depending on climatic conditions, the knowledge only underscored the romance of nature and why some wild things receive poetic names and fanciful symbolism.

Today condos bloom there.

Half of my early life was lived at home and the other half was squeezed into the scenery at the Anthonys' house.

"We need to go with him as much as we can, so that José can see Patsy more often," my mother said to her friend Betty. "He has to leave before she gets up, and he comes home long after she's asleep. Sometimes he doesn't see her for days."

The best parts of the "House" for me were the children's library and my secret garden. The children's library in the uppermost tower was reached by a twisting staircase. Here I would disappear, curling up on a padded window seat in a tiny alcove with a view across treetops and the steep hillside, where in the distance automobiles moved along Los Feliz Boulevard like pieces on a board game. I read adventure stories, fairy tales, the Oz books, and mysteries that had belonged to Kelly. Gradually, I worked up to adult fiction that had been added to a section of the junior books.

One day I asked my mother what "concubine" meant.

She stiffened quickly. "What are you reading?" she asked and instantly clamped down with censorship.

"You shouldn't be reading that!" gave me a new appreciation of the value of a dictionary.

The library's literary truths complemented the litany of living things in my secret garden. I had never heard of the book called *The Secret Garden*, but mine rivaled the classic: the shades of green in bushes and trees, the tan and light browns of weeds (eventually cleared out by gardeners) and some grass, was reached through a door in a stone wall, rarely tended by gardeners, used only by me. There I sat reading or lying on the grass comforted by green, blossoming things, soil and solitude. My father would be angry at having to search for me when he wanted to go home—still daylight and getting off early was a small treasure. But I doggedly had my way and strayed from the kitchen, escaping the sound of my father's voice, his constant "yes sir," "no ma'am," and hiding from the sight of the robot figure of my father carrying out instructions. It was his work, I knew, but I smelled the odor of servility and oppression.

"Maamaa, let's go hooome."

"Shhh, Patsy, Daddy is still working."

My mother and I waited marathon hours for him to be finished. He waited, too, for the winking red light or a special bell that demanded him alone, at which he would jump up and walk his quick, straight gait in the direction of the summons. Then he returned to resume his silent vigil. He sat on a straight chair, elbow on table, forehead in hand, eyes shut, next to a small radio that carried the baseball game, the Los Angeles Angels against San Francisco or some other team.

"End of the eighth, one on, two outs...."

The voice of the quietly excited announcer was the saddest sound I ever heard.

Ten

Like a Dick Tracy character, I led a double life as a child: half of it at the Spanish-style stone palace, the rest in our Los Angeles flat, where I felt less of a fugitive, more secure and liberated. I hated the "House." I wished I never had to go there, but it was a part of my life, as my parents and I were a triangle.

A few people of ethnic backgrounds lived below and near our flat, the top floor of a house, a white stucco rectangle turned vertically, with two two-bedroom apartments sitting plunk in the middle of a grassy square about ten feet away from other flats. The frame buildings were interspersed with dozens of empty lots, with weeds and wild flowers struggling in the parched earth.

A tall, bearded Armenian bottled-water deliveryman, who looked to me like an Arabian Nights guardian without the turban and dagger, lived on the first floor with his short, round wife. She came up once to visit, but when I asked if she had kids, she replied that she once had twins but they got lost. She started crying, and my mother tried to comfort her, but she suddenly went back downstairs. At seven I was aghast at this story, which my mother said she didn't believe. Soon, a couple whom I thought to be very, very old, with white hair and very gentle movements (old enough to be my mother's parents) moved in, and my mother became very close to the neighborly lady, Mrs. Annan.

Blood relatives whose absence loomed conspicuously in our tiny family of three in 1930s America were replaced by my parents' friends. They included Americans (Caucasians without accents), Filipinos married to "Americans" or Europeans (rarely did Filipino women emigrate at that time), and single *Pinoys*. Scandinavians lived in ethnic communities in other towns like Solvang or other states like Minnesota; the people we knew were all loners.

My parents seemed to think nationality the most important characteristic of a person.

"The neighbor across the street—the Lithuanian—came over today," my mother might say.

"The Swede said she had worked there, but I do not know," my father discussed the latest addition to the Anthonys' household.

Their opinions of people were based primarily on country of origin, and when new information appeared that conflicted with the stereotype, José would grudgingly observe that someone was exceptionally friendly or unusually generous or especially smart for his or her race. Although a gray-coated butler, he rubber-stamped the prejudices of blue-collar workers of the 1920s and 1930s and introduced innovations of his own. In the world according to José, Italians talked a lot and didn't know what they were talking about, French were cultured and stuck-up, Mexicans ignorant peasants, English educated but pompous, Jews money-grubbing, Germans hard working but uncultured, Negroes—*itim*, a derogatory word from his

Philippine dialect—always trying to rise to levels in society where they didn't belong. "Americans" were powerful and unpredictable, qualities apparently bestowed by their birth on the continent.

My Filipino father jolted me with his prejudices because our home seemed to be open to all peoples. The house echoed with accents of every description, and I learned to understand English of each shade, color, and rhythm. (A talent without practical application, it paid off in international friends for the rest of my life.)

My mother usually opposed his negative brandings. "Oh, José, they aren't all like that!"

"Oh, yes, I know!" he would counter. He had ten years in the United States over her, and she should bow to his experience.

She did grant one generalization: "Swedes really are bossy and stubborn. And they shouldn't be confused with Norwegians!"

Controlled by Denmark, in 1814 Norway was recognized as an independent nation but was ceded to Sweden and ruled by a Swedish king until 1905 when Norway received her own king. This was the pea under the mattress of my ordinarily just mother. She was particularly annoyed by "squarehead"—the derogatory term for Norwegians before the age of political correctness silenced most racial slurs. My father delighted in razzing her with the title "squarehead," rousing frowns and a peeved "don't call me that!" Put-downs for Filipinos were "dog-eater" and "monkey," but these terms were never heard in our house. Later, I heard them on the street and even read them in history books. (American politicians, urging the establishment of military bases in the Philippines in exchange for protecting "our little brown brothers," believed in American paternalism and thought nothing of using patronizing nicknames.)

Despite his prejudices, José was generous and gregarious. On Tuesdays, his day off, his first task was to vacuum the house. He didn't permit Ruth to do housework—if daily he eased the lives of strangers, how much better to slave for loved ones?

"I do not want you to clean the house—and I do not want Pahtsing to either!" he said, adding "ing" to my name as was the tradition in the Islands. Anticipating the day when I would have servants to wait on me, my father rationalized that there was no reason why I should learn household chores.

Next he shopped for company dinners, lugging home big, brown shopping bags of food in the current clean and shining old Ford (he bought a used automobile every five years or so). He then took the kitchen over like an invading army. There he stood at the sink, washing the blue-white flesh of plucked chickens, cutting *sotanghon* into shortened strands, lovingly unwrapping the most expensive meats. There he settled before the stove, roasting, boiling, or frying—throwing in separate thick pieces of fat; below, the newspapers spread over the black-and-white linoleum kitchen floor absorbed the exuberant spattering.

Carnivore concoctions shimmered with brilliant red tomatoes; juicy pieces of pork poked out from Chinese mung beans; vegetables lacking meat brimmed with butter; steaks were thick and sizzling on the stove top, their aroma of spicy fat filling the air. Such feasts augured bad news for my mother years later when the doctor commanded a low-fat diet for a heart condition. After a few weeks, she and my father wailed, "we can't do that! It tastes so terrible!"

After dining, the guests would stagger, stuffed and groaning (my father wouldn't allow anyone to stop at one helping), into the living room where he was the entertainer, saying, "now I am going to show tricks!" And, taking objects from beneath the lid of a dark green leather box, José performed feats of magic, progressing from the simplest to the utterly outlandish. To appreciative "ooohs" and "how'd you do that, Joe?" he performed, his smooth face glowing brighter with each exclamation of amazement. Striking his sleights-of-hand together with glib personal patter, he made wine flow into empty glasses, tiny rubber balls disappear from their silver containers, and a gold coin appear from behind a woman's ear. "Oh, you told me you didn't have it!" he would tease, while giggles ensued like high notes on a piano.

"People really like to see these tricks, because a magician only turns up once in a blue moon," he would comment on the success of a night's entertainment. This was the time when my father had total control, attention, and respect. He continued "showing tricks" well into his eighties, and although wife and daughter had long been lost as an avid audience, José found new eyes to bind in a spell even through the increasingly frequent fumbles of his last ten years. Until then, he was a true prestidigitator, with remarkable deftness and agility. (As an adult in the Philippines, I was reminded of my father's tricks as I watched a priest with small hands and quick fingers handle the elements of the Holy Communion. This fascinated me, but the observation would have aroused my father's hostility, an automatic response against anything Catholic. I can hear him snort, "that's all they are doing, anyway, is tricks!")

José's generosity was matched by his eagerness to give guests whatever they admired in the house, an act of hospitality typical in Asian society. Guests would demur, "no, no!" But once the gift was pressed, the recipient sensed the donor might be insulted if it went unaccepted.

"If I didn't stop him, he would give everything away!" my mother moaned from time to time. She hated appearing stingy in contrast, but she did want to keep her possessions.

"Oh, well," he would reply, "we can get another one. They liked it!"

Ruth knew, however, the replacement might be inferior and long in coming—if it came at all.

The flip side of José's generosity and geniality revealed a need for reciprocation; he was offended if a guest declined an invitation, was undecided in accepting it, or didn't return it. Because the cooking and sharing of food was an act of love that my father had absorbed in his Philippine ancestry, he would become angry, and those people were blacklisted, regarded as Untouchables, relegated to outer space. No excuses offered on their behalf by my mother changed their outsiders' status—they were assigned to hell. A dinner at our house was like a "friendly" poker game: fun, competitive, and overwhelmingly serious because honor was at stake. I later learned there was a phrase for this in the Philippines—*Utang na loob*—a concept of reciprocity reminding me of the Pacific Northwest Coast Indians' potlatch (give-away) gatherings. Social reciprocity dealt with relationships, status, and a moral give-and-take that worked well in the old cultures, but was a machine that groaned and squeaked in twentieth-century America.

Parties made up a large part of my parents' lives. Alcohol made its debut at the end of Prohibition in 1933. One night that year, the noise called me from my bedroom, and I saw my mother lying on the floor, her legs in silk lounge pants wrapped around those of the seductive mestizo playboy of the group, flirting with him as he lounged on the couch laughing, half passed out. Others lying around, howled with laughter and yelled at the intruding seven-year-old to go back to bed.

"Please stop doing that, Mama!" I begged her, embarrassed to dying.

"Go away, Patsy," she garbled drunkenly.

"Mama, please."

Late that night or early the next morning, still awake in my exploded world, I watched as my parents stumbled and careened their way to bed. I studied their glazed eyes, meaningless chat, fumbling gestures. Next day they must have made a pact to end all drinking parties, because alcohol never shook our lives again until my mother's broken bed incident much later—and when my father left his long-term employment.

Family closeness was cemented through consistency: father at work, mother at home, child at school. A drive to the country, to an area called Rosemead on my father's day off— today a city in sprawling Los Angeles, a cow pasture then—sufficed until the summer. Then, we might drive to Carmel up north, where we knew a maid in an inn who gave me brown sugar for the cereal that appeared as softly white and tan as the sand on the empty shore, or stay at Laguna Beach, where the surf pounded and all the shops were fancy, or spend several days in Ensenada, Baja California, where a skinny and garrulous street person named Candelario spoke Spanish to my father and called him patrón, flattering him to no end, twice insisting on being our guide for a small fee. Unless there was a World's Fair within an eight-hour drive, these were my father's nod to wanderlust during his one-week-a-year vacation.

José loved vaudeville, World Expositions, and Barnum and Bailey three-ring circuses; although vaudeville was dead and world fairs were a rarity, circuses thrived. He and I sat speechless as three almost-naked, completely gilded acrobats struck a pose, their metallic bodies wrapped around each other forming a human sculpture. A golden curtain flowed down from the top of the tent, then rose to applause, as another pose of the gold-carved figures materialized. Living baroque sculptures produced breathless gasps. A later, more informed age discovered that these beautiful, golden people performed an act more perilous than any of us expected—exposure to mercury poisoning.

In late March or April, we all enjoyed the ritual of cutting the first good pineapple of the season, sitting cross-legged on the newspaper-covered living room rug. I watched my dad saw off the top with the sharp leaves, then the rounded bottom, carve the outer spiked sides away, then rub the mouth-watering yellow fruit with salt followed by sugar. We devoured the fruit greedily, laughing and chattering. Later, disappointment assailed me when Ruth made José stop this ritual in the late 1930s, declaring it primitive, not in the lexicon of American manners. About the same time, she declared "Pahtsing" an unacceptable name for me. My father obeyed.

José brought us surprises. Once the surprise was a live chicken, thrashing about in the car. "I wanted to show Pahtsing that meat does not come out of packages."

After the frightened bird hopped about wildly, squawking and pooping all over, my mother shouted, "take it back, José!"

He did, realizing also that otherwise he would have to wring its neck; he really didn't want that part of the bucolic life. Sitting on the floor to eat, chickens running through the house—my father slowly became aware of the pandemonium loosed by such attempts at cross-culturization.

Other surprises lay in a diamond ring José had made from his stick-pin and a diamond watch he gave to Ruth for anniversaries and birthdays. Never a penny saved, but trust earned and love demonstrated in magnificent gifts. My parents' relationship was a love affair, until they enacted startling father-daughter roles. If he lectured her for not standing up straight, she would cry and blubber her imminent return to her mother. Then I would run to her, throwing my arms around her, mewling, "I'll go with you!"

This elevated José's pique to rage, and he would shout,

"now look what you've done!"

"Oh, Patsy, stop it!" she would snuffle, pushing me away.

The result was my utter confusion, since my goal was to be the obedient and attentive daughter they demanded. I was to be the savior of their world, fix all that went wrong, keep them happy—it was a hard job.

José's rage often carried the show. Exasperated by his employer, or a work cohort, or a political situation, he would wait until he reached the safety of his home and then swear, conjuring up all the coast guard obscenities he knew, releasing all his hostilities in a fury at the person closest to him.

"Stop it, José, I'm not used to language like that. My mother was a lady and we never heard swearing in our house!"

This sweetly delivered exhortation drove him to escalate, heady in the rise he was receiving, until he was out of anger and words. I watched and listened, swallowing resentment at this man who would yell at my beloved mother.

A volcano hid beneath his stiff butler's collar, waiting to erupt. Outspoken sarcasm at a sniveling actor on the screen, "oh, what a wonderful fellow!" or later at propaganda newsreels, "good for you, America, take them over!" seemed the only way he could air his opinions. Much to the dismay of my mother and me, he and other drivers on the highway would exchange the finger and expletives. On night he slammed on the brakes to fight it out. My father and his opponent squared off on a pull-out on the ridge of a hill; they bounced around in the crazed headlight beams, exchanging insults. Then the other man got in his car, calling out that he was getting the police, but he simply left us waiting there foolishly.

"Oh, José, let's go," my mother finally said.

The bantam rooster looked sheepish as he turned on the engine and drove home. My nerves lived on the edge of a wet, mossy cliff.

When my father's anger wasn't exploding, it flowed like hot lava in underground tubes. In the early 1930s, one of my father's favorite radio programs, one that he listened to at the "House," was Robert Ripley's *Believe It or Not!* Filled with the bizarre and scurrilous, it must have inspired the scrapbook José kept of stories and photos that hid furtively at the bottom of a column deep in a newspaper or leapt from the front page: Siamese twins marrying separate husbands, college boys swallowing live rats, men masticating glass or razor blades, a child sold for five dollars, two white men lynched by a mob and hanging from trees, a black man lynched by a mob for associating with a white woman, the fattest woman in the world stuffing on pies, an elephantine boy wearing boxes for shoes.

Next to each clipping José penciled in pertinent remarks. About a baby born without a brain who lived twenty-seven hours, he wrote, "Some of them lived 100 years and hardly had any brain." Of a Caucasian woman disowned for marrying a Filipino, "Rather to be a dark skin with a white heart then a white skin with a dark heart." From my father's point of view, these articles were simply manifestations of a world he believed ironic, idiotic, and cruel. So the scrapbook swelled with poison. I was not impressed as a child, but as a teen I lived in fear that one of my friends might see this dangling skeleton in our closet and spot us as dangerous, crazy people.

My mother tried to curb him by saying, "José, I don't think you need to do that anymore."

Later, around the time he was permitted citizenship, he stopped. His next hobby then was cutting matchbook covers from places visited and gluing them in a neat, even collage on wooden trays and end tables, gluing in pictures of the family, including grandchildren. A folksy and more benign kind of art form.

José liked to tell me old myths like the story of God who

put a man in the oven and he came out black (overdone); the next man came out white (half-baked), but finally one came out just right: brown. Another concerned a prodigal son who came home, got a slab of meat thrown at him and was kicked out.

My father exemplified his *Pinoy* folk tales with his swift punishment for my childish sins of dawdling or disobeying. His "Pahtsing, get my slipper" meant my immediate payment in hopping feet while he hit my calves with a hard, wood-backed slipper from China. Crying "No, no!" and spilling tears only intensified his anger, and I could expect a few more swats. In my heart this consistent punishment fitted the puzzling pieces of my life; I never planned to run away from home or plotted his bloody death. Personal adventures, from his childhood kidnapping to his leaving home, held me riveted.

The shadow side of his story-telling talents lay in the cruel racial and dark sexual jokes he told to laughing friends and my embarrassed mother. As a young girl, I crouched behind the closed door of the long hall that ran to my bedroom, straining to get a warped sex education.

When José wasn't busy entertaining others, he had his own brand of "R and R." One of the few entertainments open to Filipinos at the time was gambling. So typically Asian it might have been genetic, gambling tugged at my father like one of his trick magnets. Poker games at home or friends' houses could occur after dinner or simply on their own as a social evening. Hosts carefully pulled the shades down in the dining room and surrounding areas, spreading a blanket or bed pad over the dining table to quiet the clanking chips so that no one outside might see or hear and call the police. The excitement of risk-taking replaced adventures to other lands and scintillating careers denied to the working-class men. Each player settled down to overpower with skill, to bluff with audacity, and to win for status; little money was at stake.

"Raise two."

"*A-bao!* I'm out!"

"Pass-mahn." All spread their cards out. "Straight flush-la! Ha ha ha!"

"*Ayy! Ar-abao!* Ha, ha, I didn't think he had it!" My father's laughter and generous remarks made him sound like a good loser. He believed that he could afford to lose a few dollars; it didn't matter financially if he won or lost. But for *hiya*'s sake, he preferred to win. When the game was at a friend's house, my mother (who played also, even through his mild criticisms of her skill) dragged me along. Fast asleep, I would be carried to the car and reawakened to go to bed, my whining putting an end to their good times.

Gambling didn't end at a covered dining table; it moved downtown to *Sicoy-Sicoy* dens, Chinese gambling establishments in the seediest parts of Chinatown. Filipino-town was downtown around First Street, and Chinatown seemed to intersect it or at least run all the businesses and restaurants there. Home poker games involving money were just as illegal as poker games in gambling houses, but the game was more exciting as the stakes became higher, the places more mysterious, the people more dangerous.

One night my mother woke me, pushing me into our neighbor Mrs. Annan's car; the three of us drove the fifteen miles to Chinatown. My father had gone out to gamble and hadn't returned by three o'clock in the morning. We toured dark, dingy areas, my mother vaguely aware of the secret location. I saw her eyes perusing the curbs for a dead or dying gambler; I saw her expression change from one of fear to shame; she humbly asked the neighbor to take us home.

My father returned around eight o'clock after trying in vain to win back the large sum he had lost. He would have to borrow fifty dollars from George, the chauffeur, in order to buy groceries the rest of the month.

"Really, José," my mother uttered through clamped teeth, "this is just terrible! How could you do such a thing?" Her mouth could create a very firm, determined line; he knew she was angry, and in his heart he felt her power.

In reality, he didn't need her scolding. His good sense hammered him into ending Chinatown's high-risk entertainment. And to have the neighbors know your business and its shame was the fatal blow in *hiya* bashing.

Eleven

"What's a troll?" I asked my mother.

"It's a little person."

"Like an elf?"

"No, not exactly."

I was restless when my mother told the story about the three trolls under the bridge in a small village in Norway, as if she believed who and what they were. My father could go into fantasy, but she should remain grounded like a rock.

In the early 1930s, we rented the upstairs flat on Monon Street, an acacia- and eucalyptus-lined road that wandered like a ribbon over a few stubby hills near the first Walt Disney Studio on Hyperion Boulevard. Ruth had lived in the United States for ten years, and she presided over her new home with serenity. She watched me at play on the sidewalk below, looking beyond the gossamer white curtains called glass curtains because you could see through them. As a teen I would tell her they were old fashioned, but every time we moved and got new window coverings, she always hung glass curtains, with heavier drapes at the sides. Much later, I would see similar curtains in Norway and understand her attachment.

The view took in a few stucco flats and single wood-frame homes fronted by tough lawns or wide, pale weedy vacant lots that stretched to the east like little prairies. Across the street loomed a very large, ramshackle house belonging to a Mexican family of parents, grandparents, and thirteen noisy children. The eldest child, Vibiana, ten years younger than my mother, was a friend of hers for twenty years or more, and one of the youngest children was my playmate while we were small. Dark-haired, heavy-set, easy-going Letitia and I played outside their kitchen, taking turns winning board games while the piquant aroma of chili peppers stewing in tomatoes oozed from the window. Jerry, another playmate, lived down the street about half a block in a shanty sort of house, and at eight, he bet another boy he could beat him running to the end of the block—the reward, a red truck of mine I was to give the winner. When he came to the door at the bottom of the stairs to collect, I reneged, and he was stunned. The look on his face as he turned to go, saying, "You said," made me wince for many years, but at seven I couldn't part with my red truck, and I didn't know what a deal was yet.

My mother crocheted afghans addictively, read library books avariciously, and cooked simple Norwegian-style meals of meat, sauerkraut, and potatoes for the two of us, since my father came home late, eating on the run at work.

"Patsy, hand me the scissors and that pin cushion," she mumbled, her mouth full of pins. She was putting the treadle machine through its paces, and the motor made so much noise that I half expected smoke to start billowing out of it. She rapidly pushed the cloth through the narrow opening between the needle and the bobbin, pulling pins out of the seam and poking them into her mouth, since she abhorred basting. She sewed and joked, giving me unconditional love.

She was always there, unwavering. When my father arrived home late at night, they talked about his day, his problems. Sometimes they drank something dark reddish-brown from petite glasses, one or two. Songs of the 1930s tormented me. The music existed for them, with me shelved, shut up in my bedroom, screaming tyrannically, "lie down with me!" Cab Calloway and Bing Crosby delivered their bouncy or breathy sounds through the small, brown-wood radio, separated from the mahogany end table by a crocheted doily. "When the blue of the night meets the gold of the day, someone waits for m-e-e-e-e."

José rushed to her, raw from the day. Earlier she had curled up with me until I went to sleep, despite criticism from her friends. We needed, and she became for us, a large bird with outstretched wings into which we crawled, whimpering and wailing. My mother hovered like a white-feathered swan, moving slowly, matting her nest, crooning in her musical Nordic accent. And in the way life goes, as the years passed, I heard the song less and less.

I hung around her in the kitchen, watching her beat a cake batter, tarrying for the promised spoon to lick. One day when I watched her wash spinach in the sink, a frog vaulted out, and she jumped back.

"Run downstairs, Patsy! Get Mrs. Annan!" She was our fairy godmother in times of trouble.

I ran for Mrs. Annan, who came up the back stairs rapidly, and they both managed to get the frog into some sheets of newspaper. Mrs. Annan took it downstairs into the back lot and let it go. She was a very patient, sturdy lady, with a calm surface like a lake, and she knew how to take care of things like frogs with slippery green bodies that shouldn't be in your kitchen sink.

My mother's delicate, sheet-white skin, veins showing blue underneath, always worried me, and I waited for the day when she, too, would have healthy, dark-olive skin like my father and I had. For while he and I relished the warm sun outdoors or a trip to the beach—he wore a hat and I got brown as a walnut—my mother had learned to cover herself, lest her skin redden, "like a lobster," my father commented.

Her pale, sky eyes filled long, narrow shapes, lids delicately drooping, eye orbs flat, almost Asian. Her thin lips had subtle curves; her most excellent feature was her nose, long and straight with a pert lift at the end, with very narrow nostrils that could flare when she was mad at me. Sandy brown hair would gray little by her seventies, but that tissue-like skin would wrinkle and collapse long before then.

Because we looked so different in coloring, people often asked about our relationship. She was hurt that they couldn't see we were mother and child, but thought them silly—I looked like she did as a child, only darker in coloring. She preferred dark-haired, tanned looks and made such a thing about it, I came to regard her as plain, which in reality was not true. But she, after all, was just my mother—and I took everything about her for granted.

Her body was soft and rounded, even at her thinnest, though she would put on twenty more pounds in the next twenty years. I pressed my small, bony frame into hers, safe and secure. Neither of my parents ever said they loved me, but I knew. Once I was too big for laps, no hugging, kissing, or touching intruded; love was never vocal or physical, but expressed itself in good behavior towards one another. In the Philippines a good child obeyed, respected elders, and was noncompetitive. My mother's values decreed that a child must be kind and helpful; anger and discontent had to be repressed.

In Ruth's slick-paged book of Alesund she'd point out the

apothecary shop, the cafe on the look-out mountain, the hilly streets that led to her home and her school. It looked curious to me, not a bit like Los Angeles—I wondered how anyone could live in such a strange place—tall houses with peaked roofs all packed together on a tiny island, boats tied up right next to the houses, a five-storied stone school building that looked like a prison. In the centerfold of the book, fishing boats heeled on a rocky, storm-swept sea, sharks broke the water and circled closer. Maybe that was why she had left?

I would stare at the painting until I felt dizzy, an experience I loved and dreaded. I wasn't permitted swimming lessons (I might drown before learning), and the idea of deep water terrified me.

"Don't be silly, Patsy!" my mother would cry, aggravated by my citified prissiness. "When I was a little older than you, I used to fish from a little boat in a lot of water—and I couldn't swim either! How can you be afraid of a picture?" Somehow it didn't make sense to be out at sea if you couldn't swim, but I believed every word my mother told me.

Many times my father suggested she call her mother in Norway, believing that would ease her yearning. Each time she called, she swore it would be the last. "It's just too expensive, too hard to hear with all the crackling airwaves, and too hard on that old lady after we hang up." Her cardboard voice and clenched face declared it was too painful for her. She would stare at my father and me to verify why she was here and not there.

Accustomed to Los Angeles' mobility, I didn't know why she needed to call, anyway. If she wanted to talk to her mother, why didn't she go home and see her?

"We just can't save enough money to go there," I heard her tell her friend Olga one day. Olga had divorced her Filipino husband, a boxer, and was busy at an office job, earning her way in an independent, single life. She couldn't stomach wishy-washy wifely talk.

"You could save enough for you to go," the self-reliant Olga declared.

"Nooo, I couldn't go without Patsy and José," Ruth shook her head twice, as Olga frowned. Olga and Ruth's other friend Betty (wife of a hen-pecked *Pinoy*) tried to make my mother more autonomous, less house-bound and submissive, more like they were. My father voiced his opinion that they were too independent; but he didn't have to worry—Ruth was happy with the status quo.

My mother viewed her mastery of English as a scholarly achievement and was extremely proud of her good grammar and large vocabulary, vocabulary enriched through reading. She ignored Norwegian communities, preferring her small family's companionship; but when she wrote to relatives in Alesund and Oslo, Ruth was critical of her writing.

"It's so hard now, I'm beginning to forget words and phrases in Norwegian. My letters are really stilted. They must wonder what is wrong with me! I sound like a two-year-old!" Sighing, she set the pen down and balled up the paper. She had gained a family and lost herself.

At times, speech interfered with the unity of family. Since neither José nor Ruth spoke the other's language, a sign could have been hung outside our home: "Strange English Spoken Here." Occasionally each decided I should speak their tongue—for about fifteen minutes.

"*Kulrunde oyne*, the cat's eyes are as 'big as marbles'." My mother tried to capitalize on our mutual fascination with cats.

"Ha, ha, ha!" I would laugh, rolling on the couch as I tried to wrap my tongue around the strange Norwegian sounds.

"Stop it, Patsy! It's not funny!"

"I think it is!" the sassy answer came.

Diin komo kadto? "Where are you going?" asked my father in Visayan as I giggled and commanded, "talk like a man!" He thought that funny and laughed louder than I did. This was the extent of my language lessons. Both wanted me to be a good American, and they believed speaking perfect English the best way. So language lessons were dropped from our curriculum.

With the goal of keeping me alive forever, my parents guarded me like Auschwitz camp guards. Fear and overprotectiveness became my companions. "No, Patsy, seeing that movie will hurt your eyes, because you had the measles three weeks ago." Polio and drowning lay in wait at public swimming pools, broken bones and car accidents from biking, kidnapping and molestation in being away from one's mother.

Their fear said it was safer to hide from life. I hid from the elaborate Fourth of July fireworks my father hosted annually for the neighbors in front of our house. While others sat on chairs arranged on the sidewalk, watching as my father set off flares and fireworks he had driven one hundred and fifty miles to buy in Tijuana, I scrunched down in the closet upstairs trying to close out the harsh, ear-shattering noise.

My father tried dragging me out once. "Come on, Pahtsy, it's fun!"

But my fear was bigger than he was. Eventually, I graduated to sitting on the hallway stairs, some of the lights showing through the window panes in the door. I heard the muffled shouts of delight and admired the brave souls, wondering what separated me from them except a closed door and thirty feet of lawn. Once the show was over, I emerged to hold a sparkler. Years later, California authorities judged private fireworks to be a public danger and outlawed them. I felt vindicated: Hadn't I sensed the peril? But pride fell before the fact that my fear had been based solely on self-preservation.

Often I heard people say to me, "Oh! The cat's got her

tongue!" I pictured a cat with my tongue in its mouth flapping like a captured bird. I began to recognize when the cat had my tongue, and I let him keep it; a tongue could get one into trouble. I grew shy and quiet. I could speak with my mother, because she accepted me in my inadequacy.

My mother was a provincial woman, perfectly adapted to a woman's role in the 1930s. She never learned to drive. "Oh, we don't go anywhere we can't walk to, anyway. Why bother?" she would say.

"And if you need a ride somewhere, I will drive you on Tuesdays!" my father would assert.

She walked me everywhere; she walked me to school, and she walked me home. One day, she was late at the school gate, so I decided to walk home with a friend. Spying her across the street, I ran to meet her. She saw a car coming, cried out "Go back, Patsy!" and ran into the street, throwing herself between her seven-year-old and the oncoming car.

The car hit her. The driver helped her into his car, and my mother and I drove to the hospital with the frightening strangers. As we sat in the back seat, Mother's leg swelled to the size of a ham, darkened by the rush of blood within. My mouth hung open, I couldn't speak. The driver's wife looked back from the front seat, then turned, saying, "well, I guess I'll finish my sandwich."

Back at home in bed, my mother lay quiet and in pain. Visiting friend Betty shook her head and scolded me, "look at that, Patsy—what you've done."

My mother stopped her. "No, no, it's not her fault."

I figured it was, but wasn't sure why. I had seen my way clear—if only she had stayed on her side of the street. But that must be wrong. The only object of my mother's anger was the woman who ate the sandwich. The couple feared a lawsuit, but my parents didn't operate in a society of suing for money. Mr.

Anthony called his lawyer who talked with my father and determined there was no contest, even at the man's speed, due to my mother's heroic run into the street.

Once a week, my mother walked me to the eight o'clock Sunday school class. She watched for the rare car as I crossed the street, then cut through the vacant lots and went back to bed. I entered the classroom through the downstairs back door. Stories filled our ears, and bright pictures, our eyes. I especially liked the colorful story about the baby Moses and the Pharaoh's beautiful daughter who found him in the feathery green plants by a crayon-blue river. She picked him up and carried him home, accompanied by maids dressed in flowing gowns. They never said what happened to him after that, but it didn't seem to matter.

After a cookie and a sugary sweet, red drink that made my eyes blink, we went outside, and I saw my mother across the street in front of the shaggy overgrowth of tumbleweeds and century plants.

"Can we go into the church?" I asked one day. I wondered what it would be like, going up the stairs and through the front door that faced onto another street.

"No, we don't need to do that," she answered.

She had taught me a prayer in English:

Now I lay me down to sleep
I pray the Lord my soul to keep
If I should die before I wake
I pray the Lord my soul to take.

I said this every bedtime, then she said to ask God to bless Daddy, Mama, my grandmother, and aunts and uncles.

"And Jerry who's sick?"

"Yes."

Once I asked what it meant to die and my soul-to-take. She nervously answered that it meant nothing and to go to sleep now.

"Am I going to die?"

"Not for a long time. This just means you're asking God to protect you."

Later, I asked my father if we could go into the church.

"No, that's where all the good people go," he said and laughed sarcastically.

I didn't object. In some way they believed that a protecting God was somewhere around, but not in the churches that I stared at when we drove by. My parents knew the weird parts of the world and its content, and I willingly accepted fitting into their box of conclusions.

When my mother and I walked home through the empty lots, she sometimes showed me how to make "scissors" from certain weeds, glossy green after rain. Crouching down next to the vagabond plants, one bent knee higher than the other, she would knife a polished fingernail through the long, tender spear and push another pointed shoot through the opening, causing them to work in unison. Two became one, like mother and daughter.

Curled up next to her, I listened to stories she read from books of European fairy tales checked out of the library. *The Little Match Girl* alarmed me.

"You mean she caught on fire—and died—at Christmas?"

"Uh, yes," said my mother, analyzing for the first time what she had read. "They're just stories, Patsy. But it's not very nice, is it?"

So we stayed with the pretty ones whose moral was that if you were just sweet enough, nice enough, good enough, and didn't try to impose your own will, everything would turn out all right.

Twelve

Our house was in East Hollywood, close to my father's work; he could walk the distance, but preferred to drive, since he might be on call until one o'clock in the morning. A few blocks away, the Hyperion Bridge led to the neighboring suburb of Glendale, a cozy village where African-Americans (then called Negroes) performed in jazz clubs, but by law had to be off the streets and out of town by ten at night.

"Oh!" shrieked my mother, "I wouldn't live there!" My mother continued to rail, "It's only California that's so prejudiced and small-town in attitude. Our experience in the East was so good!"

California had antimiscegenation laws on its books dating to the 1880s, forbidding the marriage of Caucasions with Blacks, Chinese, or mulattos. Japanese were added around the turn of the century, Filipinos in 1926. In the 1920s, California had invited Filipinos as "nationals" to come over to work—not to emigrate—as stoop labor in the fields, until anticolor riots generated Asian exclusion laws of the 1930s.

Racist attitudes rose with the numbers of immigrants and the degree to which the local people felt their jobs threatened; the exact color of racism—black, brown, yellow, olive, white—depended upon the nationality that took root in a particular community. Deprecatory names spread across the land, following the streams of immigration like sludge; by the late 1930s they embraced Arkies, Texies, and Oakies. And when names weren't enough to satisfy the voters, laws were passed.

In 1931, a Filipino and his white bride-to-be disputed the law on grounds that Filipinos were not Mongolian. In the courts for a year and a half, in 1933, the law was appended to include "the Malay race." Earlier marriages were judged illegal and crossing to another state to wed could incur fines or risk imprisonment.

"You had to come back to California," Ruth would accuse my father when Filipino friends were excluded from job opportunities, rejected by whole communities from Imperial to Sonoma counties, by landlords from Modesto to Watsonville, from Los Angeles to San Bernardino, precluded from marrying white mates in western states of Washington, Oregon, California, Nevada, Colorado, and Arizona.

"Oh, well, no use crying," came José's philosophical answer. Besides, there was nothing he could do. "Too late now!" he would add, a truth aggravating her into silence.

Still, I often heard of the discrimination suffered by Filipino friends who worked as laborers on large farms in northern California. In 1924 a California law had encouraged Mexican and Filipino immigration to fill jobs whites wouldn't do; but during the Depression, Caucasians were willing to accept work formerly despised and vented their hatred on working Filipinos. As nationals, *Pinoys* had no consul to press their grievances. There were attempts at shipping them back—a paid voyage with a signed contract not to return—but these mostly failed, because of *hiya*: going back was to admit failure. There were fights with Mexicans and whites over jobs and over associating with white women. But for the most part, the *Pinoys* made no fuss, just accepted their lot.

"Gregorio and Tonito really put up with a lot without complaining," my mother said one evening, after they left.

"Ah, those Boys don't know anything," my father opined. "They came from nothing in the Islands, and they continue the same way." José's *ilustrado* background often fell like a shadow over his poorer Island brothers. But he didn't know what to do either, besides complaining long and loud, as if my mother and I could fix things.

"It's not Gregorio's fault that he and Kay can't get married in California," Ruth then added, puzzled. "I don't understand it; we never had trouble like that in New York!"

In the early 1930s, Filipinos fell under western states' laws against Chinese miscegenation; the laws precluded anyone with one-sixteenth or more Mongolian blood from marrying a Caucasian. The injunction included Malayan blood, because it wasn't known exactly what kind of blood Filipinos had. With so many *Pinoys* coming to do field labor, the lawmakers, led by the will of the people, banned any colored intermarriage with whites. My parents didn't care much then, but they would later.

"Augh—those Goddimn sonamabits in Washington, you never know what they are going to do!"

"José, please—shhh—Patsy's listening."

Without my mother's consent, racism entered my life everyday, slithering through the narrow opening of the steel gates, invading the school and playground. Followed by it, I crossed a great expanse of pebbled yard toward the classroom building. Five or six boys always huddled, crouched and murmuring like wolves at the entrance.

"Hey, Jap, Ching-Chong Chinaman," they called out after me from their place of solidarity.

I next tried walking inside the fence along the hill above them, body straight, face set forward, legs moving determinedly.

"Hey Jap, we can see your pants!" they expanded after getting a response by my longer route around them.

When they began to lie down pretending to see up my skirt, I told my mother. I had endured their other taunts, but not this. My mother followed me mildly onto the playground, but once she saw the accused, she turned into a tiger, untethered.

"And you just leave her alone or I'm going to tell your parents and the teachers and the principal!"

"Ahhh, we didn't hurt her."

Shocked by my mother's reaction, I felt more shame than before.

The next day, they razzed me, "you had to tell your muu-uther!" (You coward, humorless misfit, get with the program everyone knows—defend yourself in this daily struggle like we do, or just take your medicine.)

But they did leave me alone. And every day after, I walked the broad expanse of the playground, head high, breathing rapidly; the yellow sand, whose gravel leapt into my socks if I ran, loomed before me like the burning Sahara.

Later, I noticed an erotic overlay to boys' taunts, as if a love-hate exuded from them. To this I reacted with a holier-than-thou scorn, naively concluding that their new type of teasing meant they really liked me. Other kids were called "fatso," "skinny," "squinty," and anything that called attention to their worst point. To yell "Jap" and "Chinga-hoola-hina" meant that looking Asian was as bad as being unacceptable in any other physical way, but now they added another dimension I didn't understand until I became a teenager.

My social relationships continued cruel and perplexing. A pretty, blond, blue-eyed girl and I were friends until the day she looked at my hand and said, "oh! You're so dark!" Turning my hand over, she observed, "but on this side, you're white!"

I thought this meant our friendship was over. In a few days, I saw her and a light-haired friend laughing and running down the hill in great play. I wanted to relieve my aching chest by falling from the bench and sinking into the gravelly sand. Suddenly I thought, "I don't care, because I know she is one of 'those'." Our friendship was over, but it never occurred to me that she might have preferred the light-haired girl because she was bright and fun, not a suddenly sullen girl.

> You've got to be taught
> Before it's too late
> Before you are six or seven or eight
> To fear all the people your relatives hate
> You've got to be carefully taught
> You've got to be carefully taught.

Words from the Rogers and Hammerstein musical *South Pacific* reminded me as an adult of childhood wounds from which I walked away, wrapped in Band-Aids, stinging, nothing healed but certain that the world was a pit and that one must suffer it in silence. The little boy across the street who asked when I was going "back to where I belonged" made me wonder where that was. I realized in an early shock of sophistication that he was mimicking a parent; I found this bewildering because they were Mexican, despised as much as Filipinos.

Running out of friends, I made the worst choice possible, a gangly bully named Mary Lucille who had the instincts of a terrorist. She threatened to tell everyone that I liked Douglas, a classmate, unless she would be my only friend and I would go to her house at her every whim. These blackmail requirements

I fulfilled in misery, thus keeping my *hiya* intact (no one would know my unrequited desires, that I liked Douglas, especially Douglas). Finally, one day she insisted that she and I stand on toilets in the restroom and peek over the stalls at peeing girls. I was horrified—why would she want to do this? She amplified her demand, her face a grimacing big-mouthed mask; she started shrieking my love for Douglas. Terrified of the shame, I pretended to peer over an empty stall. Other girls ran to tell, and I was suddenly seated in the principal's office.

This great disgrace I bore without my tongue, which the cat had stolen again. How could I say I didn't really do what I was accused of—only pretended to—because I was so afraid of Mary Lucille's big mouth? I decided to be quiet and accept the appearance of guilt my cowardice had created.

Teacher and principal looked at me sadly when they gave me my punishment. What had happened to Patsy? The child who was always so good and an A student? Tsk, tsk. Mary Lucille sat in the office, smirking and sneaking looks at me. After accepting our daily disciplines of cleaning up trash on the playground for two weeks, she herded me onto the playground, where instead of swinging, we sat in the swings' gritty enclosure, flung sand at each other, and got into trouble again.

My mother never heard of these things. And because I didn't want her fighting my battles, the battles didn't get fought. They lay pushed aside, accumulating, enlarging, becoming more complex. But it was my mother's presence that glued me together until I began to discover—in the Philippines—that fighting spiritual wars against passivity, cowardice and pride produced transformations in the soul and character.

Thirteen

Stretched out on my bed on a bright, spring morning in 1936, I was petting my purring cat and reading a book about a boy who worked on a ship bound for the South Seas, when my mother rushed in, breathlessly talking about a trip to the Philippines. I plopped the cat onto the window ledge and rubbed the top of its nose.

"Oh, yeah?" I replied, bored. Even though my passion was adventure stories, and I spent countless hours making precise maps of voyages in books, carefully drawing lines of the routes, at age nine these pastimes were escapes from reality, with no practical meaning.

That Saturday at the "House," my father had been checking household bills in the pantry when he saw the tiny dot of the red light blinking for him. He made the trip to the living room, past the portico of Corinthian columns, through the long atrium that paralleled the swimming pool.

"Have you ever wanted to visit your family in the Philippines, Joe?" asked Mr. Anthony. He was reclining on one of the marshmallow-soft sofas set around the high-ceilinged living room, landscape oils in gold frames hanging above him, at his feet thick carpeting that stretched to the large tile-paved vestibule.

"Of course, sir—yes, sir, but no money." José spread his arms, palms up.

"How would you and your family like to go for four months?" The boss was beaming broadly, thrilled by his own magnanimity.

"Oh! I guess that would be wonderful, sir!"

"Mrs. Anthony and I are going to Europe, Joe, and we thought you might enjoy this visit while we're gone and won't be needing your services."

"Oooh, thank you, sir, my gosh." José searched for words, feeling as if he'd been clubbed on the head.

After a decade as confidential aide, demonstrating amiability, integrity, and diplomacy (available twenty-four hours a day, cleaning up after parties, and discreetly keeping the names of the well-known revelers to himself), José was getting the gold watch. He was going "back home." In his excitement, José rushed to the phone to tell my mother, who then rushed into my room to tell me.

Before we took off, my dad had to go with Mr. Anthony to Northern California's Bohemian Grove, an exclusive all-male get-away "camp" in the woods that the boss visited for three weeks every summer. After giving up our apartment, my mother had our furniture put into storage at the end of July, and she and I stayed at the "House" until we boarded the ship. George, the chauffeur, drove Ingeborg, the cook, my mother and me to the wharf where they, along with our proxy mother, Mrs. Annan, and my mother's friend Betty saw us off on the S.S. *President Coolidge*. The cabin was tiny but nice, we were in

Special Second Class, and the *President Coolidge* was a fine ship, but I was already homesick and I cried. (Every tear, sniffle, sneeze, and bottle of soda was noted in a diary I updated every night, without exception.)

An overnight cruise brought us into San Francisco Bay and past Alcatraz Island (then a high-maximum-security prison) to the docks, where my dad was standing tall and energetic. We were going "back home."

I remember running, running, running with eight or nine kids all over the *President Coolidge*, a ship like a hotel floating in the same water as whales and sharks (I liked to think with a shock) . Every day we raced all around the shining reddish-stained wood decks, up and down stairs, through the huge tan dining room, cheered by bamboo-printed wallpaper, we girls squealing and shrieking in delight. One day, a Big Girl sitting with her boyfriend and trying to look perfect glared at us, and a very old lady stared and sighed, closing her eyes as if she might drop over from weariness or old age.

For five days, past the slender railings was only the blue-green of the Pacific, gold under the sun, and black at night. Above us was First Class, below us Second, then Third, and finally on the bottom in the hold, a mysterious place called steerage, where everyone was held in a large cabin they couldn't leave. My mother was irritated at the "classes" and didn't like it because, although we were taken on tour of the conspicuous wealth in First Class, we couldn't move freely back and forth. They could come and go anywhere on board, but not the other classes. Some First Class men "slummed it" in order to gamble with the card players in Tourist Class. My mother was glad when my dad said, "I guess I won't play with them anymore—my gosh! They bet so high!"

Ruth's dresses, quickly purchased for the trip in inexpensive shops, were fashionable—about three inches above the ankle, straight enough to give a long look from waist to toes, in prints and swirling materials. My mother and father danced close together in the ballroom to a band playing tunes of the day. He looked one way, his fleshy lips smiling, his dark brown eyes warm as seals' peering over my mother's head; she looked the other way, also smiling. They had danced together when he was young and carefree, but now they were slightly out of practice. Still, my parents looked tall and slim to me in their mysterious world.

The Hawaiian Islands materialized on the horizon as mountains, glossy green with wet, succulent covering, while clouds like breath blown by giants lay in the hollows. My folks had become friends with a short, rounded Jewish couple and their thin eight-year-old daughter, Patty. The four of us drove a car with a canvas top and open windows to a mountain peak called the Pali where

> King Kamehameha,
> the conqueror of the islands,
> became a famous hero one day.
> He took a native army and pushed it over the Pali
> Oooh, eeah, aoaay!
> Ooh, eeah, aoaay!

The current hit song rang in my head over and over. King Kamehameha the First, I later discovered, united the islands into one kingdom from many warring islands, and this was the site of a famous battle. But we were tourists, gobbling up the culture in hula girls swaying and shaking grass skirts in a bamboo enclosure. The dancers smiled so broadly, their faces went out of shape, and it seemed strange to me that we had to pay to see them, and stranger yet to pay to have pictures taken with them. (Many years later my own daughter would ease my disappointment by showing me a culture on the Big Island of

Hawaii where she was living, in which the sacred hula was danced by unaffected women in unfeigned situations for everyday people.)

Another week on the ship—now called "home" in my diary—and we docked in Yokohama, about fifty-five miles from Japan's capital of Tokyo. As we neared Tokyo by cab, driving through the quiet, well organized nation, we occasionally saw women in mainly blue kimonos and white stockinged feet in clog sandals shuffling along the sidewalks, their heads bowed low. In what seemed like a palace, I hung over balconies with crystal chandeliers dripping from towering ceilings and rode amazed down wide, smoothly gliding escalators. It was Tokyo's biggest and newest department store, where pale-skinned clerks, their stylish, slick black hair swept back and piled high, sold silk dresses and embroidered robes, French perfume, and lace hankies. Their eyes swept upward at the ends like does' eyes, and they giggled as they addressed their customers.

"Look, Pahtsy, look!" my father kept insisting in excitement as if I had no eyes in my head. Through a shrouded mist the Imperial Palace of Emperor Hiro-Hito appeared. We were viewing one of many pavilions and gardens on four hundred fifty acres inspired by the Palace at Versailles, the architecture that many potentates copied to display their absolute power. In the style of Louis XIV's seventeenth-century royal estate outside of Paris, authority was here displayed in sublime white marble, in the long facade of columns and pilasters placed in formal symmetry. The palace was surrounded by a moat overlaid with lotus blossoms, surrounded by blocks of lawn compounding its isolation, surrounded by immaculate streets, continuously cleaned by sweepers in aprons; clearly, this was the site of the divine ruler, distinct from mortals.

Sailing to Kobe, we went ashore again and walked through

the ancient port city within walls, where shops attracted tourists. A French girl named Gueblene, who came aboard in Kobe, and I played with ivory rickshaws, each with a seated woman and running coolie, and Japanese geisha dolls with silk kimonos, white faces, and ebony hair. I named mine Teruko Lucille Blossom. My confidence grew steadily, and in four days I renamed the doll Little Cherry Blossom, dropping the name of my grade-school antagonist.

Within the decade these fanciful cities were to be burned shells, their citizens suffering and homeless. Doolittle's B29s dropped their bombs over Tokyo, Yokohama, and Kobe in five years and eight months, in retaliation for Japan's sudden attack on Pearl Harbor, followed up by massive air raids toward the end of the war, from March to July of 1945.

In six days the *Coolidge* covered 776 nautical miles from Kobe to Shanghai. The water was now a milky brown part of the Yellow Sea between China and Korea near the mouth of the Yangtze. We reached the noisy city by a tender, an open water taxi with wood seats like a bus. Odors of frying pork and fish and burning incense, sounds of fat spitting, hawkers calling, traffic screeching, contrasted sharply with understated Japan. In the streets, I winced at seeing the babies, sores on their large, sparsely fuzzed heads, held in one arm by cringing mothers with dark, silent eyes, begging with their free hand. I flinched at groups of men, skinny as lobsters, slumped in alleys, backs against the walls, gnarly hands cupping their bowls of rice, scooping it quickly with their fingers into their mouths.

I ran in and out of shops where jade petals hung from jade trees and carts carved in wooden chests carried miniature mandarins to court; embroidered pink silk spilled from a salesgirl's manicured hands like water.

"Oh, there you are, Patsy!" My mother rushed toward me, red-faced and panting. I realized I had been lost and found. "I've been looking all over for you!" She hugged and scolded me. I didn't understand grown-ups' quandaries—I knew I wasn't lost.

At Shanghai and Hong Kong, too, around our great ship clustered junks—small, wooden boats with wooden or thatched, rounded roofs housing whole families. Gaunt men and women called for money and extended long poles topped with nets. They deftly caught coins and dived for whatever they missed.

"Mah-neee!" they cried from their dire state.

The bellow of the ship's horn didn't alarm them. HOOOOOO!!

From a distance, as the ship pushed through the water, the boat-people's wide-open mouths seemed to call silently.

Fourteen

"Veinte trés años en los Estados Unidos," my father repeated the phrase like a catechism, his face smooth and glowing, youthful at forty-five. Family and friends sat forward listening intently considering those twenty-three years in the United States as if José were Columbus returning to Spain after discovering the New World.

"And what is San Francisco like?"

"Oh, the best city!"

"What are the buildings like?" they asked, wondering if the miracles they had heard of were really true.

"Big, you can walk for miles and miles and see nothing but large, beautiful stores!"

"And the weather?"

"Lots of snow in New York!" my father bragged. "You can get snowbound and never get out, but then they have trucks that come and dig you out. Ha ha ha."

"Have you seen movie stars?"

"Suuure, but they are nothing."

Our hosts' questions seemed endless, José's stories were expansive, his opinions doctrine, his glory secure. How many big houses in Manila were dazzlingly lighted, bustling with activity, filled with the chatter of finely dressed, smiling people? How many hotel restaurants, awash with white table-cloths, white platters, and sparkling glassware greeted us? And at every meal, to the left of each main plate was an equally large one of rice. I attacked that down to the last bit.

"José, your American daughter eats rice?" laughed uncle León, my father's second to eldest brother, the commander of the sugarcane plantation. A wide grin broadcast his geniality; a large nose like my father's showed they were brothers. The corpulence straining his belt buckle declared prosperity. "If she eats rice, she must be Filipino!"

"Sure!" my father agreed, proud of me. Rice was about the only thing I did eat, except for soup and fruit. The curious eyes trained on me had robbed my appetite.

In 1936, my father's relatives and friends were among the Philippines' elite, plantation owners and businessmen, wealthy men who had inherited land and worked hard to maintain their position. Lazares, Lopez, Locsin, Justiniani were the big names. In Manila a newspaper announced our visit, reporting that José was part of Earl C. Anthony's radio station and automobile empire. My father, who during the interview had spoken in broad terms of being in the magnate's employ, didn't demand a retraction. (Later, head bowed, hat in hand, José would show the clippings to Mr. Anthony, a miscreant before a sentencing judge. Mr. Anthony read and smiled, and said he understood. José could have his day; Mr. Anthony would get his money's worth.)

All these caring people would have been shaken had they known José's real occupation. In the Islands, even the poorest relatives had servants. Only to his two sisters did he confide his real occupation, underscoring that in America serving meant a different thing.

My mother jumped to his defense, "but he manages other workers—he's not a servant who scrubs floors!"

In Manila, the parties went on for five days. Most evenings, my mother wore a "Maria Clara" floor-length dress of finest woven piña cloth with perky stiff butterfly sleeves and a train, and a huge, stiff *pañuelo*, a scarf that framed her face with its folds. The violet and cream gown had been measured and hand-sewn for her in a day, and when she danced with my father, I thought she looked like a film star. José had discarded his dark businessman-style suit for a white tropic-weight suit and always a white shirt and long-wide red and blue striped or paisley tie (except at the beach where he removed it and unbuttoned the top button of the white shirt). He easily assumed the role of the returning noble son, home from overseas adventure and gain.

Nanay Daida, my grandmother Enriqueta's sister, and her daughters, plump Amparo and slim Carola, dressed me in a red-and-black plaid peasant dress with butterfly sleeves and a wrap-around skirt. I noisily let my mother know I preferred her outfit.

"Stop it, Patsy! That's a beautiful dress you have!"

So, although I hated the dress, I swallowed my opinion. A Filipino-Norwegian child was seen and not heard.

Filipino generosity took many forms. Any object you admired, whether it was in the home of family or mere acquaintance, became yours; to demur resulted in their insistence that it was yours. I grasped the more obvious part of the process quickly and was soon acquiring a fine collection: a wood model outrigger called a *barangay* with striped mast and shell inlay; several lidded, woven baskets; a large nautilus shell carved with a map of the Philippines.

One night, just as we were entering yet another house, my mother pulled me rather roughly into an empty room and warned, "don't say you like anything! You know they'll give it to you!"

Father contradicted Mother, "oh, it's all right? They like to do that!"

But I believed my mother knew the correct social etiquette. With sadness, I abandoned my decadent transactions.

We stayed at the Great Eastern Hotel in Manila (destined one day to hostel Japanese soldiers), but we spent hours in the home of Nanay Daida. Large, dark, and ominous, the big house was not child-friendly, and I sat in the living room like a traveler in the waiting room of a train station, my shoulders drooping, passively listening to adult talk and sharing the solitude with another captive, the tall grandfather clock ticking in resolute conformity somewhere down the hall that led to rooms of dark brown wood filled with ornate furniture.

Uncle León was our beaming tour guide. One special place was Intramuros, a walled Spanish colonial city that filled my father with pride.

"Look, Pahtsy!" was his constant command as he pointed at huge, white stone churches, government buildings, and homes with iron-work balconies draped in green vines. Once the Spaniards hid within these walls, denying Filipinos entrance, and the Americans did so at first occupation in 1898, opening it to all shortly after occupation. Now, only certain American clubs in Manila excluded Filipinos.

"What?" demanded my father, fully aware of the fact that many clubs in his adopted home of America had exclusion rules for many reasons, not all racial, but he believed his own homeland must not exclude any Filipinos in any place on any grounds.

"Oh, it's all right," his brother assured him. "We have our own clubs!"

"No, no! That is not the point!" José countered, bristling.

"Shhh, dear," my mother said.

Eager to press on to his home in the provinces, we left Manila for the Visayan Islands, and looking forward to another reunion in Manila before we went back to the States, we said good-bye and took a very lavish white ship called the *Mayan* with two staterooms for the three of us overnight to Iloilo. In a country where cousins are connecting links, and first cousins almost like siblings, documented in my diary was my "second grade" uncle, name unrecorded, who sailed with us. My father said that he and my "first grade" *tío* Enrique, my father's brother-in-law, were lieutenants in the navy; they wore stunning dark uniforms. (*Tío* Enrique had breathtaking looks with a slim high-cheekboned face, long straight nose, and drooped eyelids; my mother said he looked like Rudolph Valentino. He would later emigrate to the United States and be stationed in San Francisco.) In Iloilo, island of my grandparents' birth, José searched out a friend who wasn't home. We rushed to board another smaller boat, the *Princess of Negros*, and in a few hours we bumped into the shores of Saravia.

Walking down the gangplank, it was as if I had suddenly entered an alien brown world: water, wood boats, thatched huts, even the people were the color of mahogany. There were no cement sidewalks, no paved streets, no stucco houses, nothing familiar to my ten-year-old eyes. I was blinded to the cerulean skies, the arabesque palms, quiet waters undisturbed by the whine of motors. A half century later, in a world run amuck with machines, materialism, and pollution, I would long for such simple grandeur. But now despair overpowered me, my head swam, my legs buckled.

I grabbed my mother. "Mama, let's go home," I whimpered.

She said we would talk about it later, so I waited with hope.

When I saw all the happy, tearful people who had met us hugging my elated, moist-eyed parents and carting our bags and suitcases into cars, I stole over to Mother's side. "You said we were going home!"

"Don't be silly, Patsy, we're staying here." My own mother had betrayed me.

In one horrible instant I knew I was caught like a lizard in a noose, and thrown into a sack. I was my parents' prisoner, struggle would only bring guilt. I bowed my head and followed all these strange people—strange because they had the ability to live here. As we approached Saravia, the modern highway disappeared, replaced by dirt roads, palm-roofed houses hovered over wooden pilings, chickens and pigs making a ruckus below.

Life in Manila had been glamorous—though not as good as Los Angeles, I wanted all to be sure of that. But there had been parties and gifts, and we were always moving on. Here, in the village of Saravia, each humid day was like the previous one, brain-shatteringly boring. In my diary, almost every day the first week began with, "We had breakfast and sat around."

My aunt Isabel—*tía* 'Sabel—spoke no English. Still, she sat on the floor playing with me and the dolls I'd brought, for which favor I believed her mentally retarded and withdrew. Too involved with my own agony, I couldn't recognize love offerings.

I longed for our white stucco flat in Los Angeles, the white concrete sidewalks so smooth for fast roller skating, white bread I could roll into balls at night in bed, and girlfriends with faces the color of whipped cream. I held my breath as I wove my way through each day, waiting to go home.

Time seemed to stop. My parents and aunts seemed content to sit on the porch, talking in the dialect, Spanish, and English, separately and confusingly, sometimes all at once. I waited obediently, in limbo.

My father, home with his doting sisters, was a boy again. Elder sister Isabel, the Religious, adored him but smiled lovingly at my mother and me. Younger sister María, the Beautiful, had eyes only for her long-lost, runaway-to-America brother "Joséling." They both hung on his words and around his person.

For my mother, the sudden shift from being his only woman and confidante to an outsider who could understand little of the conversation, except when María attempted her uncomfortable English, was a shock. In this reunion, husband and daughter were the focus and she was the white woman José had married. A good sport, her sweetness genuine, she must have nonetheless wondered when she would get her time to go back home, where she, too, might be the focus of tenderness and intimacy.

As my mother sought a way to fit in, I searched for something familiar and discovered only the shockingly bizarre. Inside my aunts' screenless house ("screens melt in the heat," *tía* María explained), small light-green lizards clung to the walls and ceilings. Every once in a while, one would lose hold and fall to the floor with a sound of firm mush, then race to a wall, climb, and retreat to a corner. (Panting in relief, I imagined.) I carried my chair into the center of the living room, reasoning that only a daring few lizards would venture out so far, and so the chances of being hit were lower. There I sat, reading again and again all the books I had brought, listening to the *sphlat!* of falling lizards, longing to go home. The meaning of going "back home" was as clear as the exposed windows.

Sometimes, the skies hurtled heavy shafts of water that crashed onto the roof for hours, flooding the neighboring thatched huts. But our wooden house, with a western-style cement basement, held fast. It could be invaded by spiders, however. My father took me to see one that seemed as big as his hand on the netting in the bedroom in the back of the house where he and my mother slept.

"Look, Pahtsing!" he exclaimed, in the Islands' term of

endearment, with the same delight that he pointed out seals on rocks as we sailed by them on the California coast. I wondered whose bedroom would get the next visitor in the night, and doubted it when my aunts assured me such exotic intrusions unusual.

My bedroom was at the front of the house, the bed with mosquito netting placed in its center. A barefoot young servant girl slept on a mat on the floor next to my bed for a few nights—a new convenience I required after she had been ordered to sleep there once when the adults went out. A mini-potentate, I liked having a slave girl to do my bidding, one I could control, a girl not much older and who looked as frightened as I.

"No, Patsy! It's not necessary!" my mother exclaimed, sick of my whiny ways and fully aware of the insidious power inherent in a society drawing its servants from such a large pool of impoverished people. She couldn't bear the thought of the girl sleeping at my feet as I feigned the Hindu maharanee, so I lost that try at control.

My father said, "it's okay, she sleeps on a mat on the floor at home, anyway."

"No, José!" Ruth wailed, "there, she's with her family!"

Now, even my shadow side sided with my mother.

Sounds of the night forest filled my room. Iguanas, as long as tables, would start up their throats sounding like engines igniting. Then in loud chants, each would cry out eight or nine times in monosyllables, beginning with a bold *tuk-kuu!* (which was their local name) and finally ending in a weak *tuk*. Lying in bed, counting the times one started and stopped, interfused by the beginnings of others in the round, I would fall asleep.

One night, while the family was sitting on the porch that ran the width of the living room, we heard a sound like clothes flapping in a wind.

"Get up!" shouted my aunts, and we all ran inside.

Before we could switch off all the lights, hundreds of red-winged fireflies beat their way into the living room, attracted to the illumination. Servants brought buckets of water, into which hundreds of the broad-winged insects dropped. The vivid creatures died answering instinct. I was frightened but terribly excited at something actually happening. For an hour, activity replaced adult conversation.

Meals were high adventure. Two servant boys, at each long side of the table, stood fanning us with giant palm fronds, a custom my dad said was a continuation of early Islamic customs for the wealthy. Servants prepared meals of fish, squid, octopus, and other seafood. They stared at me as I picked at them. My aunts noticed my hesitation and asked my mother my favorite foods. They then daily served me mixed fruit and a soup of chicken and vegetables, which they left cooling in the window. By the time it was placed before me, drowned ants mixed with taro, carrots, and fowl.

Looking up from her fish, my mother put a halt to my excavation. "Stop it, Patsy and eat!"

Her anger and my hunger convinced me I should ignore the ants and boldly eat whatever the spoon picked up. They tasted sharp.

Out of sight of the grownups, I soothed my hostility by tormenting the forlorn cat that came occasionally into the house. He looked puzzled and then terrified at this small person who had come six thousand miles to torture him.

"Yaaah!" I hissed as I crept up on him.

Never before had I abused animals, since they were beloved companions of an only child. Even I briefly questioned my behavior. But I needed control over something in my life, and making sure there were no witnesses, found an outlet in making another creature as miserable as I.

Fifteen

Under fifty-foot arching palms, beneath fleecy clouds in a crystal sky, wrapped in humid air, misery was fashioning a monster.

Then, just before I sprouted horns and a tail, I discovered the Sajo house. Across the dirt road from my aunts' house rose a white stone and stucco dwelling, a tall, box-like structure of undistinguished European style, symbolizing western power and dominating this land of palms, bamboo, and thatch. But the interior was for me an incredible fairy-tale land of delights.

Inside, three stories reverberated with the lives of three generations headed by an elderly grandmother and grandfather. Adults, teens, adolescents, toddlers, and infants created a small town of twelve or so, seeming like a hundred to me. The family ate meals in huge gatherings, took afternoon siestas, laughed and joked, worked and played. To an only child, such an abundance of relationships was seductively lavish and unfathomable. Not only that, they wanted me—the new arrival from America—to join in their swarming, thriving, jubilant business of life. And they spoke English, ate

American-style food, and wonder of wonders, they engaged in the delight of colorful make-believe and went to movies.

This house appeared to host only joy. Even the family name sounded enchanting, SAH-ho, and I repeated it over and over like a charm. I never heard any arguments, never witnessed strife, never sensed the silence of resentment. I studied them, hung around them, loved them, each and every one. Lovely eighteen-year-old Joséfina became my round-faced big sister, sewing doll dresses and combing my hair; laughing, skinny Edwin, my age, was a non-teasing male playmate; Augusto, twenty-five, came from work regularly to banter and drive us to movies. There were Pedro and his wife Mary, a soft-spoken, congenial, married couple with a baby; Aquiles, the wiry-haired eldest brother in charge of family business; Casilda, *tío* León's fiancée, taciturn and bright; slim and pretty Elisa, my new girlfriend; and her quiet, little sister, Norma. We young ones played ball in the street, roamed the huge house and—when we could talk one of the grown-ups into driving us—went the fifteen miles into town to the movie theater.

My mother had full charge of me now. José, at home with his sisters, had become the carefree young brother of 1910 and was certain that any place in his hometown was safe and welcoming for his daughter. After my disappearance for an entire day, Mother ordered, "Patsy! Stay here until 10, check in once a day, be back by 5!"

I brooded and frowned at her explanations.

"You'll hurt your aunts' feelings!" and "you practically live there!"

But I accepted the deal. Each morning, I'd put in my time at the house, then in a great rush, ran madly, wildly as to a lover, through the unlocked entry to the Sajos' courtyard, up some twenty-five steps of the inside stairway to the thick, wooden door that led to life. My mother must have wished she had a Sajo House. I noticed her face, a mask with calf eyes and drawn jaw, and knew that she missed me and was jealous of my friends, but that she would never say anything, never consciously show her feelings. Possessive of my new family, I still asked her to come visit them with me. After one call, she declined again; they held no magic for her. Growing up in a large family with aunts, uncles, and grandparents near, she had experienced satiation and had no idea of the hunger a curious only child felt about the drama, excitement, and community of many relatives. Ruth preferred her tiny, three-part family.

The Sajo boys treated me as an equal. They taught me their ball games and showed me how to shoot their rifles. There, in the big living room—above the basement that cooled the house and quartered small animals and birds—through the open second-story window, I sighted some white dots in the crosshairs and fired into the yard beyond; in my undiagnosed myopia I knew the feathery blobs must be birds.

"That's the way!" Edwin said.

"Oh, my gosh, *ai-abao!* She shot one!" yelled his friend Arturo.

They pulled me away from the window, laughing at the chicken slayer. I was surprised the gun had bullets in it, aghast at killing an animal.

"No, I didn't!"

"Yes, you did!"

"No!"

"Sure!"

Soon we tired of the debate and ran off to do something else.

We played cards at a thick, round table, glossy with arms rubbing it, raised on a massive central pillar. One day, while shuffling the cards, Augusto impishly suggested that when I grew up, I return and marry him. The kids all looked at me and laughed. He laughed too, but I felt a curious stirring. I watched him deal. His long, delicately muscled arms were a lustrous brown, not a speck of hair grazed them. I tagged after him for a couple of days, wanting more attention, but it never came.

For me, the Sajos' house was like a private amusement park. The flat-ceilinged top floor stored boxes, furniture, knick-knacks, scrapbooks, and every kind of memorabilia rejected from the living quarters. On the uppermost shelf was a large glass jar that held twins who had died at birth, embalmed in fluid. They were plump and perfectly formed; they had squeezed, infant faces. I stared, entranced.

"Come on!" Elisa would call, "look at the stuff in these boxes!"

"Wait!" I'd answer—costumes and games would always be there. The babies seemed to hold each other tightly, wrapped together forever in embrace. But, I wondered, how long was forever? Would they drown in the liquid, if already dead? What was death? Nobody would ever hold those two babies— did they care? Do you care after you're dead? Where was their mother? Was she sad? I wanted to see them again and again.

"No, we weren't supposed to show you," the kids giggled.

"They shouldn't have showed you," my mother said in disgust, when I finally told her of the secret.

Why not? I wondered. Such big questions arose from the sight of those babies: why wouldn't everyone want to see them all the time? Why couldn't you talk about them? I had run squarely into life and death, and nobody would discuss the issue.

In my diary I noted the gifts of family jewelry given to me and my mother by *tío* León, diamond necklaces and rings in flower and star-shaped gold settings, places he took me, and sensed the heartfelt love he gave me as a childless bachelor. But I ignored his caring since I had abundant fathering. Instead, I impatiently awaited the time when I could gravitate toward the new sensation of independence and freedom that my new family offered, unwittingly. I became a village girl. I was like the contented *caribao*—the sweet-faced, curved-horned, water buffalo that labored in the nearby water-flooded rice fields, allowing myself to be yoked, but always ready to break away to the Sajos' house. I ate my soup affably, went with my aunts and mother into town amiably.

A visit to the public school culminated in the idea that I attend, submitted by the smiling teacher and confirmed by my mother. Confronted with a roomful of children looking and speaking differently from me, I stared at the floor, my body twisting in my own death throes.

My mother, who avidly wished for this or any variation from my days with the Sajos, nonetheless sympathetically began to make excuses for me, "well, she really is on vacation now."

But the teacher was a family friend and had already made a desk ready for me. One day, when I rebelled, my father used the Chinese slipper to make me obey. Faithfully recorded in my diary, school days folded up in my memory like the tiny *huya-huya* plant when touched by a meddlesome finger.

During a *pangingi* game at my aunts' house one day, the mood grew heavy with tension and muffled whispers; then my father's girlfriend of 1910 was introduced.

Jovially and tactfully, José greeted her, *"Ai, abao—kumusta ka na?"*

Violeta said she was fine and glad to see him again. She was plump and pleasantly attractive with a smooth complexion—and I didn't tell my mother I liked her.

"I didn't think she was very pretty," my mother said later.

Violeta didn't enter our lives, but her attractive twenty-year-old daughter Nita did try to attach herself to my father. On our first meeting, she boldly let it be known that she wanted to go back to America with us and subtly showed that in some way, due to the fact that her mother "almost" married him, José was somehow her father, too. From then on, she regularly stopped by my aunt's house. Each time, she would grab my father's arm, pressing close to him. Finding him flattered but not encouraging, she bypassed my threatened mother and concentrated on me. Already taken by the Sajos, I wondered why she hadn't found a satisfying life like I had. I hoped she would. But not my life.

"Let's pretend we're sisters," Nita purred one day.

"No, I don't want to," I answered.

My parents, *tía* María, Nita, and I had all walked to a farm. On our return, the skies darkened, thunder bellowed, and suddenly trees were hidden in a blur of rain, the path before us a running river. Holding newspapers over our heads, we navigated our way cautiously over dirt roads now shiny, slippery trenches. Soaked and upset, Nita ran ahead, then slipped and fell backwards into the chocolate-brown muck. Mortified, she rose out of the slime like a crocodile. (Good! I thought. That's what you get for trying to steal my father!)

"José!" exclaimed *tía* María, at home one day, speaking in English, not in *Ilongo*, so that my mother would understand. "Did you hear that an important Japanese army officer was stabbed to death around the time you began your trip to the Philippines?"

"I did," my mother said, "And I read in the paper that their War Minister Hayashi was making changes in the army to promote unified opinions—he even is investigating writings of professors and making sure everyone thinks identically in the whole country!"

"Yes," *tía* María went on, "José, do you think we need to worry about Japan so nearby? But we have the United States government, of course, taking care of us."

"Oh, no," interrupted my father, "don't worry about all that—it's just propaganda. We've had enough wars here already. Let me tell you about when I was in the Coast Guard and went to Alaska! It's a good story!"

As in other small towns, when talk about personal experiences slowed, gossip about other people's affairs accelerated. My parents and aunts discussed relatives, friends, neighbors.

"Yes. Manong. The city. That woman. Ooh, Rosa. No doctor. Yes, so young. Patsy looks like her. Our father. So sad. Buried in...."

Unaware that I was listening, they whispered that one of the local girls had run away with a lover. My mother believed children didn't hear, couldn't understand, and wouldn't care about adult talk anyway, unless it was about sex, and then she whispered, giggled, and reddened, so I got especially interested. When her father and brothers found her in another part of Negros, they beat her and dragged her home to live a repentant life. Apparently this was typical Spanish procedure to keep young women pure, allowing them to marry well, and guaranteeing respect within a family. Once disobeying the custom, these girls were marked forever and married off to whatever man would take them or shunted off to a convent. Intrigued by the absolute nature of her sin, I carefully watched Penang—a slim, bronze-skinned girl with a heart-shaped face—searching her face, but she only smiled back, placid and peaceful. I liked her more than ever.

The women gossiped that one of the elder men had been a business cheat, another unfaithful to his wife. I studied these men, so kind and generous, relatives who had children out of wedlock—lost in deprivation in Manila—were cast out of the family. It was known that one of the town's leaders had been fathered by a priest, a common occurrence. I wondered if only the people in this room lived correctly. And how could everyone else endure such failures and inadequacies, recover, and appear tranquil and trouble-free? Where was their *hiya*? As an adult I would discover that this was *hiya* in action—as I, too, wore the serenity mask, the storm raging within.

As a break from village life, we drove to the bigger towns of Silay and Talisay or to Bacolod, the capital city of Negros. While my parents enjoyed restaurants and touring, for the Sajos and me city blessings materialized in American films shown in a movie palace, where a man climbed a ladder up to the marquee to change letters in the slots announcing the next film. It looked exactly the same as the small neighborhood theater my mother and I went to almost every week in Los Angeles, a kind of streamlined Hollywood kitsch. Movies of the 1930s showed the Filipinos a cheery, affluent American life of big houses and cars for all, with handsome men and stunning women with stars glistening on their white teeth and in their huge eyes. Particular favorites were Joan Crawford, with her cold femininity, and Franchot Tone and his forceful boyishness. Everyone wanted to go to America and take part; if that was out, movies could substitute.

Newsreels spun off their reels first. Once, I heard about a Prince of Siam committing suicide and after that saw a man with straight, black hair named Hitler, whom everyone was supposed to "watch." I didn't understand these stories and thought them boring, but I liked the scenes of the Prince of Wales visiting the London Zoo, looking at the lovable animals.

The night drive back to Saravia jounced us into another fictional landscape. For hours, we traveled, only occasionally seeing another car through a wilderness of jet skies flickering with stars in fantastic configurations. Sometimes thunder and shots of white lightning prefaced rain that wrapped our car and carried it along as if greased. Packed stands of trees rose up on the flat earth—one they called a "haunted forest" appeared suddenly on the horizon like an outlying hideout for Robin Hood. The smell of skunk possessed our nostrils for miles. I didn't ask what it was; I simply expected an outlandish odor to issue from this outback landscape.

As we neared Saravia, we would place bets on whether the lights would be on. If the generator fared well, houses greeted us with bright yellow eyes; if not, we all yelled, *Wala' Suga'!* No lights! A village blackout set off laughter. At home the adults and older children would scurry to light candles and hurricane lamps, their waves of warm light washing up on the walls and dancing on the ceiling as we prepared for sleep.

Some days, *tío* León's big car and driver picked us up and took us to his house, the old hacienda of my grandfather Florentino. Here León ruled the sugarcane plantation. My parents walked through the house in awe, and my father's memories overwhelmed him.

"Oh, my God, here was the place where my father sat." José lowered his head, and my mother put her arm around him.

"It's all right, dear."

The house seemed to be an animate being, with a life of its own. Hadn't *tío* León had its portrait photographed and framed, just like a person's? A portico in front of the entrance of the two stories held a balustraded balcony; each window was underlined by columns; striped, green awnings and an overhanging roof sheltered the white-with-green-trimmed facade from sun and rain. The authority of nineteenth-century neoclassical architecture achieved lightheartedness in the wood of a Pacific island.

At a distance from the house stood a large barn and the thatched houses of the cane cutters. A stalwart mestizo foreman, arrayed in riding pants, polo shirt, and rifle, oversaw horses and laborers when *tío* León wasn't doing it himself. He brought out a *caribao* with giant brown eyes that pulled us around the estate in a two-wheeled wagon. Back at home I drew pictures of that soft-eyed animal and the wobbly car, curious that my crayons couldn't recreate the scene.

Tío León would soon marry Casilda and fill this great empty house, never with children, but with a woman, to me a forceful, dominating presence—calm, speaking softly, and hiding a machete. Her dark hair smoothed back into a bun, one deep wave near an eye, carefully surrounded a long, narrow, plain, pale, and intelligent face; about thirty years old, Casilda would turn her head to one side, her wide mouth smiling all the way to turned-up corners, her eyes dissolving into slender, curved moons. Her delicacy and simplicity evaporated as she drove us to town by herself, despite *tío* León's protests that she use his driver, always coming up with some place new to shop, another person to visit. Wherever she went, she glowed with an independent power. Stimulating and articulate in English or in Spanish, she would not become my *tía*, but my aunt Casilda.

One morning, Casilda called me over to her car. "Get in," she said, "I'm taking you and your mother to a new shop in Talisay."

On the seat was a newspaper I picked up as I sat down. On the folded-over front page, standing next to the Italian king, was a bald, pouty-mouthed, big-jawed man who had sent thousands of soldiers to Africa in one day and who "liked light tanks." That was funny. My mother was getting in the car.

"What's Musso..."

"Never mind that," she mocked, tossing the paper into the back seat, "We're going shopping! Move over, Patsy!"

Aunt Casilda started the car, and we were off, laughing.

"To buy, to buy, in Talisay!" I rhymed.

Since Spanish times, the Catholic Church controlled customs of life and the life of the mind. My parents, traumatized by the bureaucratic churches of their youth, bearing grievances they reinforced in each other, evaded contact with the family's field commanders of the church. My father's complaint to me, "why do you want to go there?" in front of his sister Isabel became: "That's nice that you go with your *tía*, Patsy." A clean slate, I slaked my curiosity by walking with *tía* 'Sabel to mass.

The church itself was a supernatural personage. We entered through an ancient wooden door (heavy and crooked). It closed (creeeaack!) and we sat enveloped in the shadows of a stone room with a dirt floor, encased in the smoke of hundreds of candles and the scent of incense, while a priest in white robes murmured the liturgy in Latin. *Tía* 'Sabel sat praying the rosary, worshipping in another dimension. Seated on a wood bench, without a baby Moses to admire, only a God in agony on a cross, I encountered the Invisible. I had never been in a Protestant church or a Catholic one, only the Sunday school punch-and-cookies class, and this was a long, drawn-out affair in semidarkness, countered by a rush of candle power, the intense smell of incense, a foreign language that no one listened to, the whispered rosary chants, while I was left alone in the midst of it all. I had nothing to do but meditate on the nothingness, the invisible, the mystery behind the visible. I wasn't frightened, I was bored because I had nowhere to go within the contemplation, no special words, no teachings, no presence, nothing to accept or reject. But at least nobody made me do anything, and what I learned was patience and acceptance.

At last, the huge door would open. We passed the high stone font where *tía* 'Sabel dipped her fingers in water and touched my head, shoulders, and chest bone. She was smiling at me, and I sensed her blessing me.

My visits to church were frequent, though not with the daily routine of *tía* 'Sabel's. When I wanted to sleep and miss mass, I was excused. Without obligation, the mystery behind the world burrowed deep within my bones.

Sixteen

My mother liked walking through Saravia in the evenings; the cool nights renewed her Nordic body. She would stroll with my father and his sisters through bamboo and palm groves, the sweet smell of *sampaguita* flowers permeating the humid air. Sometimes I would slump along with Elisa or Joséfina.

Home from the fields, men and women relaxed on the wooden porches fronting their small, open-windowed houses, thatched with fronds from surrounding nipa palms. In the navy-black nights, under a *capiz*-shell moon, men played guitars and the sixteen-string *bandurria*, a hybrid of the Turkish oud and the Spanish guitar that has a distinctive tinkling, vibrating timbre. Their families and friends joined in Spanish-style folk songs, some spirited, others sentimental. As we sauntered down the paths—clearings, really, in forests of towering tropical trees—the musicians smiled in greeting, inviting us to a *belación*, a celebration of a religious or secular event.

My mother was won over "oh! They want us to come and

join in celebrating their wedding anniversary! We don't want to bother them! But aren't they wonderful people!"

That was in the evenings; days played to a different tune. Ruth wanted to belong to her husband's home and family, but a barrier existed. As she sat in the shade of the porch on those scorching bright days, villagers walked by, sometimes going out of their way to take a look at the new sideshow celebrity in town, the white woman plunked down from America on this island in the provinces where no flesh was lighter than coffee with cream. She was a pale phantom compared to these sienna figures, and she must have frightened the least sophisticated. Such blank white skin: what was the matter with her? They stared boldly, unblinking, and unrepentant.

To locals she met, she kept protesting, "I'm not really an American—I'm Norwegian!"

Their eyes replied, "You came from America, speak English, and are white: you are American."

To her further objections, they would smile, nod, and repeat, "Oh, Norweegeeahn?"

Here, too, racism existed, racism accompanied by class distinction based on property ownership, grounded in Southeast Asian hierarchy, strengthened by the traditional Spanish caste system. Peasants, their skin darkest from working the land, formed the base; aristocrats with European blood and lightest in color occupied the top floor. Negritos, the small, black mountain people, and other ethnic tribes who had bolted generations before into the interior mountains, fleeing the various Spanish and American invasions, weren't even in the class system. ("Oh, those people who live in the mountains," my father later said to me with amused detachment when I was researching Philippine arts in the 1970s.) Even with what he called my "moon face," a sign of Mongolian stock, my father approved when I looked Spanish and frowned when I got suntanned or black. In 1900, when he was a boy, being Spanish was the ideal. By 1936, the model was American (white, that is), an even harder breed for the indigenous peoples of the provinces to mimic.

Although Ruth embodied the white world for the locals, in her mind this town on a Southeast Asian island was equated with her hometown on a fjord. She wrote in her journal of "the quiet days," "the delicious food," "the gorgeous moonlight," "the nicest people who can't do enough for you," denying any discomforts. She brought no new ways to Saravia, no rebuff to the culture, no expectation that she should be copied or imitated. Yet, she represented America. Seldom seen in the Visayas, her white skin suggested that she was the overlord; as wife she was clearly a mark of José's having succeeded in the West.

When we were back in the States, she said, "I got along better with Isabel even though we didn't speak the same language!" Then, with a sharp breath, she added, "do you know what María said to me? That I had green eyes like the *tuk-ku*!" Her soft face stiffened at the insult.

Their stilted relationship masked the fact that, likely as not, the comment had been an amazed observation rather than a transparent slur. Sensitive Ruth became even quieter and more tense. Photos often caught her in a mood of irritation or confusion. She had fallen victim to culture clash and had found no creative way to deal with it as I had; she had not become bicultural.

American rule in the Philippines glowed with the same dark ambiguity as had Spanish occupation. By the time of our visit, the United States had administered the Islands for thirty-seven years; despite talk in school of democracy, the poor were still without hope and without land, the rich, apathetic in their unchallenged rank. But sugarcane plantation owners and other land owners were pleased, their markets protected. They were leery of Americans leaving. The Philippines had become a commonwealth, with a trade relationship on a graduated scale over a ten-year period, pointing to independence in 1946. Osmeña (and in the future Quezón and Rojas) wanted total freedom but not in the revolutionary style of 1898; they would work within the system. A commonwealth gave them autonomy, even though a few radical anticolonialists would call them puppet governments. The spirit of Lapu-Lapu, who was said to have killed Magellan in hand-to-hand battle proclaiming "Imperialists out!" was far from our house. From 1907 through the 1920s and 1930s, even as late as 1967, the Sleeping Hero myth, anticipating the return of a resurrected José Rizal so that rich and poor would fare alike, proliferated among the peasants and tenants; politico-religious cults, embracing the myth, rallied against both the United States and Philippines governments, leading into Communist movements.

But there was little talk of politics, certainly not in our house in Saravia, because we were affluent and used to our privileges. The only mention of Island politics was polite, *merienda*-time chats by pro-colonialists who dreamed of statehood. Invariably, these were the well-to-do who saw such a possibility as a way that they could make more money and that their children would be more easily able to attend school in the United States.

"Yes, we are doing fine with the Americans here, Joe," *tío* León told his brother, "Americans have brought new technology, paved roads. Hospitals and immunizations have doubled our life expectancy. Childbirth deaths cut almost in half! And we are an American commonwealth now!"

"No, no! I mean, what happened to the idea of independence our father and uncles fought for?" José spat on the Commonwealth, which meant self-government but still gave Philippine power to a protectorate six thousand miles away. "The Islands should be free to rule themselves! What about the words of Rizal, del Pilar, Aguinaldo? Why are the Islands like a child clinging to the father—like a small child who always obeys the commands of others?

"They kicked Spain out, why not America? And even Roosevelt wants freedom for the Islands!" With great pride, my father showed his relatives the letter received in answer to his own, in which the President favored Philippine independence.

On Executive Mansion-Albany, New York stationery, dated December 9, 1932, the typed letter said:

> My dear Mr. Justiniani: This is the first opportunity I have had to thank you for your congratulations and good will. Our Democratic platform advocates independence for the Philippines, and you may assure your Filipino friends that we shall ever have a compelling sense of obligation toward them in the days to come. I shall look forward to hearing from you again some time. With all good wishes, Yours very sincerely,

It was signed "Franklin D. Roosevelt."

José was getting hot now, warming to his subject.

But idealism was beside the point in matters of present lifestyle.

"Oh, Joséling, we're doing fine!" León assured his brother. His business boomed, his acreage thrived, his field hands were content. Why would he complain, when all was going so well? Even though it was an enforced friendship, the United States gave hints of freedom like the Commonwealth system and the promise of independence in a decade to loosen any tight screws.

"Better not argue, dear," cautioned my mother. "They don't understand it from your point of view—and we do live in America." Although my father and his family alternated in English and in the dialect, my mother, blessed peacemaker, understood words and tones and feared estrangement during our short stay of two months. (It could have been longer if they would have given up over three weeks sailing each way plus stopovers, but they would never fly—too new and risky, said my dad and, "nobody needs to get anywhere that fast anyway!")

In calling for independence, José was reliving a childhood tossed about in a sea of wars, divisions, martyrs' deaths, continuous loss of freedoms, and adjustment to new masters; he thought Filipinos able to bypass any consequence of immediate freedom, and he believed his family would always be secure: they had risen from *principales* and would always thrive. But since he lived in America, all were certain he must agree that the American way was the best, else why would he stay there? *Pinoys* returning from America carried only the good stories of wealth, freedom, and equality for all, none of the debris of name-calling, exclusion, race riots escaped from their lips—that might bring about the contest of pride and shame one had undergone. At this impasse he choked off his plea and decided to forget politics for the time being. He accommodated, in order to enjoy his visit home.

"I don't know," he finished weakly, "I would like to see the Philippines free."

The *Tai-Pe*, a small, open mail-boat, took us to the neighboring island of Cebu, site of Magellan's conquest. Huddled together in the middle of the craft on a bench surrounding a raised bump that must have held engine or steps into the hold were the suitcases and cartons raised in a mound on top. Beside our suitcases were boxes of clothing for relatives, bananas and papayas, gasoline, bicycles, packages of cloth, bags of letters—piled high as parcels sent to Cebu or for the travelers. My parents, *tía* María, the servant girl Ana, and I were off to see my *tío* Ramón, their youngest brother who sold cabinets and bed frames. While we were waiting for the boat, wet winds had pulled at our bodies and luggage on the rickety wooden pier. Split bamboo outhouses were tugged to their tolerance, seeming about to break off and take wing.

Aboard, my mother cast a look at her husband; he manfully smiled and said, "Oh, no, it is okay—always like this." This was an extension of the Sulu Sea that ran north of Mindanao and between Negros and Cebu. Then with only horizon circling our craft, wet winds became a mild typhoon that ruffled the water into peaks and attacked our ship like a monster, at least to me crouching low. It wailed in defiance, jerked and dragged on everything slack. Once during a big pitch, luggage and boxes above poured onto me. I peered out, puzzled, while my mother fretted and my father checked, found me well, and hands in pockets, tried striding around the deck, laughing and faking indifference, returning quickly in a crouch to scrunch up on the seat with us. No one needed to be tied down, but we all nestled together for a few hours, and then it was over.

Taking a truck over crooked mountain roads, we arrived in Cebu. Here was a city with big buildings of stucco and broad highways, not the wood and palm landscape of Saravia. Stores and offices lined its streets where horses drew a few old *caramatas*, buggies.

Tío Ramón had a smooth, Spanish-style face, with regular features, looking like a smaller, quieter, more handsome version of my father. *Tía* Margarita was a beautiful dark-hued Spanish *señora* (where was her comb and mantilla?), and I was spellbound by them. Seven-year-old Conchita of the fine, narrow nose and delicate features captivated my father. Jealous, I loved the music of his scolding her for minor misdeeds. Aghast, I watched adorable four-year-old Flory (named for our grandfather Florentino) defy new management, deliver tantrums, drink only creamed coffee for breakfast. But six-month-old Rudy simply opened his rounded baby mouth continuously, saying, "Ba!" and I decided that grown-ups had babies so they could play with dolls. At Rudy's baptism, my parents became his godparents.

With one of Margarita's brothers who was very tall with very large features in a narrow, smiling face and an uncle who was short and wore a white bush suit and big-brimmed hat, we all drove to the Talisay hot springs for the curative powers of the mineral water. The women exchanged their calf-length, rayon-silk print dresses for swimsuits and the men donned long trunks and went into the baths. It smelled so bad I wanted to leave. This was supposed to be an exhilarating event, but by now my mother wasn't feeling well and *tío* Ramón's wife, Margarita, had to be hospitalized for an appendectomy.

The next day in the hospital, my parents were invited to watch.

"Well, I don't think that was really necessary," my mother later commented in a prissy way; watching doctors cut and pull bloody stuff from inside of *tía* Margarita made Ruth cringe.

Tía María spent the night with her sister-in-law, and my parents offered to help Ramón with the children. My parents baby-sat, while Ramón tended his below-stairs store of wrought-iron bedsteads (in Spanish-Asian designs, each holding a metal loop high above, from which cascaded piña mosquito netting). I then endured my dad's heavy fathering of Conchita and seethed.

"Now, let me see, do you want me to read to you, Conching, or would you rather go to the ice cream shop?"

In the newspaper I saw pictures of the English princesses all done up in white as bridesmaids; Elizabeth was about my age and Margaret was younger and had the dainty, pretty looks of my cousin Conchita. Tall in my fourth grade, I felt like a large, overgrown clod.

Three days later, *tía* Margarita was still in the hospital, but we had to keep to our schedule and leave. My mother by now wasn't well—she seemed to have given herself over to help-lessness and hopelessness. She always looked strained, as if something were just out of reach. She no longer resembled the happy woman in an ankle-length print dress dancing with my father on the ship, smiling and slightly breathless.

Their stone house had a store-front below, among lots of brick and stone houses, since Cebu was the second largest city in the Islands. In front of one of the many houses we visited built on a hill, my mother missed a step and plunged down some fifty stone stairs. She crumpled, rolled for a while, slowed, then fell again as she tried to get up. For a few moments, everything seemed to move in slow motion: her fall, our scramble toward her to help, the shouts of surprise. Then, when she had finally stopped rolling and we had ascertained that she was not seriously hurt, my father was mad at her for falling and scaring us all so much.

"Oh, Ruth—don't do this now!"

This was her second fall recently, a passive capitulation so different from her aggressive running into the street to stop a car from hitting me with her body. I watched her afterwards in a state of fright, while my father thought scolding could solve it. She looked dazed, explaining that it was the muggy heat that frazzled her; we asked if she was okay, and she said she was. Much later, I would hear about a syndrome in the tropics in which people lose their balance and fall frequently—mere-ly because of inability to adjust to the heat. Maybe it was just that simple.

Back home in Negros, preparations for the Catholic Eucharistic Congress kept hundreds busily engaged. It was the first time Bacolod would be so honored. My aunts took us to the splendid stone church where dignitaries would consecrate liturgy of the faith for large, provincial crowds. Outside the cathedral, through hammering, pounding, and shouted orders, seating and aisles were emerging, and banners of white with Christian symbols flew in the soft breeze.

"The bishop himself will give the communion wafer to everyone making the pilgrimage from all the Visayan Islands," *tía* María said, exuberant. My aunts watched the activity rapt in anticipation.

Suddenly, the family *bon ami* turned oppressive; the feeling was familiar; I had steeled myself to it before. My father was so annoyed by the religious preparations, he was planning something to express his contempt, something that would mortify my mother and me. I held my breath as he quickly walked to the bishop's ensconced throne on a high platform and sat in it, his arms dangling on the arm rests; he crossed his legs and was grinning wickedly. I stood glued to the spot, hoping my father would come to his senses and stop the behavior that matched the little-boy show-offs in my classrooms. Usually delighted or slightly flustered by their brother's jokes and teasing, now my aunts were horrified, their faces clouded with the enormity of the transgression.

I saw my aunts for the first time as others might see them: two thin, middle-aged ladies, their frail bodies shapeless in their long, plain dresses. Unmarried, childless, pensioned from teaching, aided by profits from the family plantation, their lives were to my ten-year-old mind melancholy and boring. María, once the belle, had aged into a sad-eyed, elderly waif; Isabel's shadowed cheeks warned off further hurt. They looked like two lean fawns who had spotted the hunter and paused paralyzed in gait, wondering which way to bolt. They only knew that José must get out of the bishop's chair! My mother didn't need any translation for this look and flew like an avenging angel over to my father.

"Oh, José, stop this nonsense now! Your sisters are so hurt they don't know what to do!" Her outrage placated him.

"Well," he laughed, dawdling another moment to show

his authority before getting down. "What's the difference? I have a bald spot on top just like the priests do!"

To my aunts, Ruth shrugged and said, "he's always joking, you know."

At first, the two women were distant toward their heretical brother, but shortly both melted under his charm. Soon they would lose him to the death of departure; they mustn't let any bad feelings spoil their time together. Then they would join in this impending gala church celebration, their usual source of happiness.

My tenth birthday was celebrated by another village *belación*. All day my aunts and parents anticipated the celebration, doubly special because September seventeen was also the birthday of my grandfather Florentino. José and his sisters looked at me as if I were an oracle born to make us remember their beloved father. The entire town had been invited.

The party planned for five o'clock, by four showed not a sign—except for the *lechón*, the huge pig that would become roast pork, slowly revolving over a fire. First, the animal looked like a demonic version of itself, red and angry. I stayed out of sight of the creature, hiding behind a tree.

"What's the matter, Pahtsy?"

"Nothing."

Finally, after hours had passed, the roast was brown and crisp, no longer so thoroughly identifiable as a barnyard animal, and I left my hiding place.

My father announced, "Four-thirty!"

Tía María laughed, "Don't worry—this is Filipino time!"

Around six o'clock, over a hundred people arrived, carrying a banquet. Women strode into the area, baskets on their heads, some filled with banana-leaf packages that held rice and fish, rice and chicken, rice and vegetables, and sweet rice cones. Others had baskets overflowing with white coconut desserts, yellow mangoes, orange papayas, cakes and puddings, and bananas in a dozen different sizes and colors. Men toted seating mats, wood for cooking, gifts and *tuba*, the Visayan fermented alcoholic beverage culled from the sap of a tree. Children, bathed and dressed neatly, bounced along beside them.

The feasting seemed to take a long time. But finally around twilight, I could open my birthday gifts. They were mainly bolts of piña—pink, red, or blue, with inlaid designs shot through with an occasional silver thread, woven by the women presenting them.

"Aren't they beautiful, Patsy?" gushed my mother.

"Uhuh," was my unenthusiastic reply.

My mother profusely thanked the women, realizing as a needleworker herself how long these lengths of cloth took to make and how precious they were. Once woven on backstrap looms, they were now woven on narrow European floor looms, but still required ages of time, patience, and skill.

I dutifully wrote in my diary of their beauty, but mainly involved myself with a cloth doll or small baskets I immediately filled with a ten-year-old's collected shells, colored stone rings, picture cards, junk. Almost a decade later, my mother would use these rare and exquisite fabrics, first to make my high school prom dress, and then, when I was in college, exotic formal dance gowns. In the 1980s, I would curate and display the rest of them and more recent weavings for exhibits in universities and museums in San Diego and Los Angeles.

My father, overcome by such generosity, decided he must reciprocate; he would give my dolls away.

"Not the dolls," my mother said.

Then he thought of my books, and suddenly he was handing out Jack London's adventure tales, *Cubby the Bear*, and other companions printed on pages. I watched all these strange, dark, thin children, whom I didn't know, had never played with or even seen before, glowing with happiness at their gifts. Knots in my throat burst into sobs at losing Cubby, a support in my transformation from beleaguered child to comfortable child. (Cubby was a bear cub whose owner packed him under one arm when he spilled the honey jar, his chubby paws flapping like a child's, his purity warming an icy world.) Recognizing his error, my father made a grand search, exchanging Cubby books for dollar bills. The Filipino children expected Americans to do unexpected things and calmly accepted the substitution (some delightedly). When I saw my father doing this, I regretted it and felt as big a brat as he was sitting in the bishop's chair.

I looked at the smiling kids and thought, "they're so much better than I am. I'm so dumb and so bad." But I did not give back the books.

And then two months after we had arrived, we left Saravia.

"Can't you stay?" pleaded my aunts.

No, we couldn't; my dad had given his word to return.

You should stay until the Eucharistic Congress, they suddenly thought up.

Were they serious I wondered, after his performance? What might he do at the real thing?

Yes, we certainly hoped to see them again one day.

In Manila, farewell parties were anticlimactic. They were the backs of the welcoming ones now swiveled around sadly. My ancient Nanay Daida who feted us in her ancient stone mansion when we arrived from the United States, seemed tired; the darkened old house sat vigil; dinners were quiet, as if someone had died.

Although José's eldest brother, Manong, had been to see us a lot in Saravia, a quiet presence in the background, he was home now where he really lived in Manila. We went to find his house on the outskirts of Manila.

When we approached, my father said to my mother and me, "I guess you had better wait here."

We could see, in the distance, within a two-foot-deep, yellowish sea of water, a lot of thatched-roof and bamboo-slat houses rising on high stilts, their two rooms dry and cool from the flooding. José pulled off his shoes and socks, rolled up his trouser legs, and waded to the house among other people going to and fro in this passageway of water.

After a while, he and *tío* Manong came sloshing through the water, suddenly stepping out onto higher, dry ground where my mother and I sat waiting. *Tío* Manong was tiny, wiry, and old. He laughed and cackled a lot through his toothless mouth, speaking the dialect with my father and grinning at my mother and me. Manong's eyes twinkled as he said José had a pretty daughter, but she was afraid of him with no teeth. I couldn't deny that, even though I could see his amicability. My mother and I weren't invited to his house—as somehow his house was considered a great shame. I didn't understand, really, but I thought we would need a boat to get there, and I couldn't see any boats around. If we walked there, we would need a bath after, because it looked like muddy water. I didn't understand why he lived there. There were lots of things about *tío* Manong I didn't understand. All I knew about him I had heard in whispers—he had no ambition, didn't want to work, lived with a woman, was not married, they had children, never invited to my aunts' house. Some things that happened in a Spanish-bequeathed, American-oriented life were unspeakable. All of a sudden my father and *tío* Manong hugged each other, and we left. My father was wiping his eyes, and my mother had her hand on his shoulder.

His time in the Islands coming to a close, my father looked for the house of Mr. F. Theodore Rogers, a supervisor he once had in Saravia. Mr. Rogers, turned newspaper man, had helped him get passage to the United States on the transport *Thomas* twenty-three years before, and without Mr. Rogers, José may not have gone to America.

My father wanted to find him so badly we drove all around the hills of Manila searching for his house. We finally found it, but he wasn't there, wouldn't be until next week when we would be gone, and so that was that. José just stood there wondering what to do next as I watched his face become very sad. It seemed almost as hard on him as leaving Manong.

"Mr. Rogers, do you know if there is any way I can go to the United States?" he seemed to be remembering.

"Yes, José, a bright young man like you would like it there!"

"Come on, José," my mother said, breaking the silence, "you can't see him. Let's leave."

My father was thinking hard and got the bright idea of going to the *Manila Free Press* where Mr. Rogers had worked in 1913. He had retired, but still was an administrator of the publication. My dad told the staff that he regretted missing Mr. Rogers and wanted to express his gratitude for all he had done for him. The staff recognized the human interest of José's story. After we got back to Los Angeles, *tía* Maria sent us a clipping from the *Free Press* that my father would pass around to friends sitting on the couch as part of stories told after dinners for years. The newspaper's proud description of their philanthropic Mr. Rogers who had launched José into an American career lauded Mr. Rogers and gave my father a life that now sounded like a Homeric Odyssey. With a passport photo of the three of us, my mother and I were also briefly mentioned. His wife "of Norwegian origin and their daughter...fell in love with the Philippines and on reaching Manila the girl began pleading with tears that they return to Saravia." True, I did cry when we left Saravia, and I could easily have remained, but I certainly didn't beg like a little baby to stay.

"Oh, that's nothing, Pahtsy," my father said. "This is a nice thing for you to keep as a remembrance."

Seventeen

At the Escolta, Manila's shopping center in the 1930s, my mother bought me a gauzy white voile dress that flowed like dandelion seeds from a yoke tightly embroidered with red, yellow, and blue flowers. The delicacy of the design reminded her of Norwegian needlework. Showing through this nostalgic dress were two dark circles like chocolate kisses, signs of a ten-year-old girl growing into womanhood. My mother apparently couldn't see the spectacle I was making of myself when I wore the dress. I had to walk bent over with a sunken chest, arms hanging by my sides like a gorilla's.

"I can't wear this dress!" I whimpered. "You can see through it!"

"Oh, that's nothing, Patsy. Don't be silly! And stop walking like that!" My mother intended to have her way now, after the independence I had seized during our two months in the provinces. Below on the dock, my godfather Fred, aunts Amparo and Carola, and the Lazares family waved farewell. At the blast of the warning whistle, my parents turned away, my father waving good-bye to his life as an important man, and they headed below deck. I didn't understand their bleak looks; I thought we were going to have fun.

But we didn't, nor did anyone else. In November 1936, the world was reeling from strained international relations. Our storm-tilted ship in its icy covering was a microcosm reflected in the stunted passenger list, the head purser's grim look, and the unspoken thoughts that often clouded passengers' faces. There were few children and no one danced in the evenings. The winds blew like ghosts, I thought, while doors banged and waves splashed against our porthole. It was like the hush before a tornado touches down.

On the tender, we speeded toward Hong Kong, where everyone stepped out and up onto the landing, except for a woman carried on a litter, her bound feet useless, tinier than her young daughter's who walked beside her. The woman wore clothing of the high-born Mandarin, satin heavily embroidered with birds, flowers, and butterflies. Her neck was long, her face white, unlined and precious, but her feet were merely rounded stubs. She was one of the last to carry the custom of foot-binding of a high-born woman, showing the grandeur of a woman who needn't toil and needn't walk.

Buildings were tall and white and packed together; the theatrical, once-royal white porcelain urns and black-lacquer boxes in Hong Kong's shop windows matched the dramatic city. From the ship at night, the extravagant colored lights gave Hong Kong the look of a candlelit, rectangular cake in front of a shining mirror.

There, my parents shopped, fanatical warriors on a mission. They purchased two deeply carved mahogany and teak chests lined with cedar, one for us and one for the Anthonys. They also bought them a jade tree with green and pink jade leaves, two satin embroidered robes, and small ivory figurines.

All of this amounted to about twenty-five dollars, the price of their monthly rent at the time.

"José, don't buy anything else. They won't want you to spend so much on them!" my mother worried.

"No, it's all right! I want them to know how much we appreciate this trip."

"Of course, but we can't carry much more back. It's true we aren't paying any rent now, but still." My mother was the voice of reason. She liked to shop at the small markets near the ship, all lined up along the pier. There were probably better prices in the city—but she hated bargaining.

Kobe was in war mode. Japanese soldiers came aboard, outfitted with sabers and wearing tight-fitting khaki uniforms crushed by knee-high leather boots whose heels you could hear as the men walked on the deck. They set up tables, ready to inspect documents of passengers wishing to go ashore. When my mother's and father's turn came, the officers interrogated them, contesting my mother's citizenship.

"You are American?"

"No, I am Norwegian," she replied sweetly, as at a PTA meeting.

"Married to a Filipino?"

"Yes," she agreed.

They then declared my mother an alien anywhere in the world (*stamp, stamp, stamp* on official papers), as she had married a Filipino or "national" of the United States, who was not allowed United States citizenship. Since she couldn't have his, had not become a United States citizen on her own, and was no longer a Norwegian subject after they married, Ruth was, in their eyes, a woman without a country.

I watched silently, fearing something might happen to my mother. Final conclusion: "Not to leave the ship." The uniformed men decreed she must remain aboard ship (such duplicity might indicate espionage).

"Not on your life," my dad murmured, and at both Kobe and Yokohama, he sneaked us down the gangplank and into Japan in a rash exhibition of his own autonomy and authority. My mother looked behind us now and then, worried that she might be apprehended for her illegal skulk into the nation.

"I was so scared the whole time! They could have put me in prison!" she would later say to friends, the mystery stories she read bursting in her head.

"No, no," my father would butt in. "They didn't care about us."

At Yokohama we drove back to Tokyo, my dad determined that we shouldn't miss the opportunity. We returned to department stores, the Imperial Palace, and watched a swimming tournament.

After the ship pulled out of Yokohama, we headed northeast into the Pacific, catching the brunt of the Arctic's gales. The Japanese navy was performing battle maneuvers in the Pacific near Pearl Harbor at Honolulu, preventing our stopover there. The captain of the *President Coolidge* feared encroaching on those waters, the head steward informed us, and we steamed considerably north of Hawaii. Stabbing winds wailed, and rocks of hail exploded like bullets on the decks. A boy named Michael and I knotted the ice into balls and threw them at each other, ignoring the burning cold in our palms.

The junior purser was eighteen, softly beautiful, and I was in love with him. He was tall and gangly, with a Robert Taylor face and boyish charm. In the dining room one day, to the delight of the few children-passengers, the older officers made him sit in a high chair, wearing a bib. We stared and giggled into our napkins. His skin, almost as white as his uniform, disclosed he spent his time below decks in an office. My complexion was coffee with cream poured in until it was mocha, and to me this was the right color. But he captured my heart, and I spent hours looking for him. One evening I was hanging around his office with other kids, talking and swinging on the half-door on hinges. It squeezed my sprouting nipple in the crack when I swung forward, blinding me in pain.

"Are you all right?" he asked, noticing my face transform suddenly.

In anguish, I looked away from him, lied "yes," and ran to find my mother. She was alone in the stateroom, and I pushed into her like a staggering newborn calf, crying and grasping her close in pain and humiliation.

She anxiously examined me and said, "I think you're okay." But she remained anxious because of my weeping and whining and took me to our doctor when we got back home.

One day we visited the engine room, deep in the ship and filled with polished and powerful machines. Outside on deck, a hold was opened.

"Look, Pahtsy, steerage!" my father whispered.

Hundreds of Chinese "coolies" pressed forward, straining for air and a chance to see from their standing and squatting positions, before the hatch closed again. They were going to the west coast of the United States to build railroads, wash dishes, work in the fields, sailing in the dark to the gold in the streets of America.

I often played checkers with an old man named Mr. Denby, who seldom let me win. He accompanied every move with long, puzzling discussions of battle tactics, with every decision he claimed victory over my army. His black troops, displaying the flag of the rising sun, would overtake my land, killing or imprisoning my red-checker people. Five years later, we would see much of his prophetic scenario realized.

Eating dinner at the same table, Mr. Denby told my parents one evening that even though President Roosevelt had just been reelected for a third term, he preferred the Socialist candidate, Norman Thomas. He agreed with Thomas that "both Democrats and Republicans supported United States imperialism by staying in the Philippines for the advantage the position gave us in quarrels in the Far East."

"Now you're talking!" my father said.

"Washington senators are talking about war in Europe and the threat of Communism," Ruth said, looking questioningly at Mr. Denby.

"Europe?" said Mr. Denby, "The Japanese Empire has just marched to the Amur River, on the northern boundary of Manchukuo. Our problem is closer than Europe."

We left the *President Coolidge* in Oakland, rode over the newly completed Bay Bridge, and took a train to Los Angeles—ships were all at dock because of a maritime strike. The Anthonys had fixed up a little cottage for us on the estate, but my folks intended to stay only until we could rent a house. My dad was already feeling he was now going to be treated to overload, and living on the estate could be overkill. We picked up our car from storage, and on the way back to the "House," a tire popped. My mother called Mrs. Annan and she picked us up. Life was returning to normal.

Eighteen

"You should become a citizen, Ruth," my mother's friend Betty scolded her. "Then you could vote and help change laws and do something for Filipinos! Give them the right to become citizens!"

Coming home to America and getting back to normal translated into this: Mr. Anthony immediately whisked my father off on a cruise ship with crew, sailing to Alaska. José was cast again as personal valet to a rich man. While he must have missed his family, he surely enjoyed aspects of the trip, since, as José often said, "I get a kick out of going to new places and seeing new things! Why not? Might as well enjoy yourself!" Serving Mr. Anthony in the close quarters of a pleasure yacht may have eased the transition from leaving his home in the Philippines. He may also have been thinking: "No use crying over spilt milk," as he poured drinks or waited for calls.

My mother, without a driver's license or experience in handling money and transacting deals, accustomed to being waited on in the Islands, unaccustomed to living without her husband, now found an apartment, hustled the furniture out of storage ("I had to get the furniture from Bekins and do everything!"). She was proud of her accomplishments. To reward herself, she bought a carton of U-No chocolate bars and gorged in the silence of her bedroom. Someone gave her a bottle of sparkling Burgundy, and to ease her own homecoming culture shock and loneliness, she drank it all at once, all alone one evening. One leg of a poorly put-together bed collapsed during the night, but she didn't know the difference, waking up with her head aimed toward the floor at a tipsy angle. It became a family joke.

When my father returned and she showed him a picture of us taken at the beach during his absence, he laughingly said, "You look like a wrestler."

She went on a diet.

"Why didn't you stay there, Joe?" asked sympathetic friends. He answered, "oh, no, I told Mr. Anthony I am coming back. It was only a vacation."

"Besides," Ruth would say, "he could never stay now, he's too used to it here."

"Oh, I don't know," his response followed, sad and mild.

"Well, this is Pat's country, so we had to come back," my mother would declare, as the problem's solution.

All quietly said and true, but the underlying fact screamed that José and Ruth were really Americans now. Thoroughly settled into the United States, its ways and meanings—even though José, as a national, couldn't become a citizen—and Ruth wouldn't if he couldn't.

"That's ridiculous, Ruth," my mother's friend Betty said, trying to push my mother into more assertive, if not aggressive, thinking and acting while José was in the Arctic. "You could write congressmen and raise some cane about injustice and discrimination!" Betty, who was married to a Filipino, was an outspoken idealist, a pre-1960s feminist, no rug to be shaken out and walked on. Her husband, Prudy, a soft-spoken, docile person, listened in fascination to her speeches. His hair gleamed in a high, shiny pompadour, and when he smiled, pink gums showed.

While giving one of her lectures, Betty would light another cigarette in the chain with yellow-stained fingers, then smooth her black hair—the color of polished patent-leather shoes—away from a stark white face parenthesized by dangling earrings. Her silver bangles clanged on her wrists.

"I wouldn't let anyone tell me what to do. Not my husband or anyone. This is a democracy, Ruth. We have to change things like racist laws." Betty simmered over the Commonwealth law of 1935 that limited Filipino immigration to fifty per year. She railed against the low pay of migrant field workers and the long hours Prudy worked as a domestic. She longed to endow Prudy and other Filipinos with equal rights.

"If someone wouldn't invite Prudy to their house, would you go?" my mother asked, in an important part of her defense.

"Of course," returned Betty. "Just to tell them how nuts they were and try to change them."

"Well, I'm not going to become a citizen," concluded Ruth firmly. "It would hurt José."

Ruth kept her life in as good order as her light brown hair was neatly curled by home permanents. Her pale blue-gray eyes calmly opposed Betty's intense brown ones.

While José was away, Ruth's Norwegian friend Ingeborg, head cook at the Anthonys' house, kept her company. Ingeborg loomed a large and solid woman, lacking in feminine charm but fueled with religious fervor. Old enough to be Ruth's mother, she exercised her might over the younger woman, longing to influence her and bring her to the light of her own spirituality.

Ingeborg would change from her crisply starched uniform to matronly wear, from heavy white shoes to heavy brown ones, and drive my mother and me to the meetings of her cult. The I AM Society, whose god was St. Germain, whose color was purple, mighty in its healing power and glowing everywhere in the meeting house, made up Ingeborg's life.

"It *vould* be good for you and Patsy to do this, too," Ingeborg often said in her heavy accent.

Wooziness set in after hours of films showing healing by colors and by the Ballards, the cult's leaders. Out of the blue— or purple—the United States government put an end to the Ballards' teachings, saying they were bilking the public and growing unspiritually rich on poor people's money.

"Oh, no," Ingeborg disagreed. "That is not true!" and continued to support them, even in their failing business. She felt my mother paid undue attention to what my father said. When he came home, my father felt his wife paid too much attention to Ingeborg and that he might wind up paying money for the Ballards' "craziness." He frowned at Ingeborg. She left Ruth alone; my mother gave a sigh of relief, and for once I was grateful that he had come riding in with his kingly, patriarchal meddling.

My parents' friends were mainly couples who had married before the western states' laws against miscegenation in 1933; some had not married due to legal blocks or total indifference. About half were Filipinos in Mr. Anthony's service: fringe people, they popped up on the edge of life like Jack-in-the-boxes with strange ideas and bizarre lifestyles. At social gatherings they talked in the dialect, or joined their blonde wives to speak in a heavily accented English. Some of the women were revolutionary in their thinking, others coolly self-confident; they married Filipino men as quiet as they were outspoken. This fed the fable that some Philippine Islands produced strong women, quiet men; other islands, dominant men and submissive women. (This pat premise was demolished by the diverse personalities of my people on the island of Negros.)

Meanwhile in California, existing alongside essentially harmonious mixed-race marriages, hostility survived toward Filipinos and their mingling with white women. White fear of miscegenation and job competition fostered racist attacks from Fresno to San Diego; Filipino rage in northern California expressed itself in knife fights (a way of fighting exported from the Islands) and fed a press eager to sell papers and promote Asian exclusion. Nothing was printed about hard working, lonely, loyal men, low paid and oppressed—of any color. *Pinoys* who were trying to find work in Fresno told us of signs blaring: "No Filipinos Allowed." The closer to the fields one got during the 1930s, the closer one came to conflicts between whites and minorities over jobs and women.

"The man was dark, probably Filipino," read the report of a robbery in the *Los Angeles Times*.

"How can they do this?" my mother would cry, outraged. "Put all this stuff in the paper against Filipinos when they don't even know for sure! In New York it wasn't like this!"

My father might simply swear in disgust at what he saw in the *Examiner* at the "House," where he followed the news in papers from both the East and West Coasts; or he might submit: "Augh, you know, Ruth—life is just one dimn thing after another!" He would set his curving lips in a tight line, wrinkle his brow, and rub the bump on his nose in the predicament of the powerless. I listened and watched, my Filipina-ness becoming dangerous. Yet it seemed to me that he didn't really identify with the Boys. Despite what he went through at work, he still saw himself as the *principal*, the *ilustrado*—and this was their problem.

My mother was typical of the women drawn to Filipino men. They seemed to be color-blind; I wondered why these women didn't know that marrying into a darker race was forbidden; I knew this, fully indoctrinated in my public schools.

Just as in the Philippines, there was a pecking order in the Filipino community, and it proceeded from the highest paid down to the lowest. My parents' close, most famous and wealthiest friend, was "Young Tommy," a well-known boxer. He was a short, muscular (and to me, cute) *Pinoy* who didn't let fame and fortune go to his head like the blows he took. Boxing was one of the few occupations open to Filipinos, Blacks, and Hispanics, and other immigrant groups. Fights were arranged according to their weight, and so the different classes were often divided along national lines: Blacks, Germans, and Italians were heavy- and middleweights, Filipinos and Mexicans welter- and bantamweights. It was acceptable if all of them got their brains knocked silly. The fans were also a mixed-race crowd with lots of 1930s film stars attending, like gangster-playing George Raft. They all yelled themselves hoarse as the fighters danced, darted, clung to, sprang at each other, blood spurting from the ring into the high-priced seats. Bantamweights were fast and cocky; the crowd was electrified watching their choreography. "Young Tommy" was a particularly successful fighter, very friendly when he came over to play poker. I don't know what happened to him—maybe he went back home. Maybe he stopped coming to the card games because the family life bored him and he found a more exciting crowd, but my dad missed him and talked to my mother about him as if he were ultimately a success story.

Closest friends were Olga and Dado. Olga's fame lay in being French and beautiful; her mother had emigrated from France and picked an exotic second husband, called by his last name, Azarcon. For her fully French daughters, she chose the names Olga and Albertine. Dado's fame resulted from his being "Speedy Dado," a popular Filipino bantamweight boxer of the 1930s. Dado, muscular and stocky, with a baby-doll face under slightly swollen eyelids, a mark of his profession, unceremoniously looped his elaborate championship belt over a hook on the inside of the bathroom door. For a while—until Dado was felled by success—the couple exuded glamour and flaunted wealth. They discussed the advantages of a Buick over a Packard, shopped at Robinson's for the latest styles, and lived in snazzy apartments in Los Angeles, San Francisco, or Australia—wherever they traveled for his boxing engagements. My parents dearly loved them, and the difference in lifestyle was far below the strength of their relationship. When they were in Los Angeles, we went to each other's houses for dinner or to Chinatown to scramble into booths or small raised-floor, enclosed rooms to eat, talk, and laugh. Toward evening's end, Olga and Dado's exchanges were erotic—he trying to seduce her, she disengaging.

"We're going to do tonight what we did last night!" he'd tease her in front of friends.

"That's what you think," she'd coyly reply with coquettish body movements.

The adults laughed.

"What are they talking about, mother?"

"Nothing, Patsy, go play."

Olga and Dado's marriage of traveling to matches, earning and spending, lasted until their son was four years old, due to their own prize-winning fights, which were loud and plentiful, and thanks to Olga's independence. She feinted to the left with nagging and complaining, moved out first, and Dado went down fast. It appeared to my parents that his gambling was an addiction, and he lost more than they spent. The crowd didn't roar because everyone liked Dado. When Olga won a TKO by divorcing Dado in the 1940s, it was a shocking move—only movie stars divorced.

I had never seen—except in the movies—anyone as beautiful as Olga, with her thick, dark hair, straight nose with graceful bump, and brown eyes with lashes like brushes. My father thought she resembled Norma Shearer.

"Oh, I don't know," my mother said.

"Or maybe Jeannette McDonald!" my father went on.

And I would stand before her, exclaiming, "you're so beautiful!"

"Your mother's pretty, too," Olga would say, having enough of my adolescent accolade.

"Oh, I know, but you're so beautiful!" I couldn't stop. Movies and magazines glorified the glamour, not the accomplishments of women. The stunning icons Garbo and Crawford outgunned the homely and sagacious Eleanor Roosevelt and the gutsy and engaging Amelia Earhart.

After their divorce, Dado just sort of disappeared. A few years later, my father and I, in an attempt at father-daughter bonding, went to the fights. One night we discovered the long-lost Dado outside the ring selling the boxing magazine, his baby-face swollen and distorted, his speech slurred. José sadly patted him on the shoulder and tried to talk to him.

"Hey, *paisano*, countryman, how are you?"

But Dado didn't respond sensibly.

José gave up, sliding extra money into his pocket. "Okay, old friend—good-bye."

My father was disappointed that I didn't become a fan; he had to go to the boxing matches alone. He screamed along with the other fans, all the Blacks, Mexicans, Filipinos, and whites, who couldn't scream at work, coming home as voiceless as the rest of them.

Olga had fared much better. Soon after she left Dado, she moved to San Francisco to live with her sister and her sister's Filipino husband (and their mother and her mother's Filipino husband). This unusual clan owned and operated a hotel near the Filmore district; it was always filled with single immigrant men and a few couples. For almost three weeks each summer my mother and I lived there, enjoying the expressive personalities of these French queens and their Southeast Asian consorts. These Amazons talked so much, a peep from a male was an intrusion, barely tolerated. Still the two marriages lasted, and I would never forget my time spent there: the lyrical language of French filling the halls, the dramatic women, the easy-going men. It was where I first met Nini, the stunning daughter of Albertine. Each time my dad accompanied Mr. Anthony to the Bohemian Grove, my mother and I stayed in the hotel for two weeks on such splendid vacations that I wanted to move to San Francisco when I grew up—until I did grow up, got new dreams, married, and moved south.

"Olga dresses like a million dollars!" my father would observe when he saw her in San Francisco, after his stint at the Grove.

"Humph," my mother answered, not a clothes horse and demurring when Olga tried to instruct her in fashion and the joys of having a job, making your own money (and being single).

It was the first time I ever heard a "humph" against Olga, and I wondered what was going on. Ruth was content being a wife and mother. For this, Olga countered with the friendship of the beauteous Marina (stuck-up, my mother said), the Spanish wife of a (whispered) philandering Spanish-Filipino mestizo named Montez. They had met when Montez was Dado's boxing manager.

Marina, her husband, and daughter lived in Los Angeles,

except when they were traveling. Their apartment was on the top of a shining tower in the fashionable Westlake area, near Wilshire Boulevard. Marina was a tiny, platinum blonde and had features of a bullfighter's inamorata, strong-boned, full-lipped, with high-arched brows over blue eyes and low-down, bee-stung lips. She talked with a Castilian accent and even lisped when speaking English. From her I learned that communication came in all forms; I felt her allure in the way she spoke, moved, handled a coffee cup. Olga left my mother and me sitting in a car one night waiting for her, while she girl-talked with Marina in her apartment. Probably about Marina's wonderfully wicked husband and what to do, I day-dreamed, but my mother felt snubbed and cleared her throat and twisted her fingers on her handbag, sure signs she was nervous.

Next on the sliding scale came movie-colony friends Gil and Beatriz. But not as high as you would imagine. You would only recognize Gil as a film star if you were in on the secret and knew that he wore a shaggy black-fur costume in B movies—he was the gorilla. The short, white *Pinoy* mestizo was very belligerent and didn't tell everyone what he did in films for fear of razzing. Once at a party at their house, he donned his ape suit and came roaring out. Women screamed, men ducked under tables and vaulted small railings—a response more from booze than fright. Often, Gil drank too much and provoked fist fights with white male guests, whom he accused of chatting up his wife. Beatriz, half Spanish and half Filipino, had large, thick-lashed eyes, and lush *Pinoy* features. My father tried to reason with him, but Gil pushed him away. Beatriz merely smiled at Gorilla Gil; she was used to him and his childish ways, and she enjoyed the lifestyle he bought her (they built a two-story home in the Hollywood Hills with a fenced deck on the garage roof—a fad in the late 1930s—that my dad seemed to envy more than he wanted to say). Beatriz

pulled Gil away to bed to sleep off his bitter drunks, and everyone would go home.

Pedro and Lou were party friends. Pedro was a rangy *Pinoy*
with a long, wolfish jaw and sweet disposition who married
Lou, an "American." He called her LouBella (beautiful Lou).
My father hinted that she was a former dancehall girl—now a
waitress, only one step up. Frustrated by his occupation, he
could be condescending to those who did the same work.

"José, stop that. She was very generous to Patsy and me
while you were in Alaska."

My mother and I admired Lou. She was practical and
warm, laughed a lot, and worked long hours. Orange freckles
danced on her pert face; she was as slim as a teen and captured
her chestnut hair in a fishnet snood.

Now and then, Pedro and Lou hosted dinners and poker
games equal to my father's. They lived in a small frame house
on the other side of Griffith Park near the train tracks, and
everybody's kids were invited to all the parties. My parents and
they were a match that fit, comfortable like poker cards and
chips on a soft, noise-insulating, white padded mattress cover.
The night air was permeated with good smelling, hot Filipino
pork or chicken adobo in sweet-and-sour sauce, vegetable
pancit, and tons of rice. In contrast, the sounds of Glen Miller
from a record reverberated coolly, as couples danced on the
poured-cement patio.

"That music is just for the kids!" my father would sniff as
he joined the poker game going on inside the house (usually
arriving very late at night due to the chain connected to Mr.
Anthony). By his late forties, my dad had lost his yen for dancing. After our trip to the Philippines, he got more serious,
focused a lot on me, my education, and what I was going "to
be." Trying to teach me his old 1920s dances that I laughed at
(because I was learning the flashy new Lindy) didn't do much

for his ego either. My mother would dance with other men while he played cards. Poker parties were slightly frightening because illegal, and Filipinos expected to get arrested for any old thing anyway.

Lou and her mother, Grace, treated Filipinos as if they were regular people. Grace's husband had died, and she was raising her son, Bud, a tall, gangly, gentle teenager, the only white man at the parties, his light-skinned face standing out against the pattern of dark male faces. Later when I was fifteen, he was drafted into World War II. We danced on the patio and his coarse khaki uniform felt strange to the touch.

Joining the Filipinos, their girlfriends or wives, and Lou's family were neighbors Rose and Tommy, Italians with dark hair and eyes, exotic enough to be fitted into a mixed-race category.

At these parties I got my first taste of reverse discrimination: voluptuous Carlotta, a twenty-year-old Filipina, acted as if she despised me. She called me the name of a fish in the Islands that was half one thing and half another.

The Filipina Magdalena, one of a few female émigrés in the 1930s, came to America to marry Custodio. In the 1920s, only seven out of a hundred Filipinos emigrating were female, while the 1930s brought one woman to fifteen males. The early 1920s' call for labor from the Islands saw men arriving to work the fields. Some were family men with the idea that their time in the United States would be temporary. They would faithfully send money to wives back home, but their efforts were usually rewarded with the loss of their land in the Philippines, grabbed by others in their absence. Other single emitters—landless, jobless, hopeless in the Islands—came in hopes of a better life.

Single *Pinoys* were lonely and longing for families. Custodio was one of them, a mild man who would forever look like a youth despite deep holes in his dark face from smallpox. He was an artist, although he probably never sold a painting and was known to only the people who came to his neat, two-room apartment. Custodio worked as a houseboy at the "House." He had sent for Magdalena from the Philippines, a sight-unseen, mail-order package, in 1933; his Philippine relatives suggested the match and helped with her passage to America. Her wide face shone in a bright, childlike way, as if she was sure she had at last found happiness by coming to the United States to be with Custodio. She smiled easily, spoke in a whisper, giggled until her eyes crinkled.

My parents said, delighted with Custodio's good fortune, "How wonderful for Custodio!"

Good turned to bad, however, when in a few years Magdalena was dying of bone cancer. After the medical doctors' death sentence, Custodio tried to overturn it, taking his compliant wife to Chinese herbal doctors, while my parents kept urging medical treatment.

"Custodio—don't you think a doctor is better?"

"No, José, I trust the herbalists—they are very good back home." In the 1930s and 1940s, any cure aside from scientific was suspect in the United States, thought to be witchery, quackery, only for the innocent or stupid.

During visits before Magdalena's arrival and after her burial, while my parents talked to Custodio, I loved to lose myself in his large painting of the Philippines. Custodio had tacked up the canvas on the only bit of wall, about two feet high and three feet wide. Before I'd been to the Islands, the painting made me wonder. Tiny figures in wrapped skirts and stand-up sleeves bent over bare-legged pulling up rice stalks in water that was knee-high. Feathery palms bowed to unseen winds, stilts held up tan huts topped with roofs of green leaves, and a blue river ran through. This was the world consuming Custodio, longing for home. He must have painted it in the

Islands, for working such long hours at the "House," he had no time to paint.

After Magdalena's death, because of the sorrow in the apartment, all of the picture's bliss faded for me. No doubt, it had faded for Custodio as well, who a few months later, with no jewelry to pawn or sell, no buyers for his paintings, gathered his meager savings, borrowed money from my dad, and became one of the few Filipinos who went "back home."

Farther down my parents' social list was a mysterious man employed with my father called by his last name—DeLeón. He was in fact lion-like, a handsome thirty-ish, somber Filipino; he smiled by lifting his upper lip. He always seemed to be thinking about something else far away, but he husbanded well his plump, flaxen-haired "American" wife. After their marriage, she converted to Catholicism and a Spanish name, Consuelo, setting up an altar in their bedroom similar to those of women in the Philippines.

"Oh, I guess that is ridiculous," my father commented.

"When they convert, they just go crazy!" my mother agreed.

They seemed to hold this altar against Consuelo. I thought Consuelo as honest as her face and wished my parents would give her absolution. DeLeón served as a Boy at the Anthonys' and gave his check to Consuelo.

Those summers, while my mother and I listened to the mellifluous tones of women chattering in French, my father listened to crude jokes and slurred language at the Bohemian Grove. The Grove was started in 1880 by the Bohemian Club, an exclusive men's club near San Francisco's financial district founded in 1872. Their three-thousand-acre property located sixty-five miles north of San Francisco became site of a two-week retreat for affluent members who could "do" something (i.e., make music, not just money). Members were the Bay Area's elite, men who had "arrived" or who had always been part of society's elite: bankers, doctors, attorneys, professors, senators, secretaries of state, presidents, upper-level executives, chairs of corporations, artists, writers, musicians, and actors. Among the campers, at various times, were such diverse men as Herbert Hoover, Earl Warren, David Niven, H.S. Morgan and son, Barry Goldwater, Bobby Kennedy, and Andy Devine.

In a redwood grove, overlooking a private lake were over one hundred twenty-five compounds, each including a main cabin, kitchen, bath, dining room, bar, and individual sleeping cabin. Scores of cooks, valets, waiters, bartenders, and groundskeepers attended the camp's amphitheaters, warehouses, wells, a trap-shooting range, and a dining area hosting one thousand one hundred men. Women forced the Grove to shut down in the 1970s on grounds of equal rights. But no one was worrying about that in my father's day. Artists were pleased to provide culture while basking in a wealthy setting that might yield future patrons. But in fact, although the liquor flowed with the exuberance of the nearby Russian River, the reigning attitude was far too conservative to be devil-may-care.

Modern art was banned from the Grove's exhibits by the board, who declared it radical and an "unreasonable departure from laws of art." In the early 1880s, a group of artists and writers had rebelled, insisting that the Grove had become too commercial and too pretentious. They were told by the board that they could leave if they liked. The Bohemian Grove was not bohemian. Later, in the 1930s, Will Rogers quipped that the drinking accomplished in the two weeks required another two in which to recuperate. The board banned his membership, since it had embarrassed a favored guest, President Hoover, who, at least publicly, ran on a "dry" platform.

"The alcohol flows like a river, and oh, my God, they are all drunk all of the time!" my father said of cronies hanging around Mr. Anthony at the Coo-Coo's Nest, his camp and treehouse at Bohemian Grove.

"They couldn't all be drunk all the time!" my mother insisted.

"Well, that's how it looks to me," said my dad, not liking to be doubted.

José went to the Grove when his boss went, almost every year since he had been hired, and while it was still work, and he was still only a manservant, José enjoyed the change, seeing famous people (get soused), and getting in on the "culture" enjoyed there. The retreat began on the first of August, when the Grove's High Priest and attendant chorus proclaimed the opening from a barge on the lake: the speech was always humorous and coarse. There would be "Cremation of Woe," a "High Jinx" play, written and produced by members. Throughout the three weeks, there were other plays, and my dad saved all the programs as if he had enjoyed these activities as much as any full-standing member. He made crib notes on small pieces of paper of the jokes—some funny, some simply obscene—so he could repeat them to friends back home.

In the 1930s, he reported sighting President Hoover, in the 1940s, California Governor Warren. My dad delighted in telling my mother and others of his experiences and overheard conversations, as if there were some prestige in them. He stayed in the boss's huge treehouse and thought it a lark. He showed my drawings to George McManus, a cartoonist who then sent me an autographed drawing of Maggie and Jiggs, his newspaper cartoon strip, which my dad framed (and eventually my mother put in a drawer).

Commercial artist José Mora must have gone simply to observe nature in the rough or possibly pick up a commission.

My dad never spoke of Mora as a drunk. He must have spent much of his time on a portrait of José entitled *King of the Coo-Coo's Nest*. My father hung the gift in the living room until my mother fussed, "do we have to have that there?"

When I was at college I took another look at the portrait stored in a closet and told my father to hang it up again. While not great art, it was amusing and decorative. Mora had emulated the Byzantine mosaic style of Ravenna's sixth-century portraits of the Emperor Justinian, with long torso, long legs, and pointy, floating feet. The painting, about three by five feet, was novel. The portrait—a surprisingly sympathetic one, considering the source—showed my father as a man still exhibiting his refinement. José is shown in profile with a Roman-bump nose and curved, fleshy lips, holding a kingly orb and wearing long robes and royal slippers. It was similar to mosiac portraits of Justinian and his forceful wife Theodora that decorate the chapel of San Vitale in Ravenna. It seems that Mora had asked José about his family name and had been fascinated, asking more and more questions. The result was José as Justinian.

Nineteen

Coming back from "back home," Ruth had picked out an apartment in our old neighborhood that rented for thirty-five dollars a month.

"*Abao*, I do not know what is happening," my father fumed when he got back from Alaska. "I guess this place is too expensive! The house on Monon was only twenty-eight dollars—we better keep looking."

The new rental fee ate up the dinners we usually enjoyed at drive-in restaurants, where shining metal trays loaded with juicy hamburgers, greasy French fries, chocolate malts, and Cokes were attached to rolled-down car windows. These drive-ins were family oriented, not the spiffy ones that appeared in the 1940s, to be patronized by dating teens. They did have carhops, but my parents made it clear that they looked down on them when I said I thought they were cute, all dressed up in skirts and tops with boleros—José and Ruth didn't want me coveting that line of work, so similar to theirs.

"This one is new and has a stove and refrigerator included,

don't forget," my mother reminded him. "I like the way the bus stop is right outside the door," she added, wistfully. (We could be late, dash out the door, and flag down the bus.)

She and I lived there until my dad reappeared from the Arctic and disappointed us by not being thrilled with the white stucco apartment, one of three that backed onto an alley. He was sure we could find a better one before the end of the month.

So my mother and I began the trek through dreary, empty hulls of houses. At last we rented a house almost at the top of a hill, looking down on a neighborhood of empty lots interspersed with small houses and some apartments. Ours was the fourth in a row of five almost identical houses, each a different colored stucco (ours was tan), with red tile roofs, about eight years old. In the living room, through a corner of the large window, if you stood on your toes, you could see Silver Lake, a pond, really, surrounded by elegant houses. A stone wall around the tiny front porch enclosed a swing that creaked when you sat on it. I could run down the hill through the empty lots to the small store at the bottom of the hill.

Most of our neighbors were working or elderly people; only two kids my age lived nearby, Miriam and Corinne. Even in this blue-collar neighborhood, there was a pecking order: the higher up the hill the house, the snootier the residents got. At the very top were the Jacksons, their large house hidden by junipers, pines, and Clarissa bushes. My father enjoyed living near the upper crust; it made him feel upwardly mobile.

Our house was about five blocks from our old place and closer to the posh Silver Lake district, where I had friends from Ivanhoe Elementary School. Visiting them, we played in the bedroom, outside, or in the dining room, never in the living room.

The empty house yawned, hungry for furnishings. We

bought a new O'Keefe and Merritt stove for sixty-five dollars and for one hundred dollars, a new General Electric refrigerator, which turned on now and again, humming and knocking like a living thing. Our old furniture from the apartment was hauled up the hill by a moving van and spread quickly around the new house. Above my father's chair ticked a cuckoo clock with a bird that popped out of a squeaky door and squawked on the hour. A gift from the Anthonys, José cherished it, but the demanding "cuckoo!" was so obnoxious that my mother throttled the bird by never rewinding the works. My dad would rewind it, my mother would let it run down, my dad would rewind it, my mother complain, let it run down, he'd rewind it, another argument. My dad thought the clock was a mark of the traveled and cultured. My mother saw it as pretentious and noisy. Eventually, he gave it to someone who admired it, and then my mother squawked, arguing that I would have wanted it for my children one day! Not actually true.

The street of shops—the same one we'd gone to before, just entered from a different direction—was notable only for its ordinariness, dressed in white wood, striped awnings, punctuated with narrow glass front doors, and patronized by our boring neighbors, little old ladies with flower hats, runny-nosed children, dowdy, colorless housewives. John's Market sold a leg of pork or beef pot roast for twenty cents a pound, two pounds of peas for twenty-eight cents, two pounds of cheese for forty-five. John, the butcher, was large and beefy looking, with a long, white apron over his great stomach and a half-smile on his florid face. Once when my mother bought cheap cuts of meat for our cat, John said, "I'll throw in some Pares green free if you like!"

Ruth was furious. "He's not very nice!"

"Why Mother?"

"That's poison, Pat! It's used to kill bugs!" she fussed.

We shopped at another market for a while.

Next door to John's was a dress shop, where a dress cost around seven dollars. Ruth told Betty, who lived around the corner, "I like to sew our dresses, but since José can get a shirt for eighty-nine cents, I wouldn't bother to make them."

Next door to the dress shop was a drugstore where my mother and I ate sometimes, getting a full-course dinner—mashed potatoes, pork chops, peas, rolls (typically drugstore fare, dish-watery, but we loved being served)—for sixty cents apiece. We caught a red bus to attend movies at a theater on Sunset Boulevard or Alvarado, my mother's ticket a quarter, mine a dime. Gobbling penny candy bars, we enjoyed each other's company. My father had long before said, "movies are no good anymore—it is all a bunch of junk. I do not know why you want to see those people, acting like smart alecks."

So Ruth grabbed me, we hopped on a bus and darted off to any movie, and lots of them. She loved the dark-haired actors and the movies where boy meets girl, they marry and become a happy family. She liked whodunits and citified comedies. She hated boy-stalks-and-kills-girl, or monster-kills-boy, or boy-becomes-a-monster films. I had to see those with my friends in later years.

At the old house, an iceman had come every day or two. It had been fun hanging around the truck and picking out freezing-hot pieces of ice to suck on. With curved tongs, the iceman would pry out a shimmering, wet hunk of ice, slide it into a canvas bag, throw the bag over his shoulder, and tramp up the back stairs, putting the chunk into our ice box. At the new house, the iceman didn't come anymore, but the milkman did, plunking down heavy glass bottles on the back porch, the clatter of glass hitting stone sounding hazardous.

Within a decade the air would become so foul that I

wouldn't be able to see to cross a street downtown without blinking through stinging eyes. When the clean-air program began, a trash truck came, and my mother quit burning trash in the black incinerator with its cavernous mouth. The incinerator was declared a guilty culprit in what the newspapers began to talk of as a strange malady called smog.

My father was so proud of the house at 2865 Avenel that he would take guests on tours. "Here is the bathroom, it has the shower over the tub, with tile all the way down." Down the hall two steps, "here is the second bedroom with windows in two sides of the house."

My mother demurred when ten years later he still conducted tours although one bedroom had loose plaster. The landlord had no interest in repairs, and my father didn't know how and refused to learn, since, he declared, "That is the landlord's business. We are not going to do his work!"

"Stop taking people through the house—it's not like it's Buckingham Palace!" Ruth finally said.

"Okay, Boss," he quietly agreed, and I heard the melancholy in his reply.

Below the house, the Hyperion Bridge led to train tracks separating us from Glendale, one of the places that banned Coloreds. Our neighborhood wasn't deluxe enough for landowners to get up a petition to ban anyone, although I never saw any Blacks or Mexicans around except for the Mexican family across the street from us. But above us on the top of the hill, looking down on us, lived Corinne Jackson, whose mother banned me, personally.

"My mother says I can't play with you anymore," Corinne said one day after coming through the bushes to our play area. "She says it's too bad, but that's the way it is. Your mother is white, but your father is Filipino, and she doesn't want me to play with you—because you're different."

With those politely spoken words, Corinne turned and walked home obediently, leaving Miriam on the empty hillside lot. Here we made up skits after school. Corinne's leaving put a crimp in our games. It had been great fun for all three of us, but now the world had changed.

"I'm surprised she said she could still play with me," mused Miriam, who was Jewish. Miriam plopped down on the weedy ground under elms and eucalyptus and pulled apart a greenish-brown leaf. I watched the traffic on the street below heading steadily out of our Los Angeles neighborhood toward the bridge into Glendale.

"What do you mean?" I asked, wanting to discuss these issues, put a name to them.

But Miriam said, "oh, nothing." She was afraid or didn't know the name of the affliction known as racism, because then it would become a real, living thing.

I watched her go toward her house, a short plump girl, bright and friendly. She had long-lashed dark eyes, a kindly mouth, and a generous, rounded nose. Her parents were Russian Jews who had escaped tyranny, and her mother had died a short while ago. I wondered if I would lose my friend Miriam, too.

At home my mother had prepared a dinner of mashed potatoes, breaded pork chops, and sauerkraut, which actually tasted pretty good. She wiped her hands on her long apron.

"Did you have fun with the girls?" she asked.

"Yeah, well, no."

"What's the matter?"

"Nothing. I've got a stomach ache."

But after her doggedly questioning my malaise, I told her I had been banned from Corinne forever. Usually I hid any wounds from my parents, but this day I must have been especially cut.

"Oh! Pat, that's terrible! I don't know her mother, but I'm going to call her and tell her what I think of this!"

"No! There's nothing to do about it, that's just the way it is—she said so. Please don't call her! I don't care anyway! It doesn't matter!" Much worse than being banned was to admit that it mattered to me, admit that they had the power to make me suffer. Deep within, *hiya* ruled.

Around nine o'clock I heard my father drive into the garage underneath the living room. Slim and energetic, he bounded up the stairs, entered the front door, and said, "hi dear, how was school?"

"Fine, Daddy," I answered. My mother was sewing, and I was gluing photos of the Norwegian film star Sonja Henie into a white leather-bound scrapbook. Mother and I exchanged looks, her mouth a firm, closed slit. I knew I could count on her to hide with me inside of this secret. She and I would never hurt my father, neither did we want to loose the anger that simmered within him and bubbled to the surface at the slightest mention of racial strife. Today had been just another day.

Miriam and I continued to play together, and she played with Corinne. Sometimes I would go to Miriam's house, and her father would say she was at Corinne's.

Owning a house was out of the question for my parents. Even if they could have saved money for the down-payment—fifty-nine hundred dollars total, with payments of thirty-four a month for twenty-five years or more—finding a home to buy was doubtful, since there was legalized discrimination on minorities moving into middle-class neighborhoods. They wanted to live near José's work and in a "good area." Without any money, they were saved the indignity of being turned down.

This funky, East Hollywood neighborhood with quiet, tree-lined streets, the gas station on a corner, old 1930s and cheap 1940s cars parked by the curb was my world. I hated any excursion into Rosemead, the mountains, any place secluded or bucolic that was away from friends my age. My mother insisted I climb the cliffs at Griffith Park with her and a friend. I wondered why one climbed a mountain. Once I looked down and froze. I couldn't go up or down.

"Come on, Pat, for goodness sake!" my mother exclaimed.

She loved the outdoors; it took her back to excursions in Norway, and she had found an eighteen-year-old neighbor who wanted to hike and climb with her. Mother also joined the Community Center's gym class at Silver Lake and went with the women to Idyllwild, Crestline, and Santa Monica beach. They donned scarves and print dirndls, danced folk-dances, and had their pictures taken, my mother's smile three inches across.

After returning from the Philippines they dumped me unceremoniously in midsemester into my class; I quickly read-justed to concrete and gravel, bells, and rules. Everybody was white except for me and a couple of Japanese kids. One, whose name was Choiye, became my friend.

Phillip, a large, loud boy in my classroom insisted, "can't Patsy tell about her trip to the Philippines?"

I resisted.

The teacher said, "we'll give her a chance to get back."

One day, climbing out from under desks after an earth-quake drill, Phillip demanded to know, "when is Patsy going to be ready?"

I shot a look at the teacher like a soldier scanning the skies for enemy aircraft.

She smiled at me and said, "not yet, get back to your book," and continued her lesson.

I was ready about ten years later. From that teacher I

learned about empathy and kindness. In return, I gave her excellent nonverbal work.

Still, I had overcome some of my appalling shyness and passivity after traveling. Mary Lucille presented no problem. When she began her bullying, I looked at her and said "I don't care."

She asked suspiciously, "what happened to you?"

"Nothing," I said, leaving the bench, but I knew my recent battles in living had won me a degree of independence from my sheltered life and frightened ways. Miracles had happened to me.

Home was a sadder scene. My father's anger hardened, his jokes got uglier, his need for approval increased. He knew he would never see his Philippine family again, never have satisfying work. Now whenever José complained about missing family, or that he might never go back, or what a wrenching loss this was, my mother would become angry.

"José, listen to what you're saying! You got to go back! I have never gotten to go home—and maybe I never will!" she wailed, more than once.

He never answered at these times, feeling her awful pain. And he soon kept his feelings to himself.

But he had a daughter who would make everything turn out all right! My dad had friends, both Filipino, Nino and his wife, Eugenia, whom we visited some times. They lived in a blue-collar section of downtown. My parents didn't like the area, made up of huge, old houses in dark streets, where ragged transients loitered, some with paper sacks, a bottle top peeking out of them. Here Filipino families had community get-togethers in their homes. Parents pushed their children front-stage-center, to sing, play music, and recite. Starting out as a soprano before these large family audiences, I saw my father wither when my voice lowered, and the bright

"Ciribiribin" came out a dirge. My dad had been to the Met in New York, bought Enrico Caruso records at one time, and owned a large, black Victrola with the dog's emblem on it. So even if I wasn't destined to be a soprano at the Metropolitan Opera, he still might have a chance for some fame and success, living through me.

My parents bought me a piano and a bookcase for holding a set of encyclopedias. Both purchases sat in the living room, intimidating presences of scholarship and virtuosity. They paid for each item monthly, and when I stopped playing, my mother took some lessons, practiced, and played with delight. Good, I thought. Later, in high school, I didn't use the books, having a better library at school, and by college I was sure they were outdated. But my mother spent the rest of her life perusing the books.

"Oh, my God," sighed the mestiza I met at Universal Studios later. "Every Filipino family has to have a piano and a set of encyclopedias!"

I, too, thought it was a Filipino custom, but part of it was the hard cultural sell given to all Americans at that time.

In my case, piano playing meant a new bid for achievement.

"Ernesto's daughter plays piano very nice!" José gushed. "I am sure she is going to do something with it." Something, in this case, meant one thing: to make money. "Let us see how Pat does." My six-year career as pianist ranged from hating to practice, playing, and performing, to, more painfully, not practicing, playing, and performing. My father persisted in making me play before friends, an agonizing recital for all. If I performed well, he was a star, bowing; if I was miserable, he slunk into the kitchen, not able to look at me. For my part, it would be thirty years before I could enjoy hearing a fine pianist.

The pawnbroker paid for whatever we needed at the end of the month after the paycheck was spent. My parents' gold and diamond jewelry from the Philippines, sentimental heirlooms, substituted for cash. These jewels pulled them out of financial holes, until the day the pawnbroker informed José that his father's gold pocket watch, chain, and other jewelry had been stolen from the shop and that having the cash to retrieve them didn't matter; they were gone. My father sat in his chair and stared into space, grieving—his father's gold watch and chain had been stolen.

"Snap out of it José!" my mother yelled.

He smiled at me, the one for whom all this wretched grabbing for money was done. He went for the evening paper without spirit, but he did snap back.

My mother did all she could to be a thrifty housewife, buying meat that would stretch, sewing our dresses, looking in the paper for sales.

One day I came home to find my mother in bed, the sheet covering her face. When she dropped it in order to spit, I saw a toothless old hag in the place of my pretty, young mother. Horror filled my heart and flashed over my face.

"What's the matter, Pat?" she asked, since I must have looked as awful as she did.

"Nothing," I answered, wondering: How could she ask? Her front teeth were badly decayed, and to save money she had them all pulled in one day. In a week or so she was fitted for partial plates, but her mouth was flattened afterwards, and she spread her lipstick into an outline above and below, trying to give herself the look of lips. Later she got gold fillings in her molars, and when those teeth were pulled, she and my father traded the gold for cash. She wasn't like Fantine in *Les Misérables* selling her hair for money—but she was saving money.

Soon after, I fled to a dentist so that I wouldn't have to give up all my teeth at thirty-seven as my mother had. Since dentists were uncommon in their old countries or, perhaps, incompetent, causing more pain than cure, my parents had no experience with this type of doctoring.

My father said, "when I was young, I had such a bad toothache, I grabbed a nail and stuck it in my mouth! Ooh, my God, then it really hurt!" That was one of the times I just looked at my parents in bewilderment.

"I need fifteen fillings," I emphasized, as I handed my mother a bill for one hundred and fifty dollars. The dentist, a cool, slim man, knew I was mad at my parents for neglect.

He said, "lots of people have cavities even if they've had good dental care. And some who've never been in, have none!" He put me in my place.

My mother was stunned that I had sneaked away and done such a thing. "It's so much, I don't know how we're going to pay it."

She showed it to my father, who looked quiet and said, "okay, sure, we'll do it, dear."

They did. I imagine now that it involved another trip to the pawnbroker.

My father never minded "living from hand to mouth" as he called his life. He didn't long for clothes as he had in New York in the 1920s, or a new car like Dado's, or more possessions like Montez flaunted. He just didn't want me to know about money worries. But I think he would have liked to own a house.

Twenty

Eleven thirty one Sunday morning, my mother was shaking me awake. "Wake up, Pat!" she yelled. "The Japanese have bombed Pearl Harbor, and the President is probably going to declare war!"

I groaned and rolled over. The war could wait, I needed to sleep.

"Wake up, Pat! Come in the living room and listen to the news!"

It was December 7, 1941. I dragged out of bed, brushed my teeth, and waited with my mother in front of the large console radio for the President's announcement. We sat in two over-stuffed chairs, me yawning and my mother looking as upset as when Corinne's mother said we couldn't play together.

It was to be an unprecedented world war, but also a bitter family crisis, the beginning of a rift between my father and me.

One of the first California-born mestizas, I knew I was officially different. My parents took a source of pride in this; I remember overhearing my father tell my mother once, "Today at the Anthonys' house, a university professor said to me, 'I hear that you have a child. Did you know that mixing the blood makes a child smart and good looking?'"

My mother laughed with pleasure, "we know that!"

So what, I thought, miserably, if the kids at school don't know.

In our white middle-class neighborhood, homogeneity was the watchword. I grew up—as did virtually all other American children of the 1930s and 1940s—admiring shades of shimmering blond hair and bright blue eyes. It wasn't until I was almost fifteen and lost what my mother termed my baby fat that I liked the way I looked. Adventure stories set in the South Pacific labeled mixtures Eurasian, half-caste, half-breed, and hybrid. I pretended they didn't mean me—the characters seemed so witlessly nasty and the terms sounded insulting.

When I was alone once trying on a blouse in the dressing room of a department store, I heard, "well, let them marry, and then what do you do with all those half-breeds running around?"

I stared in the mirror. Soon, Merle Oberon's movies made Eurasian glamorous and Hedy Lamarr's Todelayo, a South Sea exotic, erotic.

My brown eyes were almond shaped, epicanthic fold over inner lid, in a cougar-colored face that deepened to nut color in the sun's rays. My friend Margery likened my hair to mahogany. With her Dutch and Jewish heritage, she had green eyes, emphasized by arched eyebrows, full lips, a fine square jaw, and long blond hair swinging off her shoulders. At sixteen, side by side, we looked startling.

"What are you?" was the question most asked of me.

"American," I'd say, pretending I wasn't different.

"Nooo. You sort of look Japanese, but not really."

Mixed relationships were always doomed in movies and books. In the opera on the radio, I listened as the handsome Caucasian Lieutenant abandoned Madame Butterfly; in a book on early California, I read of Ramona's star-crossed love for her Indian husband, Alessandro; I saw the desperate life of the Eurasian played by Gene Tierney in the 1940s, and way beyond in 1960, the victim Susie Wong. From Hitler to the robed Ku Klux Klan, the fear was racial mixing, contaminated offspring. Reasons for mixed marriages were inevitably considered to be questionable—the general public didn't like to think that it could simply be two people meeting and falling in love. The white male finds the dark female seductively submissive, the white female a superior lover in her dark man. The dark male attains power in the acquisition of the white female, the dark woman patriarchal protection from her white man.

I felt like a native alien, belonging nowhere. I could turn heads now, and my mother's beautiful friend Olga suddenly noticed me.

"It's like being with Nini now!" she said in delight.

Nini was her stunning niece, my adored friend, a singer in small San Francisco clubs. I was flattered, but strangely offended, since I felt the same on the inside as when I was the double-chinned, thick-waisted, thirteen-year-old who had changed her name to Pat.

Sometimes Nini and Marina's daughter, Cora, and another half-and-half called Adelaida came to our house in Los Angeles to visit. I felt snug, comrades on a tight ship; there were no Filipinos or mixtures at my school or in my neighborhood. One night, joining Olga, Marina, her husband, Nini, and Cora were new American guests who brought their son to our house.

Joey was curious: "hey, how come you girls look Chinese?"

Cora sidled over to a mirror with the two of us in tow.

Nini's deep-set eyes and swooping eyelashes were thoroughly French, her skin heavier and darker than mine. But Cora and I peered through Asian eyes.

"What's wrong with looking Chinese?" I asked Cora. "I hear it all the time."

"I just didn't know it," she answered, but she looked like she smelled something bad. She attended a girl's Catholic school and never heard a disparaging word, I guessed. None of us looked like either parent, yet a combination of both. And out of these three lush faces came the hard, glib gab and wise-cracking of coastal Californian teens.

When I was sixteen, a ticket taker refused me entrance to a public pool, saying, "all Mexicans have to have a health card to get in."

Being turned away was embarrassing in front of my chubby, often surly Caucasian friend Nancy, whose goodwill I wasn't sure of.

As we waited for a bus, she said, "Maybe it's because I'm from the South, but I'm glad they're taking care of us by checking on those people."

This jolted me like an exclamation mark. Deep in our personal thoughts, we didn't talk on the way home.

At home, my mother raced to the phone to berate the ticket taker: "How can you do such a thing! My daughter is a beautiful, clean girl!" She was screaming in a blind rage; useless, I thought, since the person on the phone could care less about my mother's daughter and had no control over an administration that had decreed all dark-skinned brunettes be health-carded. "Don't tell your father! He would get furious!"

Don't worry, I mused, I didn't need that. Surprised at being thought Mexican, I was enjoying the discovery I could appear to be many different nationalities.

High school teachers' racism ran rampant. I listened to Mr.

Gordon, the math teacher, tell a girl student, "Filipinos are different sexually, and they can't help it." Some of the principles expounded in the late 1920s and early 1930s leading up to exclusion and antimiscegenation laws were that Filipinos were prone to moral excesses and, likewise, unhygienic, living as poorly as they did near the northern California fields and looking for companionship with white and Mexican women. This redheaded student nodded as if learning a new axiom in geometry.

I longed to rush up and say, "that's not true!" But he was crowded into the same desk chair a few seats forward with this voluptuous girl, and I wondered about his own purity. Why, in a math class, was he so interested in explaining people's sex habits to her, and why didn't she jump up and run away from his shoulder and arm rubbing hers? I thought he was taking advantage of her, and she didn't even know it. A few weeks later she told me and another girl, sadly, that a man she met took nude pictures of her and then disappeared. But in that classroom, I, who had been taught to respect elders and fear authority, simply sat frozen, even though this teacher was insulting my father and my relatives. Minutes after the bell rang, leaving Mr. Gordon and the student alone, I crept away, a jelly-roll of a girl who couldn't stand up for her own people.

Some time around 1943, at the height of World War II, an American history teacher explained to our class, "we are supposed to honor our little brown brothers fighting in Bataan, but, ha ha ha, they're not my little brown brothers!"

This aroused spontaneous laughter and camaraderie in the class. Paralyzed, I reddened with shame that I couldn't defend my countrymen or offend this teacher with a "Go to hell!" and bolt from the room.

But Bob, a classmate later to become a beloved, spoke out loudly, anger shaking his voice. "Do you mean those brave

Filipino soldiers fighting next to our American boys?"

The teacher ignored his outburst and continued amplifying his account.

Bob strode furiously around the back of the class, saying, "Auugh!" And then he left the room!

I sat stiffly, pretending the history teacher was invisible.

Alienation had taken hold even before I reached high school. Having been teacher's pet throughout elementary school, by the eighth grade I seemed to have lost charm for teachers and found no true friends. Disgusted with social climbers, I became a truly peripheral person.

"Why do you hang out with such weird people?" an eighth-grader once asked me, sensing I could be as normal as she was. "Mary is a Jew, and Laura's fat, and Donna has that frizzy hair!"

"We can't all be as beautiful as you are, dear," I answered, craving to jar her with cutting sarcasm.

But she just looked skyward, patted her hair in the current gag of feigning vanity, and laughed, "oh, thanks!"

I felt clubbed by her callousness. Actually, in her world she was probably too tall and thin to be acceptable, but I could never use that weapon.

I met Margery at this point and began to creep toward the light. She was a feisty girl and a fine artist; I loved listening to her and having her tell me what to think and do. Her mother was Natalie Robinson Cole, a teacher who made up for all the other horrid ones. While they lived a few miles from me toward Sunset Boulevard on a winding road overgrown with trees, Natalie preferred to teach in the downtown Los Angeles barrio and wrote books on her innovative teaching style. She slid into the gaping slot as my mentor, not only in her view of teaching art, but in the art of viewing life—humanitarian and visionary, with multicultural insights. An educator years ahead of her peers, Natalie taught me new values and enlarged my stunted life.

A large, imposing woman, platinum hair smoothed into a knot, Natalie would pass on her wisdom and impressions like Talmudic law as we discussed school, art, teens' problems. Of my father she said, "such a difficult line of work to be in—it requires so much tact, patience, and common sense." She talked as if my parents were special people; I lifted my head around her. Her friends were educated and similarly humanistic, making me feel safer around people of learning. She and her husband, Harry, held meetings at their home about causes that needed airing—like Wendell Willkie's "One World" and the need for one organization uniting all nations better than the League of Nations had been. I helped Margery fix cucumber and cheese hors d'oeuvres in the bustling kitchen and listened in amazement to the concerned speeches by writers and politicians in the simple living room lined with paintings by adults and children.

In my home, my Filipino father set the tone for teen care in the Spanish Catholic style. The customs, not religious ritual. "No, I do not want you to go there! I know what it is—we do not need the Catholic Church!" Still he taught its conservative framework, mores, and mentality—a watery soup without the seasoning. My Nordic mother agreed up to a point.

Her job was to raise a teenager with Norwegian wisdom in the American culture and to keep her husband up-to-date. Anxiously, they worked out a system. He expected her constant vigil over me, but if they disagreed, she was quick to inform him of the way things were done in America. I watched and listened.

To my parents a woman had to be a virgin at marriage. I found out that meant not to have sex with a boy on pain of parental death through embarrassment. These facts I learned through osmosis, not direct communication.

"Pat, do you know a woman's part?"

"No! Tell me!"

"Stop José! She's too young to know!"

They agreed on silence. I learned something of sex from a physiology class, but mainly from the embellishments of girlfriends as we whispered and giggled through the night. It was all about desire, temptation, and deliverance.

High school pregnancy was uncommon, but there was the possibility, since boys and girls dated and there was no Pill. My neighborhood was conservative, as was the nation, but people still got in trouble. I was surprised to learn that boys had two kinds of dates, since for them girls fell into two categories, the Good (never) or the Easy (anytime); this plan was interrupted by the Great Loves that were to last forever, or at least through high school. Whispers haunted the few who dared defy a society without the Pill. "Louise had to get married before graduation. Isn't it awful!" or "Bettina almost died in that Tijuana abortion."

Still faithful to my parents, I pushed past my fear of ridicule of being chicken to tell Margery, "I wouldn't do anything to hurt them."

Instead of laughing, she said, "I think that's very nice of you."

It wasn't virtue, but my bond with my parents that stood between intimacy with a male. So chastity was easy, and I was sure to be a virgin of Los Angeles at marriage.

"I drive you and pick you up!" my father informed me before my first date in high school.

With my pushing, my mother told him that wasn't how it was done in America. Girls went in cars with boys and seemed to get alone all right! She was pretty innocent, I thought, but I got my way.

"Do not stay out after nine!" my father ordered, "and do not drive over ten miles away!"

Curfew was stretched to eleven and we drove hundreds of miles.

"She should not go out with soldiers and sailors!" my father insisted. "I know how they are from having been in the Coast Guard!"

"José, these are not like the sailors you knew! These are just boys out of school drafted into the army or joining the navy in order not to be drafted."

Listening, I knew my mother was right, but my father was correct, also. Not a word did I say.

When my mother furtively read my mail and notes in my purse, to my discovery and rage, she said, "I need to know what you're doing!"

If a boy visited me at home, she sat the *dueña*, a Norwegian-Spanish-Philippine chaperone. Strangely, these nineteenth-century values vaguely mirrored the America of the 1940s, so my high school friends didn't laugh too loudly.

I thought it ridiculous my parents worried because I had the same ambitions for myself that they had: my impeccable future, which I didn't expect to find in the back seat of a Chevy or in a teenage marriage. I didn't trust those boys, anyway. Weren't they simply the abusive playground kids grown up? The jeering teens in history classes? Margery's boyfriend said that boys talked, and talk spread; some called my group "nice girls, neat and trim." My first love, Chris, dumped me because I wouldn't go all the way and he wouldn't have married a half-breed, anyway.

I knew if I had sex, my father would disown me and never speak to me again, or possibly beat me into extinction. Later, the first two points turned out to be close to true, when I engaged in the morality of the 1960s, but that would be another story.

So we lived the teens' dual life: the prison and protection of parents and our conscience dedicated to them and the outer world of pompous display (help the suffering masses), mundane opinions (own better furniture than in our homes), and infantile proposals (stay up all night, sleep until two, have total autonomy).

I went to my high-school prom, held in the gym, with a basketball star named Al, a very tall, long-faced Italian. It was a let-down—as soon as we got there, he disappeared, playing ball outside while I had to fill my dance card as best I could. He reappeared for the last dance and took me to a shiny, streamlined drive-in with carhops in tight slacks and high pompadours, where he and his friends threw paper wads at each other across the cars. I had accepted his invitation ecstatically because my actual boyfriend, Gary, was a high school dropout, so he couldn't attend the prom. Gary lived on the other side of the tracks in the flat lands, worked on hot rods, and drove me around in a car without a floor, its engine exposed for all the world to see how super-shiny, skillfully designed, and magnificently worked-on it was. He belonged to a club that met to discuss cars (some boys bragged of stealing parts), their girlfriends stuffed into another room. Margery, who was dating a friend of Gary's, wanted to integrate the club with women, but she was booed out.

High school graduation was a switch from off to on in my life: I realized that Gary, a dark, curly haired, dimple-in-chin, imposing-looking boy was really mean. He knew I was in pain over Chris and said, "I would marry you," intimating that this was my last chance. I used going to college as a way to break with him. He married quickly in backlash, coming to see me later, and leaving his wife in the car a half a block away at the curb.

"Ask your wife in, Gary," smiled my innocent mother, not knowing the dynamics of the situation.

"No, she's okay," he said.

My B-plus average easily got me into the University of California at Los Angeles. Ever since I was born, my parents had saved change in a small metal bank with a handle that added up to three hundred and fifty dollars; their child would attend college, even if they hadn't. That was one reason they had only one child, they told me: they could afford to send only one to college. Of course I couldn't live on campus: that would be too expensive. They didn't want me to leave them anyway; I didn't want to leave them either; and besides, Margery was going to live at home.

Even so, I was one of a few who went to U.C.L.A. from my high school. Some of my classmates went to war, some went to work, others went to Ivy League schools in the East, or to Caltech or Berkeley. Some went to junior colleges to make up units not taken at high school, then headed on to universities.

My parents insisted I start college right after high school, fearing if I dawdled, I wouldn't go at all, or might end up in a poor marriage. So I began in the summer session, at seventeen. Mother decided that I would major in art, identifying me with her artist brother Rolf, but my abilities had already decided that anyway. My father was disappointed; he couldn't see a brilliant career from art that would raise me and him up. But it seemed to be all that I could do, so what could be done? However, I did have a minor in Spanish.

"Aah, that is good. She could go to South America and be a translator," he went on in his dream. I thought there must be plenty of bilingual people south of the border already, and I didn't want to go to South America. His dreams went on, while I dreamed of a different life—living the Bohemian life in Paris while I painted great art and talked with great artists.

Meantime, I worked in the school library, weekends painted flowers on blouses, and spent summers in a defense plant. I knew of the Anthonys' great wealth and how some friends had maids or at least separate formal living rooms. But, since Margery and I had the same kind of clothes (sometimes we shopped downtown at Robinson's end-of-the-month sales), the same allowance, the same size house, the same type of parents who gave parties, the same kind of vacation experience, and had similar cars, I thought we were very well off. Margery's mother and father both worked, while my mother didn't—but then, they owned their house. Some of our friends had much less.

My father kept all financial discussions from me, but later, when he quit his job at the Anthonys', I also quit mine at the library. My mother told me, although not immediately, they were having a hard time. She said she was really disappointed in me to think I had quit my job; it was one of the few irritations she ever showed towards me. I told her I didn't realize. And I found another job quickly.

Twenty-one

At university, the general conservatism of our time curbed smoking, drinking, sex experimentation, cutting classes, and other vivid personal expressions.

"What are you?" asked a visiting waxen-faced, northeastern collegian at one of the first U.C.L.A. dances I frequented, followed by, "who do you date?"

"Only Norwegian-Filipino men," I quipped.

His interest in me was overcome by his terror. The underlying question being, if horses and donkeys produced mules, who did mules mate with? But I didn't feel like a mule, I felt like a teenager with a herd mentality, wanting to belong with my contemporaries. He reminded me of the cute boy who thrilled me by taking me home from a party in high school. After being asked in, he stopped at the door seeing my father and his friends playing poker in the dining room; he wanted to stay outside on the porch. He asked, stunned, "are those Filipinos?"

I looked at him anew and was surprised to see a stringy, slack-faced, frightened teen. How could I have pined for this zero?

Now at college, before me stood his twin. If he was right in wondering who I should date, I didn't stand a chance; the Mexican boys I knew and liked in high school preferred blondes. Here, on campus in 1944, it was rare to see Asians, Hispanics, or Blacks, but never Filipinos or mixtures. For that matter, it was rare to see boys—it was the midst of a war. I decided he had to be wrong. I danced by him with another and laughed at him sitting there staring and scared.

In 1940s California, Hawaiian was acceptable. One option was to be a sex object, hibiscus poking from my hair, printed flowers exploding from white dresses, and gooey blood-red lipstick plastered on my lips. "Can you do the hula?" asked a Navy medic when I visited a friend at the naval hospital on campus.

School dances and dating got my full attention the first semester in college. At one of the first dances, a fraternity man was sent out to test the new exotic queen. When he tried to drag me into the bushes after the dance, I cunningly pulled him, whining, back onto the sidewalk and had him walk me to the car, where I introduced him to my parents who were picking me up—smiling to see me with a nice boy I had just met at college!

"Pleased to meet you!" my mother purred.

After that ridiculous confrontation, like a cat, I could smell the rats in the garage! In a few weeks they sent another to the weekly dance, who lied that the other said I was great. At my rage, he backed off and said the other had admitted he didn't get to first base. That they didn't want to date me, just make out, shocked and hurt me. I stopped all dating and enjoyed rejecting rather than making friendships.

The hiatus led me to nice guys, waiting quietly in the background. One was Jerry, an eighteen-year-old Naval trainee on campus, his parents both salt-of-the-earth Irish immigrants. My high school friend Bob reappeared before he entered the submarine service, and my future husband, Dick. All of this while studying art, history, and Spanish, trying to ignore the screaming backdrop of a world war and another one going on at home.

On the bus coming home from classes, an agent discovered me. At her office, she tried to wrench from me Portia's powerful words from *The Merchant of Venice*:

The quality of mercy is not strained,
It droppeth as the gentle rain from heaven upon the
place beneath.
It is twice blessed—It blesseth him that gives,
and him that takes.

"Speak up, dear!" she begged, hand holding her chin up as she sagged in her chair.

I didn't understand Portia's message or know if I ever applied it; but I did know then that Asians wouldn't be in a Shakespearean play, and an Asian woman wouldn't get that strong a part. I didn't hunger for additional outward drama in my life, preferring the secret arts of painting and writing. After a few months of coaching, since this was not *Pygmalian*, she dumped me.

Then, in a hall at U.C.L.A., a film producer approached me, saying, "you are the perfect person to play the minority role in a movie we're going to shoot here, to be shown on campuses around the country. Its message is brotherhood. It says, 'Look! We help minorities in trouble!'"

I smiled: were they really serious? I insisted I was no

actress, but they insisted I was the person for this part. I finally joined four acting majors whom I watched transform themselves in a daily epiphany into four compassionate students who collect money for an operation for a minority pianist who was losing her sight. When I flubbed the victorious piano-playing scene, the director, ever there to save me, said, "That's okay. We can dub it in."

Before a cast dinner at the Coconut Grove, prefacing our flight into starry careers, we saw the finished film. I looked at the teenaged girl on the screen whose slightly foreign face never changed expression. Her countenance seemed like an inflexible mask from Bahia's carnival—not an emotion stirred. She frightened me.

In a continuous saga of discovery, a friend at central casting sent me to the set of *They Were Expendable* starring John Wayne and set in the Philippines at the beginning of World War II. When my father drove me onto the studio lot, we passed Filipino extras on strike who thumped on our car windows, demanding he take me out of there. Why? The pay was eighteen dollars a day, a week's wages in my job painting designs on blouses. Later I would protest against injustice, hold principles above money. But now I scabbed for cash.

Moviemaking was unending and unutterably boring for extras. When we weren't innocent camera fodder, I hung around. A bored Gable-type invited me to the bar across the street and when I demurred, sighed, "If you only drank."

Another weary father figure smiled at me in the day, sang to me at night on the phone from a Vine Street saloon. "What does he want, Pat?" my mother fretted.

Men and women, fresh or seasoned, draped around the stars. All around hovered a hollow, intangible fiction. Another mestiza, doll-like and star-struck, a beauty in the tar pits, tried to pull me into this thousand-and-one-nights profession. "Let me introduce you to John Wayne!" she cried. He sat lounging, a fawning crowd before him.

My egalitarian switch flicked on. No, I thought, I'm no hero worshipper, let him come here.

The famed director John Ford was another matter. He picked me for a close-up. (Eight dollars more—what was wrong with those strikers outside?) He labored with me, describing in detail all the emotions I should feel and feign, over and over. This was the big scene announcing the Pearl Harbor attack. While Ford directed, I noticed his intelligent eyes set within a strong face, above a sturdy, athletic body, very aged to me (over forty), a kind and decent man. I admired him and tried to become the actress he hoped to create, but I could have told him it was hopeless. My countenance was change-less; it never knew my heart. My dramatic scene never appeared.

My U.C.L.A. friends were mainly brilliant Jews, perform-ing in the arts of scholarship, painting, writing. They prepared me for ideas of a global culture; we revered Wendell Willkie's postwar, one-world concept.

"You're too nice a girl to get a morbid social conscience," Bob teased me, glad to see me awaking. He, too, was a true believer.

Many joined the American Youth for Democracy. The A.Y.D. didn't grab me, but its ideals of social justice did. These companions had all felt the persecutors' cuts; some sliced the "berg" or "mann" off their names to get jobs; others would sooner slice their throats. They yearned for equality, fraternity, and strong labor unions. I wondered why some of my friends considered them Communists. Later, amid postwar peace, Douglas, quiet Hebrew artist, unfolding friend, became a war-rior for the new Israeli state, and quickly, a dead hero. While others talked, he had tested our ideals and placed his life as a pawn for his conscience.

Connecting with the bright Jewish women and the witty Jewish men, I bowed my head when I discovered my own bigotry; I feared involvement with a Jew. While we dated, I detached. My need to escape from the prison where the peculiar were slapped with one hand, stroked with the other, won. I couldn't trade my father for another man on the edge, another man feigning equality in a racist country, another man raging in the wilderness called California.

Twenty-two

During World War II, in a unified nation fighting a right-eous war, I felt like a pinball bounced on and off my father's recollections of "American Imperialism" and the guns that strafed his homeland when he was a child. From the tenth grade to my second year in college I heard his voice, as if he had been pushed to the limit of his endurance and was going crazy.

"They should not have been in the Philippines in the first place! And now, they are sending boys to die in a war created by Asian exclusion laws and under-the-table dealings against the Japanese!"

"What about the sneak attack on Pearl Harbor?" I hurled at him furiously.

"Oh, yes? Huh! Let me tell you about what Roosevelt did to start the war! In 1935 he helped himself to more islands in the Pacific for bases to attack Japan, he talked of a blockade of the Pacific and Japan, he sent airplanes to the British! He was fighting a war since 1935! He is a war monger!"

"José, you hear all that at the Anthonys'—you know they hate Roosevelt." My mother aimed at neutrality.

"No! I know that the U.S. always was a gun-crazy, military country, even shooting in the street here!"

"Oh! It is not!" I would yell in defiance, never in my life had I seen a war, gangsters killing each other, street shoot-outs, or political assassinations, or heard of our invading another country. My country was perfect; President Roosevelt was a saint; hadn't we always sat bent toward the radio listening to every word of his "Fireside Chats"? Didn't Roosevelt personally answer José's congratulatory letter in 1932, agreeing on the need of freedom for the Philippines?

"I guess he is a good man," my father had always said of F.D.R.

But now his shouting ricocheted off the walls of our house. "What about the internment of Japanese in concentration camps, confiscation of their property and businesses by American people who kicked them out? The Japanese had been living here and working hard and at peace for years, and it is not right!" He shook his head in fury. Behind him, on top of the radio console, ticked the clock fixed onto a brass statue of Manuel Quezon, president of the Philippines. Some believed he was a nationalist, others thought he was a puppet of the United States administration. His brass hands tenderly steered the wheel of the ship of state. Tick, tick, tick—a ticking time bomb.

I feared the sudden appearance in the night of a secret group of American storm troopers who would drag away my subversive father to imprison him, or all three of us, in a cold, dark cell. He was shouting pacifist, noninterventionist, isolationist themes, unacceptable since December 7, 1941. He seemed a movie version of a traitor, or at best "un-American," easily identifiable in newsreels or cartoons, in a country united in an all-consuming war effort. I felt cold, dark fear. Hadn't my Japanese high school friends disappeared one day, and I never saw them again? John, the skinny, quietly smiling math genius, and Choiye, my round-faced, sensitive friend, whose only sin I knew of was that she didn't believe the Mikado truly Japanese. That could happen to me—I wasn't much different from them!

My father would inform me of United States attacks in the Philippines in 1891. I would inform him of my civic class readings—totally different. He raged like Rumpelstiltskin. I thought he intended to stamp through the floor. Another twenty-five years and the facts slithered through the walls of national pride into history books; but in 1942, he and I escalated our cultural and generational battles.

He sank into his dark-rose brocade chair next to the small, wooden table. He had pasted its top with match covers and cut-out photographs of us vacationing or hosting a visiting relative, all glazed over with shellac, shiny as his balding head. He sighed.

My mother would say, "Please don't José, it's her country. She needs to be comfortable here."

He would respond, "she's got to know the truth!"

"Well, I still think that America did a lot of good things in the Philippines—they brought good schools and good hygiene," my mother said; she thought realism only fair. She folded her arms, head raised high, chin aimed upward, nodding firmly. We all held to our spots as if they were marked by an X, characters in a play by Eugene O'Neill.

"Aaugh! You are always against me!" he yelled, striding into the kitchen and back again. "And that is not the point!" He seemed as black as the heavy curtains at our living room windows that we pulled in case of air raid alarms.

"Well, really, José, if it's so terrible, why did you come

here? Why didn't you go back? We could have stayed in the Islands in 1936!" His outbursts angered her; she wanted peace at home in the midst of war.

"It's not so easy," floated his voice from the window where he stared out under a cloud of resentment, standing over the chest they had bought in Hong Kong. Its deep mahogany carving matching the deep frown on his face.

Beneath the controversy lay distress over his Philippine family—and his helplessness. Helpless, too, I invented ways of avoiding him. Sometimes I hid in my room at night in the dark, hearing his car enter the garage; I lay curled in the fetal position, thinking coldly, "go away, old man!" I heard his disappointment at not seeing me when he arrived at his usual late hour. He wanted our unification, but alienation shook my world: I had to be either against my country or against my father.

Then after months of room-to-room combat, he quieted; our relationship calming to mutual passive resistance.

It was hard being reflective in World War II. The conventional classroom, the banal student, the Hearst press, the black-and-white films, voices of America, seemed so delighted in being able to openly hate the bandy-legged, yellow-skinned, slant-eyed Japs.

In a way, it was easier for Filipinos, because we weren't perceived as Japanese; they were locked up at Manzanar and other places. We were in on the personal heroism in the Philippines, if anything. It was a first.

Films and cartoons showed stiff-gaited, slaughter-mad Nazis, who while thick and stupid, could be deceptively handsome in order to carry out their fiendish ends. We Americans saw through Japan's plans of expansion, the Aryan arrogance, searing xenophobia. Along with my friends, munching popcorn and ogling movie newsreels, I hissed and booed the enemy and cheered wildly for our brave American men. Was this a football game with U.S.C.? Our classmates, little boys grown up, flew like comic-strip Flash Gordons to the rescue in Europe and the Pacific to blast—Bif! Bam! Boom!—Hitler and Hirohito! They were pledged to our safety.

We clutched onto railings of egg-shaped aircraft flung high into the air at the Long Beach or Venice amusement piers, stopping to tilt in the sky, our boyfriends home on leave hanging over the side, aiming imaginary rifles and yelling, "aak, aak, aak!" A hilarious mockery of an everyday activity.

We danced in Hollywood's Palladium, hugging to the music of Tommy Dorsey, his brother Jimmy, Harry James. Glen Miller had proved the famous could die in war. We romanced to the lyrics of "I'll never smile again, until I smile at you"; we remembered absent faces in "I'll be seeing you in all the old familiar places." We sang with hilarious disdain, "Ve hail, ve hail, right in der Fuhrer's face!" One of the young men would be gone the next day.

We built a solid community out of the virtue of this war. How could we have given our teen years to the production of munitions, preparation for blood-letting, obsessional thinking, otherwise?

At home, my mother tried to salve the wounds in our family. "Your father is only reacting to the way he's been treated—he's seen terrible things. And he comes from a well-to-do family where a lot is expected of you—and he's so smart that he could have been so much if this country had let him, but they wouldn't!"

Not in this land of the crooks and home of the sonoma bitches, he reiterated as he caustically sang the "Star Spangled Banner."

I assumed my mother was right. And yet, I wondered, what could he have done without an education or a trade? All my life he had planned for my education, awaited it like the oncoming tide of great rewards. His teacher training in the islands was worthless. Here there was no time or money for schooling. Not knowing what to study was his part in his failure to become somebody, besides a decent, hard-working man. So, he focused on my university credentials. He stood back, anticipating my achievement in the world that would complete me and exonerate his unrealized life all at once.

"That's why he's so bitter," my mother was saying. "And if I argue with him, he feels like I don't understand him." So she determined to back him, because she felt deeply what he'd endured. "We must support men, because they're weaker than we are," she finished. Her strength seemed rooted deep in the ground, beside my father's bombastic rage.

But he went too far when he suggested that "Hitler is nothing, all this war news is just American propaganda."

My mother roared like a lioness. "My relatives are being oppressed by the Nazis and suffering! Don't talk that way about that monster!" No communication from relatives in Norway crossed the seas or airwaves through four years of war, so she could only imagine their lives. As long as I could remember, she had sat at the card table writing to her sisters, her brother Rolf, and her mother, despite her awkwardness with the language. "Don't talk like that again!"

He didn't.

Many of my male classmates were under draft age of eighteen; those deemed unqualified for service, called 4-Fs; or naval pilot trainees who numbered in the hundreds, called V-12s and V-5s. They marched daily to their classes on campus in drab garb and, occasionally, dress blues, tramping in double file toward the gym and breaking up to walk separately to classes.

Studying was an escape from thoughts of the war. My professor praised my essays in Spanish, but was disgusted when I was too shy to read them before the class. "You're too old to have this problem!" In numb studio sessions I painted with women waiting for their men to return. The splendid Romanesque Royce Hall was one of the few buildings on campus, and rabbits scampered across the lawn in early mornings around the new gym and science buildings.

Bob, in the submarine service, visited me at U.C.L.A., where he talked to his friends in the A.Y.D. movement. Bob was Czech, tall with kinky blond hair, wrinkled forehead, curvy lips from which humor flowed. His mother loved me, and my mother loved him. While he was on furlough, we went to plays or jazz clubs, listening to great musicians. "Ba-ba-da-doo-da!" blared from clarinets, saxophones, and sassy voices. Tinkling pianos and drums accompanied, as Bob drank straight shots to my Cokes. Then he went back to the South Pacific or some place, he couldn't tell or didn't want to talk about it. I asked, "why subs?" Under the sea! It terrified me to disappear under water.

"You can hide from the bombs down there," he joked, deadpan.

My uncle Enrique occasionally came down from San Francisco to see us, looking slick in his pea coat and officer's cap. My dad and he had a lot to talk about, and they posed for pictures my mother took, looking sharp, my dad in a suit and felt hat. As the war progressed, my uncle didn't visit as often because he and lots of Filipino navy men were overseas in the Pacific. He came out without a scratch and lived to be ninety-three.

Bud, Lou's brother, died as soon as he donned a uniform, early in the war, in 1942, in the first battle in the Americans' North African campaign under Eisenhower.

"Our heroes storming the beaches to rout the Nazi threat,"

the newspapers said.

I recalled awkward, spindly Bud—how could he have stormed anything? Bud never outlived his name, dying before blooming to manhood. Lou's face of freckles and faded eyebrows held a strength equal to the losses of the 1940s. She worked in a defense plant; an earnest woman in pants, a riveter, I pictured her pulling up her visor for a Coke break like the ads on billboards.

Gatherings at Pedro and Lou's house didn't end, but proceeded quietly, like a B-29 seeking its target. Bud's mother walked and sat and stood like a white marble statue, serene and blank. Her closed lips smiled at me when she saw me studying her. Only in my mid-teens at the start of the four-year war, I insulated myself from the deep grief of parents, wives, sisters, lovers. But I saw the purple flags in the windows, said good-bye apprehensively to friends who went to Europe or the Pacific, and waited for this pall over our lives to end.

Summers I worked in a defense plant near my house, sanding rough edges off a new material called Lucite, a miraculous lightweight substance used in making viewfinders to better bomb the enemy. And the war went on.

When victory leaned toward the Japanese, José daydreamed that "maybe the Japanese would treat the Filipinos better than the Americans treated us." He brooded that this war on his loved ones could have been avoided if only the Americans had not stayed there in 1898—wasn't he right, after all?

No word came through from our family in the Philippines. We learned, however, that some Filipinos at first had looked to the Japanese as brothers, but they found that the Japanese felt superior to them, forced them to bow to them in the streets, and struck them if they didn't obey. The Filipinos were furious three months after the fall of Manila at the 1942 Death March following the surrender on Bataan, in which thousands of American and Filipino soldiers died of wounds, disease, and starvation.

My dad cut a clipping from the paper with two new items. The first one said that in a Tokyo broadcast recorded by United Press at San Francisco the Japanese intended to give the Philippines, which they were occupying, their independence on October 14, 1943, with President-Elect Dr. José P. Laurel as head. Laurel hoped that the eighteen million Filipino people would prepare with heart and determination for the day "which will mark the final goal of the attainment of the long-awaited independence." Below this was the headline, "F.D.R. Asks Early Filipino Independence." The article stated that Roosevelt asked Congress, in "partial recognition for their heroic role in this war" to advance the date for the Filipinos' independence to July 4, 1946. Hoping it would be earlier, Roosevelt said, "[I]t is possible that the fortunes of war will permit an earlier consummation of this joint will of the American and Filipino peoples."

But in Negros occidental, in Saravia, where my cousins Flory, Conchita, Rudy, their parents, *tío* Ramón, and *tía* Margarita had moved to be near our aunts María and Isabel during the war, the promise of freedom from Nippon didn't carry much weight. Toward the end of the war they were thrilled to see American planes fly over, bombing Japanese installations. Most Visayans were not exposed to the brutality experienced on Leyte and Luzon, and in isolated cases the Visayas witnessed soldiers showing respect for the Filipinos. Flory later told me that the Japanese soldiers had little to do and spent time playing ball with him, talking to his parents, and posing for pictures. When American planes flew over, the foreigners ducked into shelters with Flory and his family.

"Hey," *tío* Ramón said to one of the soldiers. "What are

you going to do with those guns? Don't shoot at the planes."

"No, we're not," replied the soldier. "They might shoot back at us!"

Flory remembered that as a twelve-year-old, with his father yelling at him to get back inside, he climbed up onto the roof, waving and calling to American planes that soared overhead, thrilled at their coming, representing release from a conqueror.

The day the United States dropped the bomb on Hiroshima, my father swore in outrage, and I poured my anger on him, with the cruelest ending, "Now my friends can come home!"

"That is what I want too, darling!" he wailed. "For the boys not to die!" (And our relatives to be all right, and our family to be close, and the Philippines to be free.) Tears streaked his face, his shoulders collapsed, shuddering bony and small. How could I have feared this powerless man?

After the war ended, all but two of my friends returned. José still served at the "House," but it was beginning to tell on him; he was weary and downhearted. I seldom went there, getting out of going with the excuses of homework, dates, and anything else I could think of. I refused to be connected with his ball and chains.

My mother got letters that rubber-stamped her intuition of her peoples' deprivations, persecutions, and subjugation. "They write that Rolf was badly persecuted by the Nazis. They had to leave Oslo, and they were afraid for his life. They say it was because he was a part of the intellectual artists and writers whose opinions and influence Hitler feared." Her nervous tremble spoke above the white-paged letter. "And they were so delighted to have the British and Americans come to liberate them!"

Letters from the Philippines told of their struggles against the Japanese and their willingness to fight with the Americans to oust the foreign invader. Illness permeated the family, but at least they were free. Relatives' letters didn't put a dent in my father's bitterness.

The worst news was that during the four-year period of melancholy and turmoil, my Norwegian grandmother had died.

"Why are you crying, Mother?"

Ruth spent most of the next two days lying on her bed, her door slightly ajar. At nineteen I was convinced that time, distance, and attachment to her husband and only child had made her forget such far-away places and people as Norway and her mother.

"You don't understand, Pat. She was my mother! Sometimes I think you are so cold!"

I was learning to bury emotions so deep that I couldn't identify anger and grief, and my favorite axiom was "It doesn't matter." Not exactly my father's "No use crying over spilt milk." I had mastered hiding shame, covering pain, and holding onto my pride. I had mastered *hiya*.

During the war, President Quezon and his family had escaped from Corregidor with General MacArthur, and for a while his daughter attended U.C.L.A. One day with my girl-friends in the student co-op, I noticed her sitting alone. My friends urged me over, and I became my social self, smiling, laughing, dredging up small talk. She answered perfunctorily, then stared at the rim of the table. I saw her shiny and modest straight black hair, her makeup-free, intelligent face, and became painfully aware of my slashed red lips, curled hair, flashing dimples; I wondered if she guessed my father was not a doctor or lawyer. I tried to retreat gracefully.

Back at my table, Margery said, "she really froze you out!"

then added: "She looks better than you."

"Why?"

No answer, but I understood. I remembered a year or so ago in this same Coke shop a black football player I'd smiled at from a distance who left his friends to sit with me. He made friendly small talk. Huge, his shoulders and back seemed to overhang the table in a giant mountain; his skin, incinerator black; his smile, shell-white teeth; his voice, loud and musical, in a three-quarter-fast tempo; in a word, different from me. I stared at the table and wished he'd go back to his friends. He exited graciously.

I wondered now if I had hurt him as much as Miss Quezon had hurt me. We were all immersed in a bloody war of control, culture clash, color, and class—a war that was supposed to end all wars. Would it ever end?

Twenty-three

I was on a break at U.C.L.A. and riding on a Greyhound to join my father at the Anthonys' retreat, an eight-room oasis in Palm Springs.

I'd been to Palm Springs seven years earlier when they had paid for our stay in a four-room ranch-style cottage when my dad was recuperating from a minor operation. The surrounding desert was all tan, quiet, with few cars on the dirt roads. There was a bike in the house my mother loved to ride; her pedaling made a creaking sound as she passed back and forth on the slightly mounded path past the low fence that ran only in front of the small house.

Since then, the Anthonys had bought another house in Palm Springs, and I'd heard my father talk about it since I was twelve; Mr. Anthony shipped butler and cook off to his vacation hideaway for three weeks every year. Some people might have looked forward to going—Palm Springs was famous as a playground for rich and famous movie stars—but my father dreaded the separation from his family and the hay-fever attacks that caused his face to swell and his eyes to water. But the boss insisted, and José needed his job. This year, José had called home and said I'd been invited to visit; maybe Mrs. Anthony had sensed a particular sadness in her butler and suggested it. My dad jumped at the offer. My mother wasn't invited; she would stay home, finish a dress she was making, and visit friends. I didn't really want to go, I had friends to be with, and Bob might be coming home on leave, but my mother said it would be good for my father, knowing his loneliness there. She insisted, so I went.

On the bus I focused on my dislike of going to any Anthony house, but after an hour of sulking, I began to enjoy being on my own and wondered about the newly updated desert town. From the bus I watched my city disappear into highways lined with billboards of the World War II era: "Loose Lips Sink Ships," "Uncle Sam Wants YOU," a sign of Rosie the Riveter showing her big biceps, saying, "We Can Do It!" and the ever-present dot-dot-dot-dash, V for Victory. I wondered how many gas coupons a Greyhound would have gotten; gas coupons meant little to my parents who didn't drive much, and my mother and I took buses. We really hadn't been affected by the rationing: skirts were short, saving on fabric; there was no metal for lipstick cases, but Bakelite was sufficient. The four-hour bus ride through the desert went by slowly, but not slowly enough for me. I was eager to see my father, but not in his employment. Successfully avoiding Number One Los Feliz Park, I hadn't seen the Anthonys in years.

Suddenly the Greyhound turned, laboring heavily into the driveway of the small station. My father stood there in gray trousers and black coat, straw hat protecting his bald head as the door heaved open. "Hi, dear!" he called, "I'm glad you came!"

"Hi, Daddy!" I jumped down, happy to see him.

He drove the white Packard to the Anthonys' small estate, half-hidden by bushes and trees trying to make the nonelitist, southern California desert look like a suburb. We went into a spare room to unload my stuff and immediately into the kitchen to await a call from the bosses. I perched on a stool feeling warm and uncomfortable even in the air-conditioning of their neat, fashionable home.

When the button's light flashed, I tried pretending I wasn't really answering the summoning of a servant. I swaggered into the living room, a poised U.C.L.A. woman, sophisticated and emancipated, brought in from a kitchen to meet the Mr. and Mrs. who hadn't seen me in years.

"Mr. Anthony went to Berkeley, dear," Mrs. Anthony said as she and her husband stood up from the cushioned sofa with gracious smiles. They congratulated me for attending U.C.L.A.

"We're your radical little brothers!" I said, repeating the smug line then contrasting the daring young campus in Westwood with the stodgy old one at Berkeley.

They looked blank. Mr. A.'s face shone a puffy pink and white, while his wife's pretty one was set off by sleek white hair and deep-set eyes that always appeared to be anticipating something. As I put the puzzle together, a blush fanned my face from my high 1940s pompadour to my silky blouse and sassy slacks. While my American Youth for Democracy friends would be proud of me, my father might be fired. Fearfully, I suppressed my speech. I could already sniff in the air the Red Witch Hunts of McCarthy coming in seven years. There were many great teachers at U.C.L..A., well-known historians, scientists, and exhibiting artists. Some of these professors would be summoned before the McCarthy panel to admit sorrowfully that, yes, as simple-hearted youths, they had been foolish and had joined a Communist group, hats doffed now in humiliation, in order to continue teaching.

That week I watched my father slink around, head down, yes-Sir-ing, no-Ma'am-ing in servile obedience. I was living with Uncle Tom in a Palm Springs cabin. I felt sick, got a cold, and crawled into bed. The cold became an indefinable illness, and the Anthonys had my father take me to their doctor. Mr. Anthony came in the door of the waiting room as we waited, and my father slumped down in the padded couch.

"Don't look so glum, Joe!" bellowed Mr. Anthony in the quiet, gray office. "She's not going to die!" His great size, bearing its cantilevered belly, overpowered my slight-figured father. The long-time boss could not possibly comprehend that in the corner of that couch, within that tiny, sagging, gray-coated digit he called Joe, something else had died.

In February, after another trip to Palm Springs, and another attack of allergies for José, my mother and I met the Greyhound. Its door slid back; down stepped a man I barely recognized, my father, freed but aged. He had quit and just walked away. He looked at me lovingly; here was his future; all that would relieve his heartache stood before him.

He was fifty-three years old.

"I decided that Pat was grown now, and I didn't have to stay at the 'House' anymore. I stayed all those years because we needed steady work to raise her and send her to college. But now I do not want to work there anymore where I am like a slave—oh, no! I want some freedom now to come and go as we please!"

"Don't worry, dear," Ruth told him tenderly. "We'll work something out. You tried to do it for a long time. Pat's grown and I'm strong enough to work, too."

After that, my father would be standing in the kitchen cooking when I came home from school. Cooking, drinking cooking sherry, and crying.

"Mother, you've got to stop his drinking!" I confronted her

one day when she dragged home from the stinking pesticide plant near our house where she now worked.

"Oh, he's all right, Pat," she sighed wearily.

"But Mother, he drinks like it's his life's blood!" I screamed.

"He just feels so bad, dear. He thought Mr. Anthony would be decent to him and give him a pension one day, take care of him in his old age," she countered. "After all the long hours and taking him away from his family for so many years. He'll be okay when he gets some work."

In about three months, when he started working again, she proved to be right.

Much later, I decided that my contempt at seeing him a virtual slave had done it; he had seen himself through my eyes. Yet, it seemed to me right that he leave such bondage. I felt not blame, but exoneration.

By 1945, liberation had been decreed on our home front as well as freedom from Japan in the Philippines. Total independence was imminently due for the Islands.

"Augh, the Philippines will still not get freedom," my father declared. "Let me tell you a story." It was an old, bitter joke often told by Filipinos in the 1920s and 1930s. "One day a lady of the house said to her Filipino servant, 'Since Americans have gone to the Islands to civilize you, are you still eating dogs?' 'No, ma'am,' the servant said, 'now we are eating Americans.' That's what they think of us—that we are uncivilized, and I know that the Philippines will not get independence!"

"Stop it now," my mother said.

"Well," he laughed, "I am just repeating what I heard!" He was feeling good these days and sifted his bitterness through allegories.

Since World War II had been waged to vanquish totalitarianism, politicians now scurried to promote democracy abroad and in the United States. The President had earlier proclaimed that Filipino servicemen who fought so bravely alongside Americans were able to obtain American citizenship. Once the Republic of the Philippines was granted independence, Filipinos living in the United States could also obtain American citizenship. Memories of Pacific battles fresh in the minds of Americans and Allies spurred a requirement that the United States retain Subic Bay, headquarters of the Pacific Fleet for another fifty years. The side effect was Olongapo, a pustule of prostitutes and drugs. Although they received the gift of liberty in July of 1946, the Philippines later declared, as my father always had, their real independence date as June 12, 1898, the year that they had defeated the Spanish.

Because the Philippines were free, José was now an alien. As an alien, he was able to become an American citizen. For a few months, he said, mouth crammed with the sour grapes of pretense, "ha! I never will!" Suddenly, surprising to me who believed his rantings irreversible, he softened and applied, solemnly longing to belong. So that was why he had sent letters to each new President throughout the years, starting in 1920 with Harding, continuing with Coolidge, Hoover, Roosevelt, in later years to Eisenhower, Kennedy, Johnson, to Carter in 1977, delighting in their answers, grading each from "wonderful" (Roosevelt's personal note in 1932) to "that's nothing!" (Eisenhower's flat form letter in 1952). Truman was left out because of dropping the bomb.

"Ruth and I will prepare to fill out the naturalization papers now," he smiled at friends. After receiving books and forms and other material from the naturalization office, the two of them opened out the legs of the squeaky card table in the living room, bent over their studies, checking each other's grasp of the patterns of history and the procedures of politics in the United States. They drove to Los Angeles City Hall and became citizens of their country.

"Now we are American citizens!" José broadcast at a party at our house. The new citizens were congratulated by a few friends, Pedro and Lou, Margery and her parents, Natalie and her soft-spoken husband Harry, the plump, ebullient Vibiana (a friend since Monon Street) and her Anglo husband, the good-natured, friendly Ernest. We all raised differing-sized glasses brimming with champagne, lifting them high as they talked of Philippine independence, United States citizenship, and exoneration of a nation they believed had finally, fully, enacted democracy. My dad's sometimes gaunt, angular face plumped up, smooth and unwrinkled as a young man's. "I guess it is okay!" Okay to trade his resentment for officially becoming a part of a country where he'd lived for almost forty years—to sign away his native land, beloved Pearl of the Orient.

"We thought we might as well, as long as we're going to stay here," Ruth apologized to her relatives.

Once citizens, my parents voted as if the country's life depended on them, sure their votes mattered and that they were an integral part of a democracy. "I cast my ballot for the one who will do the most for the people!" spoke the idealism of José, meaning populist Independents or pro-worker Democrats. Ruth looked to the government for the replacement of relatives—to the party that might help them the most in their old age, without any extended family around. In the 1948 election, the first after their naturalization and my twenty-first birthday, my mother, realistic as always, rejected the third-party candidate my father and I favored. "Oh, that's throwing your vote away to vote for that silly Wallace!" Maybe we were foolhardy dissidents, but we thought Henry Wallace, a vice-president of F.D.R.'s who had launched the left-leaning Progressive party and stood by the working class was a change from the two-party system. José beamed as a member of the American political process. Long-held resentments drifted away on white-faced clouds as he read newspapers of the coming election, argued with Ernest over the choice of candidates, and read that Wallace polled only 1,150,000 votes, mainly in the state of New York.

The two worked as a couple again (after my mother tried seamstress work, sewing and altering clothing for neighbors who held their breath when she tape-measured them and couldn't fit into the finished clothing). Now, José was counting on my amazing career to complete, once and for all, his American dream. But he quickly hexed teaching as a good career for me.

"Oh, no!" He wrinkled up his face. "I was a teacher in the Philippines, and I know it is not!"

"José, teaching here in 1948 isn't anything like it was in the Islands in 1910," my mother argued.

"Let her do something else." He clamped his mouth and jaws together firmly.

I, obedient female child, said, "it doesn't matter, I don't care."

I did care. I saw Natalie Cole as my mentor and role model, she roused my activist soul. But teaching was pushed aside as a rebellious desire.

Simultaneously, my mother axed any ideas of art assignments that might take me away from home. I was deeply dependent on my mother, even though Margery and Barbara, our mutual friends, wondered why. It seemed perfectly normal to me—they should be with their parents more. On my interview for a fashion design job, my mother accompanied me, since we went everywhere together. I discovered the job required living in Wisconsin. At home our discussion coiled in a pointless spiral.

"Pat, you don't want to leave the state, do you?"

"No. I guess not." How could I leave my parents? Why would I even think of such a thing? It was incomprehensible to her and inconceivable to me. Filipino-Norwegian children just didn't leave home.

"The woman in the employment office took me into another room to talk—away from you," I reminded her. "She asked me if I wouldn't like to have this job to get away from my mother."

"What a terrible thing to say! What did you tell her?"

"I said I didn't know." What I knew was that I was twenty-one, had no ideas, no ambition, no foresight. The commercial art job I was offered in Los Angeles, painting newspaper ads for patent-leather shoes, was a soul killer after my ivory-tower training. A few years later, after I had married and had no children yet, I would work as a commercial weaver of delicate fabrics, as ephemeral as spider webs, which my father sniffed at, but by that time I was out of his house and psychological reach.

But now, I got down to earth into the grimly practical life of post graduation. I searched the want ads, visited the U.C.L.A. placement office, got work in an insurance office, and my father went berserk.

"Why are you doing this?" he demanded. "What about a job using your Spanish?"

I ignored him. He quieted down but he broke into a rage every time he talked to me. My failure at becoming a successful "career girl" was shaming him. His longings conflicted with the mores of the post-war culture: marriage and family. I needed a regular-as-the-tide paycheck for my coming wedding and my husband's last year in school. My biology was my vision.

Twenty-four

I first met Dick Haynes during the war when gas rationing ruled the lives of the young. I was in a car pool going to the campus and took the bus home, getting an hour's homework done, even as I joked with girlfriends who rode until they got off at Beverly or Vermont. I had gone to the university car pool office and of the choices of rides in my area, I liked his name the best and called him. We met on the corner of Hyperion and Rowena on a Monday morning. He was driving and Jim, his friend and alternate driver, sat in the passenger seat next to him. In the back seat, I kept staring at his high cheekbones with hollows, his high straight-nose profile. Mmmnn. In a few days I caught him eyeing me in the rear-view mirror.

Our affinity was decisively chemistry. But in about six months he went into the Air Corps, and we met when he was on furlough once, though we didn't spend as much time together as I thought we would, since he had a secret that would come out later.

I dated other men on campus. I never met any Filipinos or mestizos; I couldn't imagine where they were. Filipinos I met were older—old to me, maybe thirty-five or more and poor, uneducated, forlorn types who came to visit my dad on his day off. I remember my mother beginning to get nervous when they talked to me at Lou's house and look upset when one field worker visiting us hinted to her he might date me.

"Oh, no," she blurted, "she's only a child."

I had lots of company my own age from school, and this appeared to be one of the best times of my mother's life, socializing and bantering wittily with my young friends, male and female. During those years my father was hardly ever at home, working as usual.

When Dick returned, at nineteen I gave up all others. I sensed that he was as wounded as I. His older brother, Terry, had died in the war, a blow that left him dazed. Through the furlough and letters, we became so close I dreaded that Dick might go overseas. But like an answered prayer, a law was passed near war's end that kept sole-surviving sons out of active duty, just as Dick was preparing to go to flight school. When the war ended, he returned with a new sophistication. Away from his conservative parents for a while, he had started to drink beer with buddies, play the drums, and sing in a bar near his camp in Wisconsin. His basic conscientiousness made him worry whether his coming back to camp late one night from the nearby town and throwing a cigarette into dry weeds at the base of a barracks had been responsible for its burning to the ground by morning.

Before he confided in me, friends who had known him in high school told me that he and his brother were buddies; they easily got high grades and triumphed in school politics, but Dick stopped all activity after Terry's death. He just sat for months unproductively in class, and teachers promoted him on past performance.

We both swam against the mainstream. I didn't care to join a sorority, thinking the girls rich elitists, and worrying that I might be rejected. Besides, I couldn't afford to live on campus; I craved individualism, a lifestyle that fit in with other art majors and my friends in the A.Y.D. Dick's loner leanings were due more to introversion and a dislike of a crowd of any sort. We imagined ourselves standing together against an alien world, protecting each other. During hazing week at U.C.L.A., any shaved guy had to walk the plank and be sprayed with water. One day after class, Dick had visited his mother who was in the hospital for a minor operation; shaved, he became a target of the youthful vigilantes. Dick and I harbored no lighthearted views of the world that permitted such foolishness. I yelled at these child-boys as they dragged Dick away. My insults dampened their enthusiasm, and they let him go.

Once, Dick took me to meet his mother, Janet, at their home in Glendale. His father worked as an accountant at the *Examiner*, a conservative Los Angeles newspaper. Highly delighted, I walked with him up the brick path to his white two-story house with red-tile roof. Inside, the rooms were all newly painted, brick-a-brack and knick-knacks covered highly polished wood side tables.

Dick's mother said, "oh, hello," as if she'd met me before or heard about me—and never looked at me again. She got on the phone, kept her back to me, hung up and then, holding Dick's hand, said that Terry's former girlfriend was spending the weekend, no dating for Dick, therefore.

Some time later, on our way to a nearby miniature golf course, I suggested we stop and see his mother. (Dick was so good at golf that he was being groomed for a professional career, which eventually duffered out.)

"Oh, we don't want to do that," was all he said.

I thought it part of his antisocialness, and I knew that his mother was mourning her first son.

On my birthday, I called Dick to see when he would be arriving. He said he would be late picking me up for a celebration with Margery and her boyfriend, Doug. We had to hurry, so I asked my father to drive me to Dick's home.

"It's a nice house!" my dad said, impressed.

"Wait here, I'll be right back," I called, as I jumped out and ran past the thirty feet of green lawn and red rosebushes (all tended by Dick and his father) to the front door. Dick opened the door, and I smelled tension and panic.

"They—just found out—I'm dating you." His mother, and then his father, had discovered that we had been dating for eight months. "They didn't know—they said that I couldn't— that we," he stammered, after being caught in a lie as big as his house. "They say I shouldn't go with you."

"Let me talk to them," I said, pushing by him, going up the stairway immediately in front of the door. I could take care of things. I was going to explain the situation to his parents as if I were in an anthropology class. ("Oh, yeah, great!" Margery later said.)

But at the top of the stairs it seemed that I was standing on a rug on fire, the edges curling up in smoke, the heat reaching into my head. To the left in her bedroom, I saw Janet prone with her straight white legs stretched flat on her twin bed, her feet in short white golf socks, her white golf shoes being removed by her husband, Ted. She was holding her hands over her eyes and moaning. Ted went past me to the bath to rinse a washcloth in cold water, then passed me again without looking. He snapped at Dick to get his mother a glass of water. My heart was racing, body trembling, mouth dry, not a word could I utter. I backtracked down the stairs, saw Dick at the bottom looking like he'd just lost his brother.

"I'm going," I said. "Call me."

In two days I saw him.

He had kept his parents' disapproval to himself and hadn't told me because he thought I would leave him.

"Why don't you?" Margery asked me when I told her. "You don't have to put up with that!"

I was used to it.

"Do you like to suffer?"

I knew discrimination would always be there. Why should it separate us?

"We're sorry," they had told him, "but it's just not right to mix the races."

"Why isn't it?" I asked. I wanted to hear the definitive reasons, not just because it's always been that way, or you're different, or your children will be morons; I wanted to know the precise problem. Dark, dirty, slant-eyed, stupid, all of the above?

"Oh! I don't know! That's just what they say!" Dick was as angry as he would ever show. "My dad is a pretty good guy. He said, 'stay away for six months, and after that if you still feel the same, I won't say anything.' But he sees I can't do that."

They had placed a roadblock before us that we were going to circumvent with secrecy and aplomb. Parental disapproval bonded us. In our young minds, we were the American resurrection of Romeo and Juliet. Our lustful meetings tasted like bittersweet, forbidden fruit.

I finally told my mother, who told my father, and then hell didn't break loose, just sadness. When Dick was over, which he often was as he seemed more comfortable with my parents than his own, my father very nicely got him in a corner in a shot-gun situation.

"I heard about your parents' decision," my father said. "What is your intention?"

"I don't feel that way. And we're going to get married." Dick said, while I stood nearby, embarrassed, flooding red at having him questioned, as if we were children. Peevishly watching my independence fly out the window, I realized I was my father's child, and he father was fearful for me.

Tasting victory, Dick's parents told him that an antimiscegenation law wouldn't allow us to marry in California.

"You couldn't even marry that girl here!" they triumphed. "This should convince you that we are right!"

My parents were enraged to discover that the law they had heard about from their mixed-race companions covered me, and was siding with Dick's parents.

My father called the Anthonys' lawyer who told him, "yes, that's true. That'll be twenty-five dollars, please."

Not only parents but government got involved in our love. Dick and I agreed that as soon as he was twenty-one, we would be free to marry without parental and institutional blocking.

"Don't worry about it, Pat," Natalie soothed. "It's one of those stupid old laws that hasn't been brought to light yet. You and Dick just drive over to New Mexico—it'll be a nice trip."

The antimiscegenation laws of California were sending us six hundred miles away to New Mexico, the nearest state for a legal marriage. If a person had one-sixteenth amount of Black, Indian, Mongolian, or Malay blood, marriage with a white was out. The previous year in California, the character actor Dean Jagger and an exotic half-Chinese woman were refused a marriage license in Los Angeles. Flying to New York to marry, he laughed the law off as an archaic holdover from the past. Also in this era, the Black blues singer Lena Horne decided to marry her white fiancé in Paris, where they remained, having found that even if she might be able to, her musicians couldn't patronize hotels and restaurants in the United States; she opted for a country she found more welcoming. These cases brought attention to the California law, and by the end of 1948 it was dropped. By 1967, it had been officially booted off the books in all the remaining states with similar laws during the civil rights movement.

But we were heading off early in 1948, and my disappointed parents sagged in despair. More than anything they wanted to see me married in a long, white dress with a big wedding, lots of friends, and a big celebration after.

I hid my hurt pride saying, "it doesn't matter." We knew we couldn't fight it.

In fact, I was excited by our flight. I couldn't have cared less about a big dress and a crush of people. Marching down the aisle looked corny. I was struck with wanderlust. On Saturday, my mother bade us good-bye and gave us each a sweet smile and hug. We packed my bag into Dick's tan Chevy coupe which his dad had helped him buy before he knew of us. In a wave of excitement, we drove day and night, stopping to eat and window shop, heading towards Gallup, New Mexico. The night was so dark, so long, it seemed as if it would never end. Once, I saw an illumination backing a mountain range—a town at last! But after crossing the range, the light turned out to be the moon, a tremendous and brilliant silver dollar with a face laughing down on us as if it had pulled off a good joke. Without a sign of human habitation, I felt a thrill almost as big as my fears. We were heading to our wedding ceremony, sure to be my fulfillment. I would never ask for anything more from life.

Meanwhile, my mother cried into her white hanky and nursed her hurt; my father cursed the United States government and swore vengeance. At the same time Dick's mother lay on her bed, her head resting on her lace-trimmed pillow, nervously fluttering her eyelids, and his father denounced the selfish son who would so deceive his own mother.

Gallup turned out to be a house-here, gas-station-there, chaparral-surrounded town. We splurged on a postcard-pretty, slightly pricey hotel to balance our tawdry banishment. Dick signed the register, explaining what the arrangement was; we brought our suitcases to the room, decided to nap in spite of our nerves clanging, disagreed on whether to consummate first or not, and avoiding an argument, we slept. We got dressed in our best, and playing it by ear we asked the desk clerk where a Lutheran minister might be. Clearly other couples had made such petitions because he knew the directions by heart and told us where we could get a license first. My mother had baptized me Lutheran, and Dick had attended Presbyterian services, but he didn't care, so we drove to a nearby Lutheran minister's house.

A late afternoon sun was shining on a rosy adobe house behind a long front porch with supporting wood posts. The minister's wife, Mrs. Tanner, a pleasant, middle-aged woman, came outside to greet us, two youthful refugees from Los Angeles, as we tentatively approached the house. A glance told her what we wanted.

"Please come in," she widely grinned.

We stood awkwardly in a living room with Navajo rugs and Pueblo planters holding *nopal* cactus. Dick was as handsome as a chiseled Greek statue in the dark blue suit he had bought while flying to visit his dying brother four years earlier. A red-print tie and crisp white shirt accented his square jaw. My mother had sewn a white rayon-silk suit from a McCall's pattern for me after we had sat in the yardage department of the Broadway, studying patterns and walking around handling fabrics for hours. She hand-wrapped the tiny buttons with silk.

Snow as white as my dress capped the ground; it was ten degrees. I was chilled to the bone, my tawny complexion frozen, flaking, and blotchy red by the only lotion I had,

Dick's shaving cream.

Before the ceremony, Mrs. Tanner said, "You look lovely, dear."

She reminded me of my mother, and I thought she was trying to fill in for our lack of parents and friends. I relaxed, but she couldn't fool me; I felt grotesque with skin like a shaggy dog. Mrs. Tanner and a silent Indian maid with long, black braids were witnesses during our short ceremony.

"I liked the way Reverend Tanner finished by saying the wedding ring represented the unbroken circle of our lives together," Dick said as we walked away.

"Yes!" I agreed, but I couldn't help being chagrined that even pushing and shoving I couldn't get the ring on Dick's finger, and he had to do it. We didn't know it, but these signs forecast our future.

After the ceremony, we drove back to the hotel and celebrated with colorful daiquiris and Mexican dinners. Then we sat on the stone seat that circled the fountain in the middle of the lobby, staring as people swirled around, talking so fast, laughing so loud. Anyone who noticed us would have thought we didn't know each other or were in mourning. In fact, we were frightened, unsure of what we had done. We didn't talk. We had loved each other only last week; I thought, it must still be true. I worried Dick was unhappy, thinking about being thrown out of his parents' house, while I grieved at the thought of our being thrown out of our state. A hot, velvety-yellow humiliation enveloped me, the color of the light in the lobby.

After about a half hour, Dick said, "let's go to our room."

We went upstairs to our intense virginal bed.

We began our life together driving back, taking three days through light snow, then under clear, iced-blue skies, over the empty Route Sixty-Six in frosty vast space. We combed gift shops, peered into Meteor Crater, studied Hoover Dam, in a tourist honeymoon. In Arizona we watched a Navajo woman walking through the chaparral to her hogan and here and there a lone Navajo man striding the great distances on the majestic, silent reservation. The Indians seemed remote from civilization but linked to one another. I felt close to them, since Dick and I had linked up as loners. This landscape was ours.

I had found my golden boy, the white man who would let me enter into that American world where everyone was okay, affluent, protected, and accepted. I believed that only with him would I find peace and a place to fit in. Aside from those infantile notions, Dick was good and kind and totally color-blind.

On a visit later, my uncle Enrique told Dick he was interested in living in Los Angeles and asked if there were restrictions on home building in a certain area.

Dick answered, "no, there aren't. You can build whatever size you want!"

I wanted to belong to such innocence, a world in which there were no worries or cares—except about how big you wanted to build.

Living with my father had been eventful, if not for the parties he hosted, for his political harangues. Living with Dick was quiet. He was as silent as the Indians in the 1940s B-Westerns. "Ugh!" would have been a long sentence for him. After a beer, however, his tongue loosened, and the more beers he popped open, the more loquacious he became.

When Dick's parents realized they had lost, they wanted us to forgive and forget.

"Never," I said.

"I don't blame you," Dick sighed.

"You must for Dick's sake," my mother insisted, and I did.

At first we lived with my parents, a house of our own unaffordable on my salary and Dick's G.I. Bill. This delighted my father, who thought we would remain with them forever. Then Mrs. Jackson, an aunt of my childhood friend Corinne, whose mother had forbidden us to play together, invited Dick and me to move into the apartment over their garage in the big house on the top of the hill.

José was distraught.

"They have to start their lives!" my mother bellowed. "That's the way they do it in America!"

My dad couldn't see why and continued to drop in when I was home as if it were another room of his house.

"Make him knock, Mother!"

"He misses you so much, Pat, it makes me a little jealous!" But she fixed it, and he adjusted.

Dick admired my dad, his conscientious ways, his humor, and his good health. When he saw his Victrola and Caruso records, Dick decided we should take my parents to hear a Swedish tenor who was being compared to Caruso. At the theater in Los Angeles, my parents walked in shyly, staring upward, left and right, as we climbed the stairs and heard glorious *Don Giovanni*. A few years before, at my graduation from U.C.L.A., I had been mortified to see the way my father had gaped at the buildings as we walked to the commencement, but now I thought him sweet.

We moved again and again, each time up in size and neighborhood. Dick turned out to be fussy about where we lived. As far as we knew, our neighbors liked us. The only flack we got was from one of his friends warning him away from marrying me and a possible slight from a coworker who didn't invite us to his party in a chain of get-acquainted parties when Dick went to work as office manager for a big corporation. When we moved to our beach town near San Diego, I didn't know that there was a two-street area for Blacks who worked in big houses and that Jews were not allowed to buy homes at all.

My parents gasped when Dick got a promotion and we moved to San Diego. Ruth and José planned to move close to us right away, but then decided we might be transferred back and they couldn't keep following us around.

For about eight months after our move south, my parents visited each week, staying from Saturday morning until Sunday afternoon, unless my in-laws were coming down. It was wall-to-wall family every weekend, and Dick finally complained: "Do they have to come down every weekend?" I must have looked crushed, because he said, "oh, it's okay."

I was homesick for about a year; then I wouldn't have gone back for money.

In the 1950s, there was a new wave of immigration from the Philippines. But my parents took no part in the growing community. They worked, saw me on weekends (visits both ways were less frequent as they grew older and we had more children) and that was about it. They didn't seek out new friends and seldom saw old ones: Olga had remarried and moved to another state; Nini married and lived in Colorado; others had gone back to the Islands.

The divide was traumatic for my parents. They had nothing to replace our three-some. Attempts at getting close to the Filipino families they knew who lived in downtown Los Angeles failed.

"They are always wanting to borrow money, and then they can't pay back," my father complained. He had his part in the division, with his snobbish attitude, "they don't know how to talk about anything."

When Daria was born, my father seemed to forget his frustration with me. The dark haired, delicately featured, gracefully built little girl climbed into his lap and heart. Even though all was quiet on the home front, he would go outside to stand guard over her. She was the independent one, off and running every chance she got; my father could never change that quality any more than her exotic looks and the small, straight nose he admired. He smiled proudly when a Tijuana salesgirl said, *"Mira, que bonita es la nariz!"*

And though Daria looked almost as Asian as I, my mother-in-law was taken with her immediately, showing her off to relations, pushing her in her carriage, and coming back with the news that at the drugstore on the corner someone had said the baby looked just like her!

After my marriage, my parents went to work as temporary domestics, sent by agencies to jobs lasting from three days to three weeks. They decided that Ruth would quit the assembly plant weed-killer job near our house, quit alterations, and they would work together or separately as domestics as they had two decades before.

Ruth did have one engaging job. For three weeks she worked for a studio executive in Beverly Hills. A young Eastern politician who had just undergone back surgery came there to stay as a guest, to rest and recuperate. "He was so sweet and nice looking," my mother bubbled, "he was very polite and thoughtful. And when he left, he thanked me very much for such good service and gave me three hundred dollars! Never do any of these rich people tip so much! I was thrilled!" In a few years she recognized Senator Jack Kennedy as the sweet, ailing boy.

After a series of temporary jobs, José and Ruth worked together as a couple. One job lasting five years was for a woman named Theda who lived in Bel Aire, an art director and an heiress to her father's oil fortune. Upon hearing of my art degree from my parents, she graciously offered me a chance to do an advertisement for her agency. In my tiny living room at the beach, cluttered with toys of two toddlers, I did a black painting on white board with meticulous lettering. Leaving the room for a minute, my heart stopped when, on returning, I found my one-and-a-half-year-old Maria, blonde and plump, always clowning to get a laugh like my father and my grandfather, painting on the ad. I tried to paint over her scrawls, but I was never rehired.

If I disappointed my father in failing to pursue a significant career, grandchildren made up for it. Once he gave me a compliment: "Keep up the good work, he said, after a visit when the children were young—the twenty-ninth of June 1957, engraved on my mind's calendar. This was the month Lisa was born, the sprite with hair like a Raphael angel.

Dick had been transferred to Fullerton. It was closer to Los Angeles, and my parents visited more often, bringing with them one time Turi and Trond, who were visiting them from Norway. Turi was my mother's niece, the daughter of Rolf, my mother's favorite sibling. Their blond son, Trond, was born in the United States. With dual citizenship, he returned a generation later to live and work a while.

"I love it here, just like Norway!" said my mother when next we moved to Corona del Mar. My parents were now working for a family called the Bowles, who had four children.

"Daddy is really good with the kids," said my mother, who had never been comfortable around a lot of bouncing children. "We have to watch them at cocktail time every day. So many of them!" Still they worked there for a decade.

The Bowles were very friendly, gregarious, and sincere; they always invited me when I was in Los Angeles to visit as friends. In a sense, the Bowles became my parents' second family. Ruth and José joined the Bowles on trips to Lake Arrowhead for two weeks; Ruth was animated the entire time. Once, she and the eldest child explored the woods, much as my mother had done as a child in Norway. "We got lost!" my mother laughed later. "It was terrible, I really didn't know how to get out—and Kelly Louise was along!"

José and Ruth tried to hang onto old roots, still renting the house on Avenel, coming home every Saturday morning to rest and feel free, to see my mother's dear cat, who was fed the five days in between by neighbors. It grieved her. They needed proof they had a home of their own.

After a few years, my mother brooded, "We just can't keep it anymore. It's so expensive for less than two days a week. But what can I do with Fluffy?"

They sadly gave up the house and cat and lived permanently at the Bowles' elegant home in Beverly Hills. My mother started writing to a niece, Einy, and their correspondence continued until Ruth died.

"I'm writing partly to keep up with what's going on there and to get to know the young ones," she told me, "and to keep them from forgetting me! Also so that when you go one day to visit them, they will know you!" It must have been a crushing blow to realize she would not see any of them ever again—or her mountain and stream country—but so many of her brothers and sisters had died, it wasn't so desperate anymore, and she began to live through the thought of my going back in her place.

Dick and I were transferred back again to the seaside near San Diego in a lateral move. In 1959, we bought a house on the hill overlooking the ocean.

"Thanks for treating my daughter to the style in which she's not accustomed," joked my mother.

He laughed, too, in appreciation for her compliment. Starting with a three-hundred-dollar down payment in 1954, parlaying it into five thousand dollars by 1959, meant a ten-thousand-dollar start on the house we wanted next, if he could keep up the payments, all of which began to make creases in his forehead. He was easy-going only on the outside.

On visits my father was still the patriarch. "Is Daria going out again tonight? *Abao*, they should stay home sometimes!"

"Maria, are you chewing your food a hundred times each bite?"

"No." Her hair flowed like caramel down her back.

"Oooh, I thought I told you to do that. That's the way to have good digestion."

She mimicked someone chewing grotesquely and giggled.

"That is as good for you as the way you save money!" he went on. "Hah! She is going to be the millionaire!"

Even amiable Lisa joined her siblings in deploring their grandfather's fussiness. "When we stay with them at their house, he watches us all the time!" He would follow behind them when they went to the corner store. "We know he's hiding there behind the bushes to make us think we're alone!" she fretted. "Make him stop, Mom!"

When they visited, my mother, never before being very involved with a bunch of kids, loved watching her future stream. She sewed for them, babysat, and worried—how could I possibly do so much? She never meddled. But she did want me to perform as if each one were an only child, while I settled for treating each child as an individual.

"They need to learn independence, Mother."

"That's why your father and I had only one. We thought we could do our best for you that way," she continued. Somehow that statement made me feel more guilty about satisfying my wish for numerous offspring than the basket of dirty wash or the sink full of dishes.

We had a piece of the good life. Dick and I took our children to the desert or the Gulf of Mexico in Baja, California. Fishing, swimming, photographing the kids in the great open spaces gave Dick the glow of health. Often we'd park in the middle of a 102-degree desert, and I would watch as my husband, slim and athletic, stalked off, disappearing in *ocatillos*, *nopales*, and saguaros that hid lizards, snakes, and centipedes. The children and I sat, heads thrown back against the seats, breathing in the quivering hot air, pulling another Coke from the cooler, playing board games until one child would whimper in boredom, "when's Daddy coming back?"

An hour later, Dick would appear, a wavy mirage, bringing a wriggling lizard he'd caught with a tiny string noose, showing us the small beast and then letting it leap, dart, and disappear.

This was the face we turned to the world.

Twenty-five

My parents still occasionally went to poker parties at Pedro and Lou's house. And my father continued to bet on the Irish Sweepstakes every year. In 1958 he won three hundred fifty dollars and felt he was on a winning streak. He then began to play the horses, giving his money to a bookie who promptly left town.

"Oh, well," José said fatalistically, trying to cover his shame. "You know how life is, you never know what is coming next. My old friend Nino told me about this bookie, name of Alfredo. He was okay; lots of *Pinoys* used him. Well, gee whiz, what happened? He ran faster than the horse!"

"Yes," Ruth chimed in. "You and your lucky streaks."

"I still play the races, though, you never knooow!"

My husband's American pastimes of swimming, fishing, and tanning on the beach were monotonous to my Filipino father. He never learned to swim, last had a fishing license in Ben Lomand in 1925, hadn't worn a bathing suit since 1930 when tanks were in, and didn't need a tan. When my mother,

Dick, the kids, and I swam or sat and sunned by the ocean, my Dad sat above the beach on a wooden bench, dressed in a suit, polished shoes, and straw hat, looking snappy.

"Come on down on the beach, José," invited his son-in-law, thinking he could be more part of the family that way.

"No, thanks, Dick," my father always replied. "It's too sandy for my shoes, and I'm going to go back and start the adobo pretty soon." He blinked in the brilliant sunlight, enjoying the warmth of the southland.

When Dick's father, Ted, visited, the two men stood high on the rocks, hurling their lines out into the ocean to catch the big one.

By this time, Dick's drinking had become an addiction: one beer had become a six-pack, then bourbon, then the odorless vodka. Physicians diagnosed Dick's "down" periods as clinical depression, a hopeless prognosis since antidepressants would not appear for fifteen years.

"Nothing they give me helps as much as one drink," he apologized sadly when I nagged. "And then I can't stop."

I was helpless. When we married, I genuinely believed that only minorities had problems; a white middle-class man must have crystalline skies overhead, straight sailing. And so I tried to control my world in various ways. I entered the 1960s revolution as precinct worker. I joined women friends picketing grape farmers for unfair practices, marching for civil rights and demonstrations against the war in Vietnam. I was pleased to discover the United Filipinos under the Agricultural Workers Organizing Committee, and joined with Cesar Chavez' Mexican laborers, creating one of the most well-supported strikes in history. Filipinos were making their voices heard.

I got a surprise from my father when I told him of these activities.

"Oh, we're okay now," he shrugged. "What those people

want gets tiresome."

Where had I learned to care? At his knee. Yes! Wonderful things had happened for Filipinos, independence of the nation and immigration for educated professionals to America. "But there is still work to do!"

"No," he said. He was finished and tired of all the rage.

My niece Marie Lou had recently arrived in California to teach in the Whittier area. Now more Filipinas immigrated than men, receiving a warm welcome and good job opportunities.

"Ha, ha! I guess that's funny!" my dad laughed at his wit. "Americans used to go to the Philippines to teach Filipinos English, and now Filipinos are coming here to teach Americans English!" He took pride in Marie Lou's success as a teacher, but would not discuss my initiation into high school teaching. I was miffed.

Like my father, Dick never knew what it was like to enjoy one's work. I never knew whether Dick hated his work and got depressed or was depressed and so hated his work. The latter, decided a psychiatrist, who promoted electroshock treatments that stunned Dick into silence and relaxants that weakened his facial muscles. When he returned for help, depressed still, that doctor had been sizzled by his own machine and was a blob of wobbling jelly. "You have troubles? Look at me!"

When we had our fourth child, I wondered why, since I knew my husband was sick and getting sicker. Our son had crawled from the womb, howling to the skies, while his father lay curled up at home in an immobilizing depression—what Abraham Lincoln had called his Black Beast. My seventy-year-old father had driven me to the hospital. On the hard gurney, my arms strapped down, I stared at the illuminated ceiling. Dick always said he loved our three daughters and didn't long for a son. I just believed it my traditional duty. The nurses scrupulously checked the name tag before handing my son to me: he was blond and light-skinned, and I was sunburned-olive and black-haired.

"Is this your baby?"

"Yes!" I exclaimed, as I had at Maria's birth, too. Couldn't they see the similarity in features; was relationship only in the coloring?

My bliss matched the country's elation at the first American in space. But I plummeted to earth as I waited for Dick to come to the hospital. Looking forsaken, he came, with a name for our son: Matthew. The sound was strong and melodious, and I found its meaning later in a book of christening names: Gift of God. But when Dick was leaving, and I crooned, "isn't it wonderful?" he only said sadly, "it's too late now."

I reported Dick's behavior to our family doctor.

"Oh, he's just a psychopathic alcoholic," he informed me, moving some pencils on his desk. "Get him to AA."

But even the kindly physician didn't seem sure of what to do. Alcoholics Anonymous and twelve-step programs were not yet a priority on the popular culture's agenda. They were for weird street folk, not so-called normal people like us.

Dick insisted he was not an alcoholic. "I send people to AA in my job for the company!" he told me scornfully. A counselor did not need counseling.

In our therapy sessions, the old stereotype of the Asian woman—gentle, malleable, obedient—appeared one day as what Dick felt was the perfect wife for him.

"Ah, so!" the psychiatrist joked.

We all laughed, but inside I questioned the stab, because I believed I was a modern, enlightened American woman.

Mornings after his blackouts could seem normal. In a black-humored way, Dick once suggested we send out Christmas cards with our own breathlessly happy form letter describing the joys of family life: "Hi! How are you? Dick just got out of the mental hospital again, one of the kids flunked kindergarten, and another broke both legs." We bent double laughing, adding every misery and pain we could imagine.

My father never faulted Dick when he was drunk and disorderly. If he fell on the floor, threw up, or wandered out into the night, my father said, "Oh, that's only the drinking. He has been working too hard."

"But the children shouldn't see this, José," my mother worried.

"The doctor says he should go to AA," I fretted, wondering who could help us.

"No, no, he's okay." My father had seen so many rich and famous people fall down and disgrace themselves at the Anthonys' house and at the Bohemian Grove, he considered drunken behavior a sign of a man's arrival as a person of stature. "I saw them drink all day, get sick, cry, and then get up the next morning and go to work!" His conclusion was that money was an amazing cure.

When it got frightening at home because of guns, I would pack and run, throwing clothes into bags, pushing the children into the car, driving to my parents' house in Los Angeles, three hours away, the kids asking, "isn't Daddy coming?"

"You must return to your husband," José, traditionally my protector, would declare.

"She needs to stay here for a while until he calms down," my mother interceded.

"Noooo, no," he would protest. "Dick wouldn't hurt anybody."

I agreed: "He would never hurt me, but by accident?"

"Look at his sports cars and your new station wagon! Your big house and his important job! My God, a man has a right to a drink when he comes home!" The small apartment my parents had rented when they retired was bursting at the seams with all seven of us crowded in, and arguing made it seem to shrink.

"A woman stays with her husband. What are you doing here? Go home now!"

My mother-in-law said, "At least I'm not to blame. I never allowed drinking in my house!" Her husband, Ted, had died at fifty-five of a heart attack on the golf course, and she had married their family doctor, traveling worldwide annually. "Stay with him," she urged. "He's not going to live much longer!"

Of course! my heart agreed. Why should I? my survival instincts screamed. I was running from his madness.

The last time I bolted was serious. I checked out a cheap house on Sunset Boulevard near Alvarado intending to do substitute work; it was back to the basics but a relief from insanity. Dick called and promised to change, threatening catastrophe if we didn't come back. After two days I capitulated, and we headed home.

His friend, Marvin, said, "I was glad you left, but you should have stayed away longer." My loving husband and father of four became a white-knuckled sober-drunk for a year.

One day, about ten months after Bobby Kennedy's assassination, which Dick took hard, and two weeks after a stroke Dick had suffered, I drove home from my permanent job of high-school teaching to find our son and two of his sisters on the porch, unable to get into the house.

Before I could call out to him to stop, seven-year-old Matt loosened a screen and scrambled in through the bathroom window. The two girls and I hurried after him. Matthew found his father in the kitchen-family room, lying in blood and brain tissue.

I dragged the children across the street to a neighbor's house. Glynnis phoned my parents, while another neighbor called the police and Dick's mother. In a few days my mother and father cheerlessly took a train and then a cab to my house for the funeral. Janet and her husband, Harper, drove down from Los Angeles. I just sat on Glynnis's couch, wondering what I should have done differently.

•

Twenty-six

Without my husband, I bitterly believed that being virtuous and twenty-five cents bought you a cup of coffee. One might as well escape through the world's pleasures, I thought, until I too was dying—from lack of meaning, absent hope, vanished faith.

Sam, a boyfriend of Daria's turned evangelist, came to me, introducing God's ideals of love and community. I read how Christ had forgiven the adulterous woman and asked anyone without sin to throw the first stone. I became part of Sam's small community.

"Pat! Don't go crazy!" my mother cried. "My sister got religious and sent me letters filled with Scriptures!"

"It probably helped her," I said.

My mother looked at me out of the corners of swimming-pool blue eyes, terrified. "I know you've been through a lot— why don't you take a trip or something?"

"I don't want to go anywhere," I said calmly. "Really, I'm a lot happier now. Maybe you'd be interested."

She gathered her defenses. "Oh, your father would never let me do anything like that. And anyway, I think a smart person can do without it." She drew up her body, with that typical head-nodding when she was sure of something.

"Well, I can't," I said.

Cliff was an artist whose work I had admired for years, and soon after we started up a relationship, he was staying with me and my children. But I hurriedly asked him to leave when my father visited and found us living together. My father shouted that I was a whore and no longer his daughter. Sam, Daria's husband now, and my mother held him back from hitting me. José swore he would have the children taken away from me. Under this dark mantle he went home vowing never to speak to me again. I had brought shame on the entire family—he couldn't tolerate it or me.

My mother's voice on the phone was hoarse and slow, coming from the depths of hell. "How can you do this? When your father went away, I didn't go with another man!"

"My husband is dead, Mother."

"Yes, I know, but still, why do you have to do this?" Her accent was especially thick in her worry. "Your father won't even talk about you! I'm afraid he's going to die."

I knew I had committed a terrible act of *hiya*. But I didn't realize the extent for almost thirty years. Later, various family members emigrated to the United States, but they remained shadowy. "Who are they?" I asked my father.

"Oh, just cousins—nobody," he sniffed. My father refused to discuss a half-brother who was born to my grandfather Florentino before he married Enriqueta. Even though José liked his grand-niece, he withheld recognition of this nephew, a cousin twenty-five years older than I, who eventually became a friend and role model.

When Cliff and I married, my parents didn't know whether to laugh or to cry.

Cliff had dark, curly hair, a swooping moustache like Dennis Hopper in *Easy Rider*. He sang and played guitar—like Dylan, I thought—and had a madcap sense of humor, making pratfalls for the super-eight movie camera and jokes about everything.

My parents had a hard time with just about everything: Dick's death, my second marriage, aging, dwindling finances, seeing their grandchildren leaving. Children should stay at home!

By the end of her sixth decade my mother was an erupting volcano.

She had pointless tiffs with neighbors. "No, Pat, I'm not taking it any longer. I've always been so goody-good and let people walk all over me! Now the Hungarian (neighbor) wants me to pick up her mail when she could do it herself!"

I was in the dark, but it was clear to her. She fussed with my father over trivia. José was now like a small boat, bobbing on the swells of my mother's anger.

"Sure, Boss—everything is okay."

They reminded me of characters in a Hindu allegory in which forceful young men turn tranquil in old age and submissive young women, tempestuous in theirs.

Ruth fought illness, feared dying. "Dr. Blaine scolds me for coming in with so many symptoms. He thinks I'm a hypochondriac, Pat. I'm not going to see him anymore! But I have this weakness, and sometimes I can't get up in the morning."

"Go to another one!" I insisted, "you're not supposed to feel like that!"

For a while, she didn't go back to him—or any other doctor, fearful of more rebukes. She studied the encyclopedias for solutions to her symptoms. When she finally did go back, scientific diagnosis was colon cancer.

After a successful operation, her fears quieted, and she luxuriated in the three-week hospitalization.

"Make your father stop taking three buses every day to come to see me, Pat. He's so old now I'm afraid he can't take this."

"Maybe the trip is good for him to get out and around, instead of staying home and feeling lonely," I suggested, knowing he wouldn't listen to me anyway.

Supported by pillows like a queen, she was enjoying the enforced, overdue vacation. "We have lots of fun talking here, and I'm planning to take a Spanish class when I get out! I've just been staying home too much!"

At home, her enthusiasm waned. A colostomy preceded a breast lump and mastectomy. She believed cancer was stalking her. "Where will it come out next?" she asked anxiously.

"Pat, the mastectomy is so much worse than the other operations, because it's so ugly," she lamented.

"Nobody can see," I offered.

"But I can," she murmured. I wondered why my seventy-four-year-old mother was so vain until I saw the place where the breast had been—the gray-mottled stone slab that replaced a small, firm globe. I gasped secretly, reminded of the day she lost all her teeth.

"Isn't there some kind of plastic surgery?" I managed.

"Oh, no, they won't do that. I'm just glad they paid for the operation—it cost eight thousand dollars!" Medicare granted her life, not beautification.

My mother worried that José was going to have a heart attack; a doctor said it was a possibility. "He's so frail and walks so slowly. I'm afraid he's going to get hit by a car when he goes to the store!"

Yes, he walked like a sandpiper, and standing he looked like he was half-seated. He needed care. But secretly I awaited the day when she and I would be companions again; I day-dreamed our lunches and discussions, the day when she would read, crochet, and sew—recapture her old sense of humor. After her surgeries, my husband Cliff and I showed my parents retirement apartments near us in our town, and pre-pared for their move. My father admired the buildings, but his age and frailty defied any change.

I said to my mother, "Don't worry, we'll move you down here." She smiled, her drooping eyes crinkled. "I'll be so happy to live near you."

My parents couldn't bear the way their grandchildren went off, as if the world were a small town to be covered quickly, as if they themselves would never have done anything like that in their lifetimes. Daria and Sam moved to northern Idaho and started what turned out to be a long and happy marriage, rais-ing and teaching their seven children.

Maria moved to a tent in Colorado, climbed mountains in Costa Rica, lived on a sailboat in Hawaii, before settling down to marry Jim, a lawyer with the American Civil Liberties Union. They would have three sons, while she went to school and became an environmentalist. But what appeared at the outset to be an old-fashioned marriage didn't survive.

Lisa married Kip, and they moved to Maui, had a son, and Kip built a two-story, solar-heated house; Lisa joined a tradi-tional island dance group.

"Do you think they'll be coming back pretty soon?" my mother asked after they'd been there two years. "Yes, one day," I assured her.

Matthew planned to go to an Eastern school and study to become a scientist.

My father looked at his grades and said, "I guess each gen-eration gets better."

Matt would be like an only child for me, so far apart from the girls, and as a young scholar he joined me on research trips.

"You should stay home now, instead of always going all around," my father scolded me.

Relatives in the Philippines were also travelers, coming to the United States one after another. Niece Marie Lou was followed by Flory in 1970 on the high tide of Philippine immigration. A 1965 United States law had granted every nation twenty thousand immigrants a year. Immediate immigration was granted to relatives of citizens and permanent residents— men who had come over in the 1920s and 1930s; and to those with professional skills.

Flory was qualified on both counts. With an engineering degree and experience at one of the American-owned oil companies in Cebu, he was part of the Philippine's brain drain.

"I petitioned the Department of Labor, got a Green Card at Hawaii, first port of entry, and arrived in California, all within the year!" Flory said, amazed.

But he stayed with my parents for a few months, unable to find work.

"You came at just the wrong time, employers told me!" Flory said. Engineers were in a layoff slump.

Not wanting to be a burden on "Papa Joe," Flory started work at an electric plant, building switches and panel boards in an assembly line. After six months, he got his American dream job for a large engineering firm.

"Like a big family, Pat. After I was there one year, I sent home to my mother one of the first frost-free refrigerators," he boasted.

He filled in as the brother I wished I'd had. In California, he met Lucille (Lulu) from a family of nine children, all emigrating from Mindanao. She was a vivacious Filipina, taking seven National Board exams to reach auditor, and she was already an American citizen, since her father was the son of a German-American who had lived in the Islands before World War II.

Toni, a pretty, enterprising Filipina, arrived from Luzon in the late 1970s to finish graduate work in political studies at the same university where I was getting my master's degree. She had worked in a think tank for Marcos; she blamed his self-seeking cronies and Imelda for the corruption. Asked why he didn't tell the papers of the philosophical rift, he answered, "good leaders don't point the finger."

"I have a surprise for you," I told my mother. "Two tickets on the train to see Sam and Daria in Idaho!"

"Oh no, Pat!" my mother squealed, "we can't do that! We're too old!"

Time had passed so quickly. They were now seventy-five and eighty-six.

Twenty-seven

I was overjoyed to board a new, shining white ship, bound for Bacolod in Negros. The Visayan Seas were not the raging, turbulent waters we battled in 1936, but rested tranquil, a tender blue; wispy white clouds curled on the horizon. Islands suddenly appeared, like they were when Malakas and Maganda—the Islands' Adam and Eve—broke free from the floating bamboo that a seagull pecked open.

A fellow passenger tells me that just as "Visayas" is now "Bisayas," my home is now written "Sarabia," which matches the inflection of more than sixty dialects. She goes on to say that authorities renamed it "Magalona" in honor of a Senator, but inhabitants resisted the proclamation and stubbornly continue to call it "Sarabia."

Arriving in Bacolod on Sunday, unannounced, I phone *tía* Casilda and find that she is out. After checking into a cheap businessmen's hotel, I walk to the *zócalo* and enter the cathedral, where mass is being said in *Ilongo*. I stand with the overflow in the back of the huge stone church, understanding a few words, enjoying the sense of community, feeling very *balik-bayan*. I am shades browner than I was before and blend in. I think, we all look the same now, while nearby worshippers whisper, "*A Kana!*" (American).

That evening, the generator of the hotel goes out. "*Wala' suga!*" I remember the "no lights" cry from when I was ten. Through the window a radiant sunset backlights palms. Suddenly, flickering lights dance against the window, sirens wail, footsteps run downstairs, and I dash down to see the four-story building across the way a golden wall of flames. A mob stands transfixed, lighted by the inferno, laughing and directing the firefighters.

Frightened, I phone *tía* Casilda, who worries, "oh, Patsy! My driver is not here!" Then sighs, "Get a taxi, and come right over!"

I push my way through the crowd, seeking a cab.

A hotel guard walks rapidly toward me. "Mum, please come back to the hotel. The fire is almost out. Too hard to find cabs, streets are closed off, and lots of robberies lately! You'll be safe here!" He takes my bags and I follow, remembering my aunt's uneasiness about cabs, due to starvation in Negros.

I grasp the reason for the excitement. We're in the provinces, where the monotony is broken each month only by a festival. To my embarrassment, I also realize that I've misread the crowd's intent: men are standing in lines, passing buckets from hand to hand up to the roof of this hotel and back down again.

In the morning, *tía* Casilda's genial driver, Leopoldo, steers me through a new suburb of a crazy mix of Chinese, colonial, California-modern, and faux-Greek houses.

"Ninety percent are owned by wealthy planters," Leopoldo says, smiling at my flurry of questions. "You are interested in everything because you are on a sentimental journey."

Tía Casilda has a small, impeccable, modern home protected within a high wall. Highly glossed, red-brown *narra* wood flows from the entry through a short stairway to an upper floor. No geckos run on these walls, no moths fly around the imported lamps. Inside, two maids clean and polish every corner. Outside, Leopoldo doubles as gardener.

Although my *tía* is seventy-two, she is energetic and involved, as easy to talk to as in 1936. Left inheritances from her Sajo family and *tío* León's plantation, she has capitalized on her good luck by being a shrewd businesswoman, a fact I glean from phone calls I overhear. One day, her wealth will send two of her brother's children, whom she has raised, to universities in California.

The children, Seth and Sylvia, live under her bossy demands, as do the servants. "This must be done before six o'clock. Where is the work you were to do? Why did you not finish that?" she exclaims in *Ilongo*. I brace myself for her bad humor; but she turns to me with loving amiability. I must remind her of days in the 1930s when she and *tío* León were young, she a slim and softly smiling woman, he a powerful man, one of the town's leaders.

"Your *tío* León died after the war of diabetes, after too many years of hiding from the Japanese, shivering in the rushes of the river—after the destruction of the hacienda, after too much starvation, too much sadness." She presses knuckles to her mouth, eyelids lowered, eyes glancing sideways—an old mannerism that used to hide a smile. Her feelings for *tío* León are as deep as the Mindanao Trench.

"Your *tía* María died the same way. Did you know, Patsy, that a few years after you were here, she met and married a Russian who came to Sarabia?"

"He sent my father his picture, signed 'Your brother-in-law Kosenko.' A good-looking man, I thought." I remember his sepia photograph (military and proud) and one with *tía* María celebrating their marriage. My father, still possessive of his sister, wondered about the Russian.

"During the war people buried their money and jewelry for safekeeping," my *tía* continues. "This María did. After she died, we looked for her valuables, but they were gone. And so was Kosenko. We were angry—it's hard to forget."

"But if she loved him and had some good years with him."

"Nooo, he ran away!" His action was a clear violation to *tía* Casilda. "The most important thing is family."

I ask her about the billboards I have seen that declare, "Whoever works the land owns the land (Ferdinand Marcos)." To my mind, this seems just.

"No!" she insists. "We have always let the people live on the land and work the fields without charging them. Now they are expected to buy when they really don't want to. They just want to plant enough to eat! They don't work enough to earn money to pay for the land, and so it takes them generations to buy it, while we want to keep the land for our children!"

I wonder if there are some who want to move beyond that.

"No," she insists. "They are too lazy." Land reform has become a war—a way to close the gap between privileged and poor. The walls surrounding her house, topped with jagged glass, are solid emblems of *tía* Casilda's feelings toward the common folk who skirt their exterior. Even I feel protected in the company of the family matriarch. It represents the shelter of the Sajo house of 1936, the security of Justiniani status in a noisy, provincial city where most people are just scraping by. For *tía* Casilda and her peers, there is no way out except to disappear behind high walls. Beep the horn, a steel gate opens; drive in, the gate shuts, and the street clamor is closed out. Inside it is easy to imagine that everyone is as cozy as we are, with running water, flushing toilet, air-conditioning, television, maids, and a week's supply of food from the open market.

At the end of the century land reform still baffles Philippines presidents. Too few wealthy families for a true democracy, but too many for any politician who likes his job to lock horns with. Feudal landowners of the pre-Hispanic Islands didn't have to break their heads over democracy, as my father would say, and the modern-day *ilustrados* don't either.

Now *tía* Casilda sits in her bedroom sifting through her memorabilia, showing me pictures, giving me a fine cloth of piña and unused, gold-sequined dancing shoes with low-heeled, hard soles, Philippine-Chinese style. From the coffee table she gives me a ceramic plate she bought in Italy. I forget the rules of Asian generosity and admire it. Beaming, she shows me a childhood card I wrote to *tío* León: "I'm sorry I won't be seeing you for a while, but please give my love to everyone there."

"Why did you never marry a Filipino?" she asks. I think a minute and say, "I guess you marry who you grow up with." How can she understand that a country that prepares the Philippines for democracy doesn't really practice it? My towns are socially separated if not actually segregated.

"As a child in Los Angeles I lived on the edge of an upper-middle class neighborhood close to my father's work—I had only Caucasian classmates. As an adult in San Diego, neighbors and teaching associates, same thing. Not even in higher education have I met Filipinos or mestizos."

"Your father never told us." *Tía* Casilda accepts it.

The Sajo family makes its pilgrimage to my *tía*'s house, ghosts from my childhood dreams. Aquiles, Pedro, Mary, Elisa, and Norma. Absent are my playmate Edwin, who died in battle on Bataan, and my friend Augusto, who died after the war from hardships suffered. "Big sister" Joséfina is a nun in Manila. In a whirlwind reunion, they treat me like a movie star.

"You look exactly the same!" Elisa gasps.

"Like a ten-year-old?"

We giggle in renewed friendship.

Lunching in a cafe, I experience preharvest starvation. A man, bones pushing his gathered skin, treads from the door to *tía* Casilda, who chatters in scatter-shot *Ilongo* to her sister-in-law Mary. My *tía* nods at him, and he drifts off to sit crouched at an empty nearby table. The quick, brown waitress pads soundlessly over aged linoleum serving rice, heavy noodles, and bland fish. The man who has been ominously watching us finish comes over to silently slide all the leftovers—even from our plates—into a paper bag.

"For his children, he says," my armored *tía* smiles, "but I think it is really for him."

So skinny and bent, I hope so.

On the way to Sarabia and my appointment with the past, a man and water buffalo stand waist-deep in the vastness of watery rice fields. Finally, I am standing in *tía* 'Sabel's house. At ninety, *tía* 'Sabel is a beautiful, little old-lady "girl." We hug and cry, my childhood memories looking through adult eyes. I'm a woman returning to say hello and good-bye for my father. He will die in a year, *tía* 'Sabel in two, and *tía* Casilda, who in my mind is a survivor, even now is concealing an illness and will die not long after her sister-in-law. Everyone from my 1936 dreamworld has grown old and prepares to die. Many have already.

On my second visit, *tía* 'Sabel is out of bed, in the living room, waiting. My return both stuns and accelerates her. "Why did you wait so long to come back?" she demands through *tía* Casilda's translation.

"I had children to raise," I say blithely, realizing I had no need in the midst of my life to return.

"Does José still tell his stories?" *tía* 'Sabel asks.

"Of course!" and we all laugh.

"In contrast, *tío* León was very quiet," they recall, smiling.

As I did years before, I look through the windows, through the foliage toward the Sajo's house where I plan to go. Gone! Only weeds blow in the breeze. *Tía* Casilda sees my surprise and says, "The guerrillas blew it up during the war to keep the Japanese from using it as headquarters, but we think they really did it out of vengeance. They did the same to your uncle's hacienda." The great houses symbolized the disparity between rich and poor, forever and everywhere in the Islands.

With *tía* Casilda translating into the dialect, I tell *tía* 'Sabel that during the trip in 1936, she was the one who introduced me to a spiritual life. She is delighted, and her bony hands grasp the photographs I bring, searching the faces of brother, sister-in-law, grandnieces, and grandnephew. The old clasp memories. When *tía* 'Sabel dies, I'll clasp them too, but I'll have a new picture of the Philippines: it is a *tía* 'Sabel, with a feisty spirit that survives through all the ravages of war and disappointment.

Tía 'Sabel aches for me to stay. But as during my first trip, I fight the claustrophobia of her rustic house, her small town, our lack of direct communication, by escaping with *tía* Casilda to greater spaces. Leaving, we drive by the old stone church where I knelt with *tía* 'Sabel—gone, too. Hacked apart to make room for a modern one. I think of the heavy door opening, the crack of light that invaded darkness. I think of the Sajo house, the babies in the bottle on the top floor, my childhood concern with their lives and deaths, and their final destruction in fire. Since then, I've had experience with the struggle of death, and I accept the fact that life deserves one's full attention—no wallowing in remorse, as my father would say, no crying over spilt milk.

The morning of my flight to Cebu, rain clatters on the tin

roof of the washroom so hard and continuously, I'm sure we won't be flying.

"Oh! This is good weather," airport officials say. "Wind is bad."

I don't know how to leave *tía* Casilda; I just hold my umbrella before me and push through the downpour. *Tía* Casilda, Seth, and Sylvia stand behind the rain-washed window, waving good-bye.

In Cebu, I wait in my cousin's living room for Conchita and her husband to return home from their offices. Before he enters, Rudy looks through the screen door and exclaims to Conchita, "You didn't tell me your cousin was American!" (I'm finally an American.)

Conchita and Rudy are an attractive couple.

"You were seven and so little and pretty. I was jealous of you because my father liked you so much!" I blurt out, but Conchita doesn't even remember.

They wonder why I've popped over out of the blue. Busy people, they look relieved when I say my mission is to research the Spanish-period basilica for my thesis; had they envisioned a tourist to pamper? Here in their neighborhood, in the handsome city of Cebu, set like a jewel in a backdrop of a glistening floral jungle, is the Basilica of the *Santo Niño*—the legendary statue Magellan brought from Europe over four hundred years ago.

In the basilica, elaborately carved *narra* wood gleams in long benches and on the wide staircase leading to the monastery. In the church stands the twelve-inch *Santo Niño*, given by Magellan to Chief Humabon's wife, who placed the woodcarving on her altar, alongside stone images of nature spirits.

"After the arrival of de Legaspi and the conferring of

Christianity, the Sainted Child kindled a worship throughout the Islands," a dark-blue mantled sister tells me, "every church has a copy."

I've heard stories of its magical cures. Each pilgrim kisses the name plaque attached to its glass case. Over them the Child raises a hand in blessing, the other holds the Earth. The statue is startling in its ornate clothing—it looks like a doll from Woolworth's!

"That's not the real one!" Conchita explains. "The real *Santo Niño* is locked in the vault under the Basilica." The huge wooden cross left by Magellan is also hidden away, protected inside another cross, outside the church.

"How do you know it's really in there?" I ask, my western skepticism surfacing.

"Oh, sure it is," my relatives answer. Pure faith is better than tainted doubt.

Back home, we sit down to a delicious dinner of squid cooked in its black ink. We pass dishes and discuss Marcos.

"There's no incentive for the middle class to make money—that's why so many want to go to America," Conchita says, noting the poor job market.

"Flory likes it there," I say, as we discuss Conchita's energetic brother and my first cousin who lives an hour and a half drive from me. In the 1970s, the United States has opened doors wide to Filipino engineers, doctors and nurses, some thirty-five thousand Filipinos immigrating annually from 1965 through the 1970s, an opening that narrows in the 1980s when the American economy stalls and there is a flood of home-grown doctors and lawyers.

I show Conchita my childhood passport photo, enlarged and decoupauged onto wood cut in the outline of the picture. "*Tía* 'Sabel gave it to me. Our aunts had one made of you, too!"

Conchita has never seen it. Although all my life has been lived six thousand miles away, I am closer to *tías* 'Sabel and Casilda than my Cebu cousins, an island away.

As Flory told me, she says her father, my uncle Ramón, died about eight years earlier. She contradicts our *tía's* account of Kosenko—he was very friendly, built their air-raid shelter in Saravia; they had been good friends. After the war he came back, returning María's things, saying, "it was all a misunderstanding."

Their mother, my *tía* Margarita, the pretty Spanish *señora* of 1936, is a vigorous and relaxed grandmother who gives me a pair of beaded slippers for my mother, "so she will remember us!"

Saturday night church services allow families to spend Sunday together. Seizing the opportunity, we drive to Mactan across the bridge and rent an open, split-bamboo beach house with nipa roof, one of dozens clustered along the surf. But no one goes near the water. I insist and find myself sprinting across fiery sands, accompanied by children only. I search out tiny, delicate conchs, circles, spirals. The kids help, finding perfect ones, chattering in *Cebuano* and giggling at the bizarre activities of "*Kanas*." We hop like rabbits back to the shelter.

Huge picnic baskets keep us busy for two hours, barbecuing *lechón*, fish, crab and eating candied coconut and unripe mangoes in Indonesian hot sauce. The men laugh and think I am macho to eat it without flinching.

"I'm used to Mexican food," I brag.

My cousin Rudy, a six-month-old infant during my first visit, is as cool as his wife, Baby, is friendly. A bottle of the famous Cebu-brewed San Miguel beer puts me in a drinking-buddy category, and Rudy and I are suddenly friends.

Hearing of my plans to visit Mindanao for my research on textiles, Baby warns, "if you go to Mindanao be very careful. It is different over there!"

"Yes," Conchita says, "a Japanese tourist has just been kid-napped!"

Rudy laughs that "often there are Christian-Muslim wars in that place. They are just as bad as the old *Moro* fighters of your father's time!"

From their jocular tone, I know they are half jesting.

I love my cousins; they are the brothers and sisters I never had. After eating and drinking, members of the party, both young and old, curl up on benches to sleep. Others read the papers, while large mongrel dogs warily enter our hut and sniff around for scraps of food, only to be shooed away. These mongrels are distant cousins of the powerful ones Conchita and her neighbors keep as watchdogs, that growl with murder on their minds.

A few days later, I'm warily off to Mindanao. On the way to the airport on Mactan, Rudy drives us to the site of Magellan's death. I stare ahead at the sea, the barren land at my back. I wonder if, in that final battle, Magellan wondered what he was doing so far from home. Or did his explorer's curiosity, his Christian faith, his own ego keep such questions at bay?

From Cagayan de Oro in northern Mindanao, a day excursion bounces me along pot-holed, two-laned roads, past a passenger-filled bus sunk in mud, and past the beginning of a four-lane highway. Here Filipino neighbors are working together rolling back their houses on top of huge logs away from the expanding road. I was delighted to find more relatives in this place too. As one of my cousins had said, "almost everyone in the Philippines is a cousin." The Willkoms family is related through my cousin Flory who lives in Orange County, California. They very generously took me with them for a day of visiting some of their vast landholdings.

One place we visited was their long-ago first house, open-windowed to the tangle of palms and other trees all trying for control. From a massive lunch basket we pulled dried fish, peeled papayas, and *lumpia*, (stuffed, fried roll-ups). Mosquitos tasted us in the bargain. Suddenly Mr. Willkom, a big German mestizo whose mother had been a Filipina, brightened with an idea: "We are going to Marawi city!"

"Oh, really? Do you think we should?" Mrs. Willkom demurs slightly.

"Oh, yes!" He had been there many years before, and thinks this is the time to go again. Their children, seventeen-year-old Carol and fifteen-year-old Jingo, take turns navigating the corkscrew road.

High up, where the jagged rim of the world reaches the skies, the Maranao people have fashioned Marawi, a Muslim enclave within a rich forest. At the entrance, military constabulary with rifles at the ready, demand our precise business. "Just to look around! Haven't been here in a long while!" from Mr. Willkom in Chabucano, his imposing bulk now at the wheel. A uniformed guard motions us on. Roads ply through outlying areas on the way to the town. Two-story houses, the hue of huge old trees, are lacily draped by the leaves of living ones; over every long porch railing silk-blend malongs (wrap-arounds) in peacock blue, emerald green, shimmering yellow, and the one-time royal gold and purple, hang like banners, high above the ground of dirt and wild plants. Passing deep wooded areas, houses spaced at long intervals, we pull into the town. Aside from a few modern buildings, Marawi seems to take pride in its surrounding forest and has no need to lay concrete everywhere.

In the town, another gun-toting soldier stops us, questions Mr. Willkom, goes off. Intimidation inhibits our curiosity. But I see that in Marawi the women are the glory! Wearing brilliant malongs decorated by bands of backstrap-woven, Islamic flower and tendril, they carry bright matching parasols. Their hair piled back and high shines slick and black. Complexions pure, eyes dancing, they throw backward glances at the men as they stroll, laughing, answering in aplomb, drifting away, swaying as they go—lighted by the sun, with a background of forest. Less plumaged men, some wearing western garb or printed malongs over matching draped trousers, languish on the porches of the stores, or go their way.

We are obviously tourists, suspicious characters, and they stare at us. Although headbands, turbans and aluminum mosques abound, something about Marawi reminds me of the Old American West, from the simple wooden storefront porches and colorful costume, to the simultaneous easiness and edginess of living isolated and accompanied by gun-slingers. The Marawi people are artists in brass, wood and weaving and connected to their land. I feel that the Willkoms have given me the great gift of seeing indigenous people in their own setting and putting me in touch with my past.

Twenty-eight

As soon as I returned to the United States, I drove to Los Angeles and gave my parents gifts of piña, wood, and shell I had brought back, showing them my slides on their light beige wall.

"No, that cannot be 'Sabel—my goodness, she looks like a ninety-year-old woman," José said.

"They all thought you looked very young in your pictures," I told him, as he expected they would.

"Yes, I have very smooth skin," he agreed. "People are still surprised that I am eighty-six."

"Oh, just look at him with his skin," my mother taunted.

"And there is a picture of *tía* Casilda," I went on in my slide show, "and here are Norma and Elisa. Remember how we were children together in 1936?"

"Did you see the Maravillas and the Lazares families?" asked my dad.

"No, I don't know them," I replied.

"Mnnnh," he murmured, disappointed; they were his old

cronies, the rich upper-crust of the 1930s who entertained us royally. I had a whole different set of friends, people my age, who were my cousins by blood or marriage, the new middle class, as well as curators of museums and professors in universities.

"See," I pointed out, excited. "These are the brassworks of the Bagobo, the weavings of the Bontoc, and here are the Muslim mosques in Marawi in the mountains of Mindanao. See—only the elderly women wear the *patadyong* in the Visayas now, but in Marawi the women wear these purple and gold wraparounds."

"Hmnnh," José mused, disinterested. These were the mountain tribes whose photos had helped keep the Philippines from their independence in 1901. He believed them barbaric, too.

"You must have had a lovely time!" I could count on shared interest from my mother. "I'm so glad you're back now. I hope you won't be traveling for a while. Would you like lunch?"

My parents were at home in America.

On the phone with my mother, about eight months after my trip, I was greatly encouraged. My husband and I had shown them a sparkling, inexpensive senior apartment nearby, we were making plans for their move, and Ruth sounded wonderful, strong and happy. Referring to their train trip to visit, the last thing she said was, "we'll see you next week!"

Four days later, my daughter Maria's husband, Jim, called. Gently he told me that my mother had died. A sudden heart attack. I planted a sob onto the refrigerator door. Jim said calmly but urgently that my father was now alone in the apartment in Los Angeles, trying to understand what had happened, and that I should go there at once.

My mother died in the same way as she had lived: quietly, pleasantly, never asking for help or attention. To me she resembled a cat—just going off somewhere and dying. I stood rooted in their small apartment that they had rented at their retirement some thirteen years earlier, just a few blocks from the Monon Street house. I looked out their window at the stone, Islamic-style fountain—the thing Mother "liked best about the apartment." Across the courtyard was "the Swiss" woman's apartment and her three-foot, green iguana—off its chain it ran about like a child.

Clutching her scarf and now her sweater, my father kept pacing and asking, "Ruth, where are you, darling sweetheart?"

Cliff and our son, Matt, got a U-Haul, and we lugged their things out of the apartment to bring my father home to live with us.

At the funeral and brief religious service, José sat with a grimace of doubt and disbelief, which I thought might be directed at the minister and religious rites.

On the way to San Diego, we stopped at Flory's house in Orange. My dad, broken and bent like a twisted wire clothes hanger, was carrying a bottle of wine in a sack.

"He shouldn't do that," I complained to Cliff.

"He won't keep it up," Cliff assured me.

Three of Lulu's pretty sisters who played and sang in a band were there. "Come on, let's dance!" they called to my mourning father, turning up the stereo.

"Oh, no, not me," he shrank back, swaying.

"Yes! Come on!"

They pulled him off the chair and made him dance, now with one, then another. Suddenly he was standing straight, dancing a little, then smiling, then laughing, then dancing in a one-two trot, still dancing at eighty-seven and half dead with despair. Someone snapped his picture, dancing his two-step like a young man.

"That's enough," he said after a while and came back to mourn.

Mother wouldn't mind, I told him.

At my home, he kept going over the morning of her death. "She got up—said she was not feeling well, packed a small bag because she thought she would have to stay a while. We took a cab to the hospital. How can it be? She was laughing and making jokes. They put her in a wheelchair, they got into the elevator—and then I don't know! Her face got all red—they closed the door and went upstairs." He never saw her again, but his mind rejected the loss.

A week later he found a silver bracelet among her possessions; for hours he burnished it with silver polish to take to a nurse who had tended him in the hospital when she told him of my mother's death. I drove him to Los Angeles. He entered the hospital and exited as quickly. The nurse wasn't there, but it didn't matter—his features showed he had faced the fact that his wife of sixty years wasn't in the place where he last saw her—she was dead.

While my father tried his best to cope, his slender frame stooped with anguish, the corners of his mouth drooping, his despair creating an angry look that may have been fact. He wanted to talk about my mother, and so he told me stories. He described how he and Ruth had met.

"That's how you met?" I couldn't believe it.

"Sure!" he exclaimed, cheered in discussing their first encounters. "Your mother's aunt, *tante* Tilla, had this lunch counter where she lived in Bridgeport that was part of the house. It faced the street, open to the public. I used to go there to get a sandwich and cold drink. Then your mother came from Norway and worked there."

"Friends didn't introduce you?"

"No, I told you, we met at this lunch stand." The old man

crossed one leg over the other and came to life, involved in his story. "She served me sandwiches, aah—cheese and chicken, I guess, and something cold like sarsaparilla to drink. So I kept going there every day to eat—and to see her. *Tante* Tilla was very nice. She liked me. Ruth and I went to Coney Island soon after we met." He laughed in contentment.

Oh, Mother, I thought, why didn't you tell me this? Why did you keep such a sweet story from me? Did you think I would think you had been picked up—and that would allow me to think meeting strangers on the street permissible?

My father moved into our home in May. It struck me that I was very American in that I often found it hard to cope with José's presence. I was used to a modicum of independence, and now, here he was, the grand patriarch, dispensing what he considered helpful criticisms of my marriage and my parenting. He wondered why Cliff painted pictures all day and why I spent money shooting photographs for articles I wrote for magazines that paid so little. I didn't know where to start in defending artists' and writers' pursuits with my father.

His attitudes, stuck in the 1930s, could still inflame me. One day, my father told me that, when my mother was fifty, she received an offer through an employer to do fashion sewing, a well-paid, secure position, but that they had decided that at her advanced age, she should stay home and rest. I was furious since that was the ploy he was using on me, now. In my venerable old age of fifty, I was getting an advanced degree so that I could teach art history instead of studio arts.

My father was the soul of discouragement, "Augh, it is too late now. You should stay home and rest!"

"I don't need rest. I need to do work I love!"

"Oh, no, you are too old for that now."

I pretended not to care and tried to ignore his comments.

José, who hadn't had a close friend since my godfather, Fred, decided to meet Filipino seniors at their community hall downtown. We made the twenty-minute drive to the hall where mainly poor, elderly men gathered for breakfast, lunch, and dinner in cafeteria style, played pool and cards, sat quietly, or talked to each other about their ills, their pensions, their shared past. With no common history save for their immigration to the United States, those elderly had no pull for my father. One man, gracious and charming, formally dressed in sports coat, joined us drinking Cokes at a table, expounding with authority. My dad couldn't get a word in edgewise. I was fascinated by the ex-navy man who had been in the United States for forty-five years. He remembered San Diego as a navy town in the 1940s, had served in the Pacific at Iwo Jima, returning here to live. Most of the men were field laborers (with no pension) or former navy personnel who had served in World War II, still waiting for the pension due them. Lonely, usually unmarried, called the *sacadas*, the survivors of the pioneer generation of the 1920s and 1930s. Without the senior program, they might be wandering hungry and abandoned.

"He is Tagalog" was José's summary, translating to: I know all about him already. José was bored and wanted to go home. He was not getting what he considered the appropriate respect. He was still the same old *ilustrado*. Without my mother, he was destined to be lonely. I didn't recognize that at least José had me and my family, and he didn't seem to notice either.

In August, he and I drove the thirty minutes to Tijuana where we walked all day. Back at home his feet cramped all night, but it was okay; he laughed at the pain, remembering his pleasure during the day. In Mexico he found an earthy country reminiscent of the Philippines. I thought of our family outings, when I was a child, to Ensenada, where a local "guide" named Candelario attached himself to José, calling him patrón, accepting small tips my father paid him, more for his deference than for his information. So José and I shopped and ate in the bright, busy mariachi din; he spoke Spanish to bored merchants and looked like a young man sightseeing in Madrid.

After several such jaunts, I ran out of steam, so my father found the bus stop and took trips on his own to the seniors' club or just downtown, where he walked around for hours.

Stephan, Cliff's twelve-year-old son, was with us alternate weekends and with a sweet spirit and sociable way easily talked with my father. It was a touching boy-old man relationship in its quiet, simple questions and answers about the weather, Stephan's kites, what my dad was reading in the paper. José admired his grandson Matthew's mastery of science, and sometimes Matt went to dinner with him when Cliff and I were out; Matt never forgot his grandfather's pronunciation of bege-tables. But at seventeen, Matt was showing signs of the depression his father suffered at the same age, and I became frantic, now deciding to practice tough love, next deciding total permissiveness, running him to doctors and hospitals.

My father finally found an audience in a young doctor who, eager for patients, had accepted José's Medicare case. After a checkup, the doctor said José was in great shape, except for a heart condition down the road. Otherwise, the doctor said, "he's very healthy—and he's a very interesting old man." He had given José more than a physical exam, he had listened to him, enjoyed his account of the 1918 Spanish Flu, his anecdotes of New York, and respected him as an elder. If only my father could have narrated his experiences daily to fresh audiences—gone on tour as a living chronicle of the twentieth century.

One day, I drove by the bench near the house where my father sat waiting for the bus. Whew! I thought, my child is playing, and I can do my work! At the same time, I was touched at how handsome and dignified he looked, sitting so straight, his straw hat at a jaunty angle, one leg crossed over the other, hands clasped over his slim middle.

We had taken my dad, Matt, and Stephan to a beach house in Ensenada for a few days, and my dad had enjoyed such tremendous well-being that by December, we thought it safe to leave him alone for a day and a half while we flew to Berkeley so that Matt could check out the campus. On our return Sunday night, he was overjoyed to see us, but in an hour, he was hit with a stroke. We ran him to the hospital, and in the emergency room the doctors gathered around him, listening to him and laughing at his stories. José came home that night, but stopped eating; again we hospitalized him, but the doctor said we might as well take him home—he had lost his fight. He didn't even want to sit in front of his television in the chair padded with pillows I had slip-covered in his favorite paisley design. He just crawled into bed.

Jim, Maria, Flory, and Lulu came to celebrate Christmas Eve with us. After a dinner of turkey, mashed potatoes, cran-berry sauce, peas, and apple pie, we sat around the big wood coffee table, opening gifts (still retaining the Norwegian cus-tom of celebrating the eve, not the day). Declining to eat, José was entrenched on the couch, wrapped in his burgundy robe.

"How are you feeling, Papa Joe?" asked Flory, solicitously.

"Just fine, Flory, how is your job? And how is Jewell?" Jewell was Flory's bouncy, curly-haired daughter, at home with aunts. Their conversation was family, my mother's name intro-duced several times.

After Flory and Lulu left, my father went to bed, and Maria and Jim sat with him for a long time, maybe an hour and a half, inviting more yarns; José glowed with life. "Let me tell you about the time in Manila." They were rapt listeners, and he relished this time.

José spoke little the last week of his life. Lying in his room one afternoon, he philosophized, "I guess if your mother had not died, I would have lived to be very old!" This reflection from my eighty-seven-year-old father was lost on me, and I gasped with the ignorance of a younger generation.

What are you now? I wondered. I didn't realize he was dying.

I fed him oatmeal; he stopped taking his medications. One day he seemed to be thinking over events that he couldn't fix, for he said as I entered the room with his food, "I guess no use crying over spilt milk, huh?"

"Oh!" I breathed, caught off guard. "Are you lying there just thinking about sad things? We all do good and bad things. It's okay." I was repenting for him.

He said nothing. I sat on the bed and thanked him for sending me to college. Instead of responding with what I longed to hear, "You did well with it," he said, "Your mother and I thought it was the best thing we could do for you."

I begged God to help me, but I had so much unresolved resentment I didn't know how to deal with. I could only rack my brain for another compliment as he lay there. As I spooned cereal into his mouth, he said, "Ah, das berry good."

I told him the latest news; he removed his false teeth. I washed his hands and face; he spoke of whirling sights. Cliff bathed him in the tub; he became incontinent; he lay in bed, trying in frustration to explain his thoughts, describe a feeling, or tell me something. I did recognize that the elderly should live and die at home with loving family.

Another day, he kept pointing to the ceiling cupboard and gesticulating; I later wondered if he had hidden something there—his gold coin worth one hundred dollars? In Tijuana he had had it evaluated and was delighted to have another pawn.

But he took it with him; I never found it.

New Year's Eve day, he asked me to take him to the bathroom alone. I couldn't support him and called for Cliff and Matt. "Oh, I think you can take me alone," he argued.

"No, I can't," I insisted. But I stood by, handing him toilet paper around the corner of the door for his privacy. Then he stopped taking it.

Now I see that he did die in the most dignified way possible. He put his last ounce of strength into the long journey from the bed to the bathroom, from the unreality of his dying thoughts into the literal world, his last act immaculately completed, so no one would have to clean up after him. His head slumped forward. He was at last autonomous and free.

My cousins Flory and Lulu came to his funeral.

Flory was astonished. "What happened?" he asked. "When we saw Papa Joe, he seemed fine!"

"I don't know," I answered dully. But it was certain that my father didn't like life without my mother. For him, I was incapable of filling in for her, too busy with my own life. José was following his own destiny—by the name of Ruth—seven months after she died.

Later I thought about what he had said to me, just a week before on Christmas Eve, "In 1921, your mother was the most beautiful young girl in New York—and I was the best dancer!"

Epilogue

Instead of my mother, I was the one heading 80 miles an hour toward Oslo, in search of my Norwegian family. The trip—on impulse, really, in 1988—had been inspired by my close friend, Kari. I had met her five years earlier at a poetry reading; she too wrote stories and poetry and she too had a Norwegian mother. She was the second person to think of me as Norwegian—the first being my mother. Kari wondered why I had never gone to Norway. Categorized as Filipino or Asian throughout my life, I had never thought to investigate the Norwegian branch of my family. Although many Norwegians came to the United States at the same time my mother made her "visit," I really had had no contact with the Norwegian community—not surprising, since immigration from Norway dropped steadily after industrialization, so that today Americans of partial Norwegian descent number only four million and migration is low. Kari's question turned my thoughts toward Scandinavia.

My cousin Turi and her husband, Trond, greeted Cliff and me at the train station. The couple had visited California in the fifties, and since that time, my mother and I had corresponded each Christmas with Turi, one of the two daughters of my mother's brother, Rolf.

During our stay, my cousin reiterated what my mother had heard after the long silence caused by World War II: Rolf had suffered. "He was among the artists, writers and teachers who Hitler feared," Turi said sadly. "They were the first to be sent off to Germany as possible troublemakers." After her father helped a group fighting the Nazis, it was dangerous to stay in Oslo, so in 1943 the family moved to a farm in Gudbrandsdal, where Rolf painted. My cousin was sure war anxieties exacerbated the heart disease he died of in his fifties.

Turi put me in touch with our cousin Reidun—someone she hadn't seen since she was eleven years old—and a trip to Alesund, by train and by mailboat, was hastily arranged. There on the docks, people from my parents' black album greeted Cliff and me: Reidun, daughter of Astrid (sister of Ruth) and her husband, Torstein, along with twenty-year-old Stig, great-grandson of Astrid, nephew of Reidun. Tall, slim Stig (my son Matt got his height and frame from Norway) translated for us.

As we strolled along the harbor, I was disconcerted by walking through pictures I had grown up with, dated 1920, 1938, 1970. Here was the same Art Nouveau architecture, mandated by the Kaiser, with modern facades and faddish shops.

"We are on Aksla, the hill where the Germans who occupied Alesund did surveillance on Allied subs and planes in the forties," Stig said, walking over to a heavy battery. "Those must have been bad times," I said, touching the bleak old metal. "You'll have to ask my uncles about that," the loquacious young man laughed. "I was born in 1968." How easy to forget the way time flies and the world goes on.

In his mother's cooperative art gallery, Stig explained that Einy was on holiday with his father and sister in the Greek Islands. "She'll be sorry she missed you." Einy was the niece my mother wrote to all those years, and now, looking at her paintings and some photos of her (a brunette beauty), I realized that in my haste to make this journey, I had missed an important family member.

My family guides pointed out Ruth's school, a dignified structure, and the corner building where she had lived on the second floor, a block from the water. This was why she always loved hilly sites, beach towns, boat cities, and why she cherished hiking through the woods.

Everyone related to Ruth, or who had known her, or who had heard about her came laughing excitedly through Reidun's door, bearing food for a party. (I remembered my mother, bent over the card table, writing letters, telling me: "When you go there one day—and I'm sure you will, they will know you.") Living my life, I had few thoughts of traveling to the uttermost ends of the earth. Now, surrounded by family, Norway didn't seem that remote. And the love of her family and friends revealed that they really did know me!

"Why did Ruth never come back?" This was the question of the day, made pertinent by my arrival. "She always wanted to, but they never could afford to, and she would never come without me or my father." I tried to untangle the mystery. It was simply couldn't, not wouldn't. Traveling had become middle-class manageable by the eighties, but my parents would never have flown; they really believed that if we were meant to fly, God would have given us wings. I watched my cousins trying to imagine Ruth's life, as the only Kongsvold in America. It seemed hard for them to grasp and I was the only child who could tell her story.

Eighteen Kongsvold relations sat in Reidun's living room,

speaking Norwegian, smiling and gazing at me. Friendly second cousin Annie-Brit, under waves of auburn hair, her sister-in-law, blonde Hildegunn, whose animated face split into a laugh over her halting English, chattered with me as if we had always known each other. A friend of the family who was four when Ruth left, insisted, "you look like your mother's pictures." I received this as the greatest acceptance they could offer.

On a wall hung a photo of Ramona, my granddaughter at age three, sent thirteen years earlier by my mother. All generations were meeting together in Alesund. We scanned picture albums (there I was at two, seventeen, twenty-eight); I designed a family tree, all their remarkable names carefully placed on proper branches. My uncle Rolf had our grandmother Kaia's family traced back to 1530! A month later, Einy and I began a correspondence, picking up the twenty-year correspondence she and my mother had maintained. Nine years later, she would come to the U.S. to visit me.

As I write, the year 1998 approaches, the centennial anniversary of the independence of the Philippines. The nation is free of Marcos' twenty-year misrule, U.S. bases, and most of its brown-outs. Already savoring economic growth, the Islands swell with 70 million people, and Manila, Makati and Cebu City show the signs of super-industrialization, with urban sprawl, traffic jams, and colossal indoor, air-conditioned malls. Pristine beaches still abound on Mactan and other islands I'll keep secret.

In San Diego recently, President Fidel Ramos joyously quoted his 1993 address to the White House: "I said 'We should reconstruct our Philippine-U.S. relations on the basis of trade, not aid.' And it's worked.... Now, professionals are finding work at home." I hear my father laughing with approval.

Still, Filipinos make up America's fastest growing Asian population, with some 200,000 emigrating annually. Today, they number over three million in the United States, 40 percent in California, and the 1998 centennial marks a far cry from the day in 1913 when my father sailed through the Golden Gate seeking adventure. Many more opportunities open to the newcomers. I have been lucky to be involved with this community since the 1980s, when I started to teach in a folk arts program for Filipino-American youth. Among the remarkable talents that the program attracted was Bayani de León, a composer-musician from the Philippines who taught music of the *bandurria*, classes in Tagalog, and the early written script of the Islands. Called by the community and the National Foundation for the Arts "a national treasure," the modest Bayani came as a result of United States policy that fostered the immigration of educated professionals.

In addition to encouraging the migration of talented people, the 1990s Immigration Act amendment stressed the reuniting of families. A model new immigrant is my cousin Flory, a prosperous engineer who came to the United States to better use his education. In a dream job, he met Filipinas in the same ratio to men, married and had a family, sponsoring his mother, Margarita, and sister, Fe, in emigrating—things José never could have dreamed, much less achieved. Flory and Lulu have watched their children speed off to universities, bright-eyed Jewell graduating from University of California/ Santa Cruz and younger brother, Jed, off to New York to study for a career in finance. Flory fears Jed might stay there. "Children should stay home!" I hear José say.

Despite new immigration laws, jobs and legal acceptance, discrimination and hate crimes have not vanished. Flory—like José in his youthful Justiniani spirit, looks and great energy—doesn't shout about it, but once he said to me,

"I was so surprised, Pat, how bad the racism was." Cluck, cluck went his tongue in Visayan disgust. "I had no idea when I came here, I thought they would be like the friendly GIs that came to my father's cafe in Bacolod!"

Photographs of a family reunion held a few years ago in our beach house capture the remarkable contradictions in our family clan. Brunette to blonde, round and almond eyed, tall and sleek, husky, petite, pale-faced and deeply tanned, we form a micro United Nations. What began with José and Ruth in 1921 has today become, four grandchildren, twelve great-grandchildren, three great-great grandchildren, three step and foster children, four godchildren, seven spouses or significant others: a total of thirty-three.

From their northern lake and woodlands, Daria and Sam bring sons Abe, Eagle, Moses and Ben, and daughters Hannah, Yellow Bird and Ramona (who, in Justiniani tradition, prepares to be a teacher). Daria keeps an antique shop and is book-keeper for Sam's businesses; others relish their wooded area and outdoor activities, as carpenters and skiers. In our multi-racial tradition, some are dating Korean or Filipino mixtures.

Maria and her husband, Rich, arrive from the Spanish-style home he built in the high desert of southeastern California. She is back from one of her ecological trips. In his father's tradition, Justin studies to be a lawyer for the under-dog, Michael has his mother's wit, John continues in the multi-ethnic vein with a Mexican girlfriend.

Lisa and Kip come from north country. Three-year-old Austin keeps her company while she works in her home office decorated by her paintings. In the newest electronic tradition, she works by modem, while Kip designs Websites. Son Mica starts another legend by enrolling at a University of California campus, and has a Native American girlfriend.

5228

Matt drives the ten miles from his apartment on a cliff above a San Diego freeway. With a Ph.D. in molecular biology, working in a world-reknowned scientific lab, he has begun new traditions in our family. While carrying on his dad's desert-mountain legacy, he pursues belts in Kung Fu.

I look over this gathering of my clan; it is one of my joys to know that we are all Americans.